To Hubert Gray
who is largely responsible
for this book

READ THIS FIRST

It's frightening how some people, though adept at walking and scrambling, have none of the mountain sense usually learned through decades of mountain wandering, problem solving and familiarity with mountains in all weather.

Learn to read topo maps and be able to find a grid reference. Turn back if it looks too hard for you, if you can't handle loose rock, if the river is too high, if you can't hack a 10-hour day, or if the routefinding is out of your league. Turn back from a summit or ridge if a thunderstorm is approaching or if conditions are made dangerous by rain, snow and ice. *At all times use your own judgement.* The author and publisher are not responsible if you have a horrible day or you get yourself into a fix.

In this book there are no dos and don'ts. It is assumed that users of this book are caring, intelligent people who will respect the country they are travelling through.

Be aware that in Kananaskis Country trails can change in an instant owing to logging and the search for oil and gas. Please notify me of any changes you find so I can make revisions in future editions. Use **Contact Us** under the **About** tab at kananaskistrails.com.

Gillean Daffern's
KANANASKIS
Country Trail Guide

VOLUME 1

RMB | Rocky Mountain Books Ltd.

rmbooks.com

@rmbooks

facebook.com/rmbooks

Cataloguing data available from Library and Archives Canada

ISBN 978-1-897522-76-9 (v. 1).—ISBN 978-1-897522-77-6 (v. 2)

Book design and layout by Gillean Daffern

Cover design by Chyla Cardinal

Cover photographs and interior photographs by Gillean Daffern unless otherwise noted

Maps by Tony and Gillean Daffern

Topographical maps Her Majesty the Queen in right of Canada.

Printed and bound in Canada

Distributed in Canada by Heritage Group Distribution and in the U.S. by Publishers Group West

For information on purchasing bulk quantities of this book, or to obtain media excerpts or invite the author to speak at an event, please visit rmbooks.com and select the "Contact Us" tab.

RMB | Rocky Mountain Books is dedicated to the environment and committed to reducing the destruction of old-growth forests. Our books are produced with respect for the future and consideration for the past.

We acknowledge the financial support of the Government of Canada through the Canada Book Fund and the Canada Council for the Arts, and of the province of British Columbia through the British Columbia Arts Council and the Book Publishing Tax Credit.

Nous reconnaissons l'aide financière du gouvernement du Canada par l'entremise du Fonds du livre du Canada et le Conseil des arts du Canada, et de la province de la Colombie-Britannique par le Conseil des arts de la Colombie-Britannique et le Crédit d'impôt pour l'édition de livres.

Disclaimer

The actions described in this book may be considered inherently dangerous activities. Individuals undertake these activities at their own risk. The information put forth in this guide has been collected from a variety of sources and is not guaranteed to be completely accurate or reliable. Many conditions and some information may change owing to weather and numerous other factors beyond the control of the authors and publishers. Individual climbers and/or hikers must determine the risks, use their own judgment, and take full responsibility for their actions. Do not depend on any information found in this book for your own personal safety. Your safety depends on your own good judgment based on your skills, education, and experience.

It is up to the users of this guidebook to acquire the necessary skills for safe experiences and to exercise caution in potentially hazardous areas. The authors and publishers of this guide accept no responsibility for your actions or the results that occur from another's actions, choices, or judgments. If you have any doubt as to your safety or your ability to attempt anything described in this guidebook, do not attempt it.

CONTENTS

TRAILS

Changes to the 4th edition

The big news is that the guide has been split up into five volumes. The reasons are all advantageous to the reader: to keep the number of pages down (who wants to tote around a 1000-page guide book), to allow for a more user friendly layout where trails are arranged by access road, to make room for more maps and for ease of adding new trails and subtracting old ones.

There have been major changes to highways, access roads, trails and trailheads. And as before, trails continue to be affected by logging, pipeline construction and the search for oil and gas. There is also a new quota of official, unofficial and demoted trails.

Since the last edition K Country has become a collection of parks: wildland parks, provincial parks, provincial recreation parks, Don Getty parks, ecological reserves, preservation zones, wildland zones, cultural and facility zones etc. each with a different level of protection and with different sets of rules—all of which makes things tricky for us guidebook writers. To avoid confusion, no attempt has been made on the maps in this edition to show the different parks. If a regulation impacts trail users it is mentioned in the text.

Since the last edition we have also been introduced to seasonal closures, permits, user fees and substantial fines for non-compliance. As if to sum it up, the word "ranger" has been replaced by the less friendly-sounding "conservation officer."

For up-to-date info, visit our web site at **kananaskistrails.com.**

ACKNOWLEDGEMENTS

For this book the following people have been extremely helpful and supportive: Heather Bates, Tracy Cove, Harry Connolly, Jim Dennis, Jeff Eamon, Duane Fizor, Ian Getty, Gord Hurlburt, Rienk Lakeman, Allan MacKay, Mike and Judy Buchanan-Mappin, Rod Plasman, John Pomeroy, Karen Ritchie and Donald Smith. An especial thank you to Don Cockerton and Alf Skrastins (as always).

All photos are by the author unless credited otherwise. Thanks again to Alf Skrastins, who gives me free rein with his extensive photo collection in the effort to get the best photos possible. Thanks are also due to Sonny Bou, Clive Cordery, Eric Coulthard, Wendy Devent, Vern Dewit, Brenda Everitt, Gillian Ford, Maurice Gaucher, Niccole Germscheid, Ron Hunter, Peter Irwin, Evelyn Ko, Leon Kubbernus, Annette Le Faive, Dave Macdonald, Angélique and Allan Mandel, Roy Millar, Bernie Nemeth, Andrew Nugara, Rachel Oggy, Shelly Sochr and Bob Spirko.

PHOTO CAPTIONS
Front cover: Upper Kananaskis Lake from Indefatigable trail.

Back cover: Summit of Midnight Peak.

Page 1: Larch on North Kent.

Title page: The crux section of Northover Ridge. Note the figure on the northernmost high point. Photo Sonny Bou

Contents page: ridge 147230, with Mt. Sir Douglas in the background. Photo Alf Skrastins

Page 17: Climbing the first and second chains between Ribbon Falls and Ribbon Lake. Photo Roy Millar

Page 320: Taiga and Sierra at Frozen Lake.

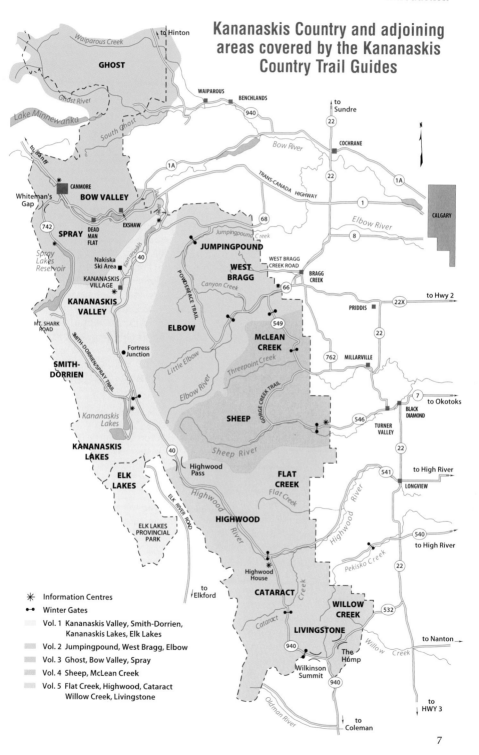

Kananaskis Country and adjoining areas covered by the Kananaskis Country Trail Guides

- ✳ Information Centres
- •— Winter Gates
-     Vol. 1 Kananaskis Valley, Smith-Dorrien, Kananaskis Lakes, Elk Lakes
-     Vol. 2 Jumpingpound, West Bragg, Elbow
-     Vol. 3 Ghost, Bow Valley, Spray
-     Vol. 4 Sheep, McLean Creek
-     Vol. 5 Flat Creek, Highwood, Cataract Willow Creek, Livingstone

KANANASKIS COUNTRY

THE NAME

Since the last edition the whole world has learned to pronounce the name 'Kananaskis': CTV's Lloyd Robertson, US president Bush, British prime minister Tony Blair, Russian president Vladimir Putin. One wonders what explorer John Palliser would have thought of it all.

The strange name dates back to 1858 when Palliser named the pass he was about to cross 'Kananaskis' ...*after the name of an Indian, of whom there is a legend, giving an account of his most wonderful recovery from the blow of an axe which had stunned but had failed to kill him, and the river which flows through this gorge also bears his name.* Possibly the Indian in question was the great Cree Koominakoos who lost an eye and part of his scalp in a battle with the Blackfoot in the Willow Creek area, but made a miraculous recovery and showed up at Fort Edmonton some weeks later ...*ready to take to the warpath again.*

THE CONCEPT

Today, the Kananaskis Passes, Kananaskis Lakes and the Kananaskis River form the heart of Kananaskis Country (or K Country as it is more commonly called), a provincial recreation area owned by Albertans and established on October 7, 1977, to ... *alleviate congestion in National Parks, and to provide greater recreation opportunities for Albertans.*

Let's give credit to architect Bill Milne, who got the ball rolling. Alberta premier Peter Lougheed and Clarence Copithorne, then minister of highways, quickly came on board and a new Hwy. 40 was built. Their vision for the Kananaskis Valley was one of strenuous physical outdoor activity accessible from a good road but with minimal services. As we all know, that simple idea turned into a grand plan called Kananaskis Country, encompass-

ing a lot more country (over 4000 square kilometres) and a lot more development, with facilities for every conceivable outdoor sport.

Many people forget that Kananaskis Country has always been multi-use, meaning it is open to logging, cattle grazing and oil and gas exploration.

LOCATION

K Country is located on the eastern slopes of the Canadian Rockies, west and south of the Olympic city of Calgary, Alberta. From the city outskirts the eastern boundary is only a 20-minute drive away.

The western boundary adjoins Banff National Park, then runs down the Continental Divide. The northern boundary is delineated by Hwy. 1A and the fringe communities of Exshaw, Dead Man Flat and Canmore. The eastern boundary coincides neatly with the Bow-Crow Forest reserve boundary, while the southern boundary is marked by Hwy. 732.

GETTING THERE

Calgary is served by major airlines, several bus companies and by train from the east. Greyhound buses run west along the Trans-Canada Highway to Canmore, but stops are infrequent. That's it as far as public transportation goes. You need a car.

The core area described in Volume 1 is usually accessed from the Trans-Canada Highway via Hwy. 40. It can also be reached from the town of Longview on Hwy. 22 via Hwys. 541 and 40 over Highwood Pass. Another way in is along Hwy. 68 from the Trans-Canada or via Hwy. 742 from Canmore.

The northern portion of Elk Lakes Provincial Park is most often reached from Peter Lougheed Provincial Park on foot. The alternative is to drive to Sparwood on Hwy. 3, then take Hwy. 43 north to Elkford. From Elkford a gravel road follows the Elk River Valley to the park entrance.

WHAT TO EXPECT

Volume 1 centres on the Kananaskis River Valley and its tributary Smith-Dorrien Creek, most of which now lies within Peter Lougheed and Spray Valley provincial parks. At the junction of the two rivers lies the heart of K Country at Kananaskis Lakes.

Radiating out from the lakes are a number of passes: Highwood Pass, which carries the highest paved highway in Canada, Elk Pass, which leads over to Elk Lakes Provincial Park in BC, and the infamous North and South Kananaskis passes to the west.

A large portion of the mid-Kananaskis Valley is taken up by the Evan-Thomas Provincial Recreation Area, which features Kananaskis Village, Nakiska Ski Area, Ribbon Creek ski trails, Kananaskis Country Golf Course and Boundary Ranch. Farther up the valley is Fortress Ski Resort (closed at time of writing).

The Fisher and Opal Ranges lining the east side of the valley are good for exploratory trips up canyons and along rocky ridges.

Separating the Smith-Dorrien and Kananaskis valleys is the Kananaskis Range, which offers something for every level of hiker: numerous lakes within cirques, meadows and passes, easy ascents and classic ridgewalks, Mt. Allan being the prime example. Logging roads often give access. In fact, the Smith-Dorrien and Mt. Shark ski and bike trail systems are based on the old roads.

In the west along the Great Divide, the K Country scenery reaches its zenith: high peaks (up to 3449 m on Mt. Joffre), glaciers, waterfalls, extensive alpine meadows, lakes, boisterous streams and old-growth forest. This is the scenario for the Canadian Rockies' most spectacular backpack, the exciting Northover traverse.

This volume also covers the north end of Elk Lakes Provincial Park, which is known for its lakes and BC bush.

WEATHER TRENDS

Generally, the hiking season starts in April in a few valleys at the north end of Hwy. 40. The Smith-Dorrien and Kananaskis Lakes area starts to open up much later, around the beginning of July. May is often a dry month, with rains starting in June. The flower months of July and August are the best for big trips, but be aware of late afternoon thunderstorms should that be the trend that particular year. Indian summers through September and October can be glorious. The mornings may be cold but the sunny, stable weather is a relief and the larches may have turned.

As in any mountain areas, snow can fall in any month of the year. In the rotten summer of 1992, for instance, snow fell on three consecutive weekends through late July into mid-August. Conversely, the summer of 1994 was consistently hot with the temperatures hovering around the mid-30s. At such times the area can be locked down to prevent forest fires. Generally, low cloud is not the problem it is in other, wetter ranges of the world and navigating by compass is an unusual event.

NATURAL HISTORY IN A NUTSHELL

I urge you to buy the appropriate field guides or Ben Gadd's all-in-one *Handbook of the Canadian Rockies*.

Mammals Most commonly seen: bighorn sheep along Hwy. 40, moose along Hwy. 742, mule deer, elk, black bear and grizzlies, which frequently close down the Bill Milne bike path. Grizzlies most often frequent the valleys on either side of the Smith-Dorrien Valley, the high passes to the west and the area about Highwood Pass and Ptarmigan Cirque trail. Less commonly seen are wolves, goats, lynx (mainly in winter), and cougars at the north end of the valley. In the wet valley bottoms are muskrats, beavers and the odd river otter. Other critters include porcupines, ground and tree squirrels, and chipmunks, picas and marmots among the rocks.

Birds Most common: whiskey jacks (the ones that gather around when you stop to eat), Clark's nutcrackers, hummingbirds (wear red), ravens, thrushes, chickadees, kingfishers, owls, grouse in the forest, ptarmigans up in the alpine, loons on the lakes and various waterfowl in the valley wetlands. Dippers are common in fast running creeks. Golden eagle counting occurs during spring and fall migrations around the Ribbon Creek area.

Fish Trout in the lakes, which are stocked annually. Bull trout spawn at the mouth of Smith-Dorrien Creek.

Vegetation Trees range through fire succession lodgepole pine in the east to spruce and fir mixed with larch in the west. Balsam poplar grows in the more arid valley bottoms of the Fisher Range and are associated with dryas flats.

For too brief a time alpine meadows and grassy ridges are crammed with flowers in July and August. In particular, overseas visitors will be intoxicated by the gaudy colours of North America's Indian paintbrush. Glacier lilies cover glades near treeline.

Nibble on strawberries, raspberries, gooseberries and blackcurrants.

HAZARDS & NUISANCES

River crossings The once wild Kananaskis River is part of the Bow River's hydro-electric scheme. Flow is no longer controlled by seasonal variations, but by the touch of a button, which has led to a few people getting benighted on the opposite bank. Upstream of Kananaskis Lakes this glacier-fed river and its tributaries can be impassable for much of the season.

Smith-Dorrien Creek and the Elk River in BC are impassable during spring runoff and after prolonged heavy rain as are many creeks running east from the Divide and the Kananaskis Range.

Conversely, creeks running west towards Hwy. 742 and Hwy. 40 are much smaller and manageable.

Caribbean water it is not, as Anthony Hopkins found out during the filming of *The Edge*. If cold water makes you feel sick to your stomach, wear neoprene booties.

Bears and other beasts At all times be aware of bears, but particularly in early spring after hibernation and in fall when the berries ripen. Most of the area described in this book is a high bear area. Many hikers carry a bear repellent and bear bangers where they can reach them in a hurry.

In the paranoia over bears we often forget that elk and moose should be given a wide berth too, especially in spring when with young and in fall during the mating season when males get very ornery. Lately cougars have become a year-round worry.

Hunters Hunting is allowed outside the provincial parks and provincial recreation areas, Marmot Basin being a prime example, but generally the area covered by Volume 1 is not a big hunting area.

Ticks Between about March and mid-June (and in certain areas right through to November) ticks are abroad and are found mainly in areas where there are lots of sheep.

Loose rock In Calgary an insurance company's ad on a billboard once read "As firm as the Rockies," which made me laugh aloud. The Rotten Rockies aren't called that for nothing, the sedimentary limestone being subject to extremes of heat and cold. Of course there *is* firm limestone, but it's safer to expect the worse. On scrambling pitches, develop the technique for pushing handholds back into place. Be particularly aware of rockfall in gullies. You will run into scree—lots of it. Utilize game trails where the scree is more stabilized and watch for the occasional bounding rock from people above you.

FACILITIES

Hwy. 40 (Kananaskis Trail)

The Stoney Nakoda Resort Casino has a hotel and three eateries. Peaks Cafe is open for breakfast at 7 a.m. Closes at 9 p.m. The Ridge Buffet is open 5–8 p.m. daily. Sunday brunch goes from 10:30 a.m. to 2 p.m. Sidelines Lounge (full menu) is open until midnight Sun–Thurs and until 2 a.m. Fri–Sat.

Barrier Lake Information Centre is open Mon to Thurs 9 a.m.–4 p.m.; Fri to Sun 9 a.m.–5 p.m.

Sundance Lodges offers unique accommodation in tipis and trappers tents. Bring your own bedding and cooking supplies or rent. Attached is a coin laundry, small grocery store and gift shop. Open mid-May to near the end of September.

Boundary Ranch, run by Rick and Denise Guinn (son and daughter-in-law of Alvin Guinn of Guinn's Pass fame) is the place to go for trail rides. Rick's Steakhouse is open during July and August for lunch and early dinner until 6 p.m. on weekdays and 7 p.m. on weekends. One of the few eateries where corn on the cob is a staple. Gift shop attached.

Kananaskis Village features two luxurious hotels: Delta Lodge at Kananaskis and Executive Lodge at Kananaskis, upscale restaurants, shops and bars. Woody's Pub has the cheapest eats. At the Village Centre is an information counter, Ribbon Creek Grocery & Deli (hot and cold snacks, open 9 a.m. to 8 p.m. year-round), a post office, a comfortable lounge, and Kananaskis Outfitters (rents, bikes and bike racks, canoes and hiking equipment).

Down the road at Ribbon Creek is **Kananaskis Wilderness Hostel** with fully equipped kitchen, coin laundry, volleyball court.

The Summit Restaurant at **Kananaskis Country Golf Course** opens at 5:30 a.m. for early breakfasts and stays open until the last golfer has left the course.

Fortress Junction gas station sells gas, snacks, groceries, camping supplies, books and gifts, fabulous ice cream cones and has a cash machine. Open year-round.

Mt. Kidd RV Park has a snack bar, groceries and hot tubs.

Kananaskis Lakes Trail/Road

The **Peter Lougheed Visitor Centre** dispenses information and has a comfortable lounge to relax in. The displays are a must see.

William Watson Lodge offers accommodation and a campground specifically for seniors and the disabled.

Boulton Creek Trading Post has a bistro and grocery store and rents road bikes. Bistro is open mid-May to mid-June (Thurs-Sun 11 a.m.–7 p.m.), then mid-June to Labour Day (daily 11 a.m.–7 p.m.). Store is open May 1 to mid-June (Sun–Thurs 9 a.m.–5 p.m.), then from mid-June–Labour Day (daily 9 a.m.–10 p.m.), then from Labour Day to mid-September (Sun–Thurs 9 a.m.–5 p.m.).

Elk Lakes Provincial Park

Elk Lakes Cabin at the entrance is operated by the Alpine Club of Canada (ACC), and is open year-round for accommodation. Provided are stoves (bring white gas), mattresses, pots, dishes and cutlery. Reservations required. Pay here for campgrounds.

Nearest grocery stores: Boulton Creek Trading Post in Peter Lougheed Provincial Park and the town of Elkford, which has all amenities.

Hwy. 742 (Smith-Dorrien/Spray Trail)

Mount Engadine Lodge, expertly managed by Andrew and Sharisse Kyle, offers accommodation with meals. Non-guests can enjoy all you can eat gourmet dinners at 7 p.m., but you have to book 24 hours in advance. Walk-in afternoon tea and buffet treats are available from 3–5 p.m. on weekends only between mid-June and Thanksgiving. Also on offer: guided hikes, mountain writer programs and the popular Music in the Meadow concerts.

CAMPING

HIGHWAY ACCESSIBLE CAMPING

Campgrounds fill up quickly in the summer. It's galling to find every campsite full of campers whose idea of exercise is the walk to the biffy, so book ahead if you can. Overflow areas with minimal facilities are often available. After Labour Day the situation eases. Prices vary depending on amenities offered and the number of vehicles in your party. An RV and a tent count as one unit. Generally, Alberta seniors receive a discount.

Hwy. 68 (Sibbald Creek Trail west end)
Stoney Creek group (beginning of May to the first week in October). Call Bow Valley Park Campgrounds, 403-673-2163.

Hwy. 40 (Kananaskis Trail)
Sundance Lodges (Mid-May to near the end of September). Besides tipis and trapper's tents it also has regular camp sites. Call 403-591-7122.
Mt. Kidd RV Park (year-round). Campers Centre features a grocery store, coffee bar, laundromat, showers, saunas. Outside area children's wading pool, tennis courts, horseshoe pits, volleyball court. Call 403-591-7700.
Canoe Meadows group (Apr 11–Oct 13). Call Bow Valley Park Campgrounds, 403-673-2163.
Porcupine group (May 1–Oct 13). Call Bow Valley Park Campgrounds, 403-673-2163.
Eau Claire (May 15–Sep 1). Call Kananaskis Country Campgrounds, 403-591-7226, 1-866-366-2267.

Kananaskis Lakes Trail/road
Lower Lake group (year-round). Call 1-866-366-2267.
Pocaterra group (May 15–Oct 13). Call Bow Valley Park campgrounds, 403-673-2163.
Canyon (Jun 13–Sep 1)
Elkwood (May 15–Sep 1)

Boulton Creek (May 2–Oct 13)
Lower Lake (May 15–Sep 15)
Mt. Sarrail (Jun 20–Sep 1)
Interlakes (May 15–Oct 13)
For all of the above call Kananaskis Country Campgrounds, 403-591-7226, 1-866-366-2267.

Elk Lakes Provincial Park
Park entrance next to the parking lot.

Hwy. 742 (Smith-Dorrien/Spray Trail)
Buller Mountain, a winter-only campground, is presently closed. Call 403-673-3985.

BACKCOUNTRY CAMPING

For official sites you need permits costing $8 per person plus a $10 maintenance fee plus GST. Children under 16 are free, but still require a permit. Permits can be picked up from the Barrier Lake and Peter Lougheed information centres. The easiest way is to phone 403-678-3136, give them your Visa or MasterCard number and ask them to fax or email the permit to you or tell them you'll pick up the permit en route. In Alberta the number is toll free. Dial 310-0000 first. It will have occurred to you that backcountry camping can cost considerably more than highway-accessible camping.

Random camping is not allowed in provincial parks and provincial recreation areas. Outside of these areas you can camp almost anywhere except in a few areas which are regulated as follows: random permitted with permit, restricted random with no access Apr 15–Sep 30, no random camping and no access Dec 15–Jun 15, bivouac random Apr 15–Sep 30, bivouac random Apr 15–Sep 30 but with no access Dec 15–Jun 15. Confused? Contact an information centre for clarification.

Off Hwy. 40
Jewel Bay, regular and equestrian (Jun 16–Apr 14), **Ribbon Falls** (May 16–Nov 30), **Ribbon Lake** (May 16–Nov 30), **Lillian Lake** (late Jun–Nov 3), **Elbow Lake** (Jun 15–Nov 30).

Off Kananaskis Lakes Trail/road
Point, Forks, Three Isle Lake, **Turbine Canyon, Aster Lake**.

In Elk Lakes Provincial Park
Lower Elk Lake, Pétain Creek, Pétain Basin (bivouac). Cost is $5 per person per night. Children under 16 go free. Pay at the Elk Lakes Cabin. Random camping is not allowed.

Off Hwy. 742
(Smith-Dorrien/Spray Trail)
Rummel Lake, winter only.

For up-to-date info on campsites pick up *Explore Kananaskis Country and the Ghost Area,* which is published once a year by Friends of Kananaskis Country. Copies available at all information centres in K Country and elsewhere in Alberta.

INFO

A FEW RULES

- Respect seasonal trail closures.
- No registration is necessary for overnight trips. However, registration books are available at information centres and at some trailheads.
- Respect open-fire bans. Should you wish to report a fire, telephone numbers are listed on trailhead kiosks.
- Dogs must be on a leash.
- Anglers require an Alberta or BC fishing licence.
- There are some restrictions on backcountry camping.
  See "Backcountry Camping"
- There are some restrictions for mountain bikers. Read the trail description or contact an information centre.

SEASONAL ROAD CLOSURES

Hwy. 40 between Kananaskis Lakes Trail /road and Highwood Junction is closed between Dec 1 and Jun 14. During this time, skiing, snowshoeing,walking and biking is allowed.
Valleyview Trail/road is permanently closed between Elpoca day-use area and Little Highwood Pass day-use area. Walking and biking are allowed except at specified times when the road is used as a dumping ground for road kill. Check the K Country website.

FRIENDS OF KANANASKIS COUNTRY

is a not-for-profit registered charity that works in partnership with Alberta Tourism, Parks & Recreation "for the benefit of Kananaskis Country and its visitors." See www.kananaskis.org.

VOLUNTEER TRAIL CARE GROUP

As before, K Country needs your help in maintaining selected trails. To volunteer, phone 403-678-5593 or write to trails@ kananaskis.org

CHECK THE K COUNTRY WEB SITE

Check the K Country trail report for trail conditions. Especially useful are the "Important Notes," which among other things give warnings about bear or cougar sightings and temporary trail closures. See www.Kananaskis-Country.ca.

CHECK OUR BLOG

KananaskisTrails.com is a blog site maintained by Gillean and Tony Daffern. It covers all things Kananaskis, including notification of new trails, trail changes and trail issues.

CHECK THE WEBCAMS

Webcams in this area are Barrier Lake Station and Nakiska.

USING THE BOOK

ARRANGEMENT OF TRAILS

Trails are arranged by highway and are colour coded. Refer to map on page 16.

TYPES OF TRAILS

Official Trails officially maintained by Kananaskis Country, Alberta Tourism, Parks & Recreation, and Alberta Sustainable Resources are a mix of new and old trails, logging and exploration roads, fire roads and cutlines. Expect parking lots at trailheads, biffies and the occasional picnic table. Junctions are marked with signposts of the "You are here" variety. Some trails have directional arrows or coloured markers on trees or posts. Unless the trail is equestrian, expect bridges over creeks.

Unofficial Trails are similar to the above, but sometimes have no obvious trailhead, are neither signposted nor marked in any way except perhaps, for the occasional piece of flagging, cairn or trimmed branches. Creek crossings are the norm. For the first time, this category includes trails demoted from official status.

Routes either have no trails or have long trail-less sections where you have to navigate from one intermittent game trail to another. Often there is some bushwhacking.

Scrambles can have official or unofficial trails or be routes. They range from ridge walks to gruelling uphill flogs in excess of 1000 m to the top of a mountain. You can be sure of scree, and possibly a pitch or two of easy scrambling. There may be mild exposure. Special equipment is unnecessary *in optimum conditions when the mountain is devoid of snow and the weather is good.*

HEIGHTS, HEIGHT GAINS

These are given in both metric and imperial.

RATING TRAILS

No attempt has been made to classify trails. What's difficult for one person is easy for another. It's all relative. Also coming into play is the length of a trail, its gradient, its remoteness from a trailhead, conditions underfoot and so on. Read the introductory description carefully. If you're having a horrible time, it's up to you to turn back and try something easier.

RATING TIMES

Times are dependent on too many variables—everybody chugs along at a different rate. Some will be carrying heavy packs; some people, like me, like to make frequent flower stops. And then there are the underfoot conditions to consider, the weather and so on.

- Half day, up to 3 hours
- Day, up to 6 hours
- Long day, up to 10 hours plus. (Take headlamps)
- Backpack, overnight camping.

Some of the trips are designated "bike 'n' hike" and even "paddle 'n' hike." Biking the first part of the trail can cut down the time considerably. In this way I've often squeezed a weekend trip into one day.

DISTANCES

Distances are given in kilometres. Distances shown between each segment of trail are not cumulative, but show the distance between segments.

TRAIL DESCRIPTIONS

Trail descriptions are arranged according to the character of the trail. Most trails lead to a single destination. But sometimes the destination is the springboard for further options under headings like "going farther," "making a loop," "optional descent route" etc. I sometimes describe the same mountain with different ways up and down, or an area with a number of trails or peaks radiating out from the same access. Occasionally loop trails can be extended into longer loops. Long-distance trails, rarely hiked in their entirety, are described by segment.

DIRECTIONS

Left and right refer to the direction of travel. Skier's left/right refers to descent, climber's left/right to ascent.

GRID REFERENCES & GPS RECEIVERS

Where I give grid references you can follow along on your topo map.

Maps have blue grid lines running east/ west and north/south. Each line is numbered. The first two numbers indicate the grid line forming the west boundary of the kilometre square in which your point is located, and the third number the estimated number of tenths of a kilometre your point is east of that line. The fourth and fifth numbers indicate the south boundary of the square and the last number the estimated number of tenths of a kilometre your point is north of that line.

GPS receivers are useful when bushwhacking or for finding your way back to a trail or a trailhead.

MAPS IN BOOK

Sketch maps in the text are not always to scale and serve only to clarify complex areas where you might go wrong. Maps at the back of the book are based on today's topo maps, which come in a mix of imperial and metric. Therefore, the contour intervals vary. There are also errors like missing creeks, lakes, mountains and glaciers. Because of this these maps are intended as a guide only. Still, trails and routes are marked as accurately as possible.

- Red line: a trail, official or unofficial
- Red dash: a route
- Black line: trail in other volume.
- Dashed black line: route in other volume

BUYING MAPS

Maps in the back of this book are for reference only. You need to carry a bona-fide topo map. The latest editions of Gem Trek maps come close to being the perfect maps for the area, with contour intervals at 25 m. They show grid lines, up-to-date road alignments, official trails, some unofficial trails, and major powerlines.

Government topo maps, depending on the edition, are in both imperial and metric, with contour lines at 100-foot intervals and 40-m intervals respectively (not so good). Occasionally, features like small lakes, streams, glaciers and even mountains are omitted, which leads to exciting discoveries. Generally, road alignments are corrected on maps post 1983.

Provincial Resource Base Maps from Alberta Energy & Natural Resources are updated fairly regularly and show what the other maps don't: all cutlines, all powerlines and exploration and logging roads. Unfortunately, the reality is sometimes nothing like what is shown on the map.

MAPS FOR VOLUME 1
Gem Trek
- Canmore and Kananaskis Village: scale 1:50,000, contour interval 25 m.
- Kananaskis Lakes scale 1:50,000, contour interval 25 m.

Government topo maps
Scale 1: 50,000
Contour interval 40 m.
- 82 O/3 Canmore
- 82 J/11 Kananaskis Lakes
- 82 J/14 Spray Lakes Reservoir

Contour interval 100 ft.
- 82 J/10 Mount Rae
- 82 J/15 Bragg Creek
- 82 J/6 Mount Abruzzi

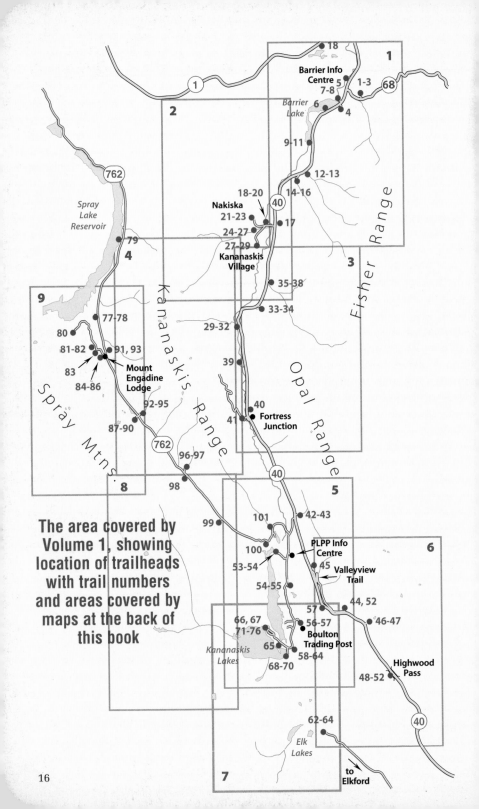

The area covered by Volume 1, showing location of trailheads with trail numbers and areas covered by maps at the back of this book

16

TRAIL DESCRIPTIONS

1 "HORTON HILL" — map 1

Short day hike
Route, then unofficial trail
Distance 1.7 km one way
Height gain 320 m (1050 ft.)
High point 1722 m (5650 ft.)
Map 82 O/3 Canmore

Access Hwy. 68 (Sibbald Creek Trail) at Lusk Creek day use-area.

"Gnarly"
"Cool"
"It took a lot of mussels to do it"

You'll have fun reading some of the comments in the summit register atop Horton Hill—the forested hill at 401562 that rises directly behind Tim Horton's Children's Ranch off Hwy. 40.

Getting to the top is not as effortless as it used to be (see TRAIL NOTE). It's a moderately steep climb up the trail-less south ridge to the saddle where you pick up the Horton Hill trail marked with yellow arrows.

HISTORY NOTE The hill was named after Miles Gilbert "Tim" Horton, a hockey hall of famer who proved there was life after hockey by founding Canada's largest coffee and doughnut franchise. After his untimely death, the Tim Horton's Children's Foundation was established to offer summer camps for underprivileged kids. This particular ranch opened in 1991.

TRAIL NOTE The Horton Hill trail starts from the ranch. But because the ranch didn't want the hiking public traipsing through their lease, they suggested another way in via a logging road which

Horton Hill (Left-most bump) from Baldy Pass trail. Going farther continues along the skyline ridge to the right.

joined the trail a third of the way up the hill. When the logging road was reclaimed in 2009, the ranch then suggested we use their disused horse trail, but unfortunately a hurricane blew through and felled a whole swath of trees over the top of it. So for now, the south ridge it is!

Sadly, the lower two-thirds of the trail is deteriorating from lack of use. A few years back the authorities deemed it too dangerous for kids, who must now use only official trails.

Summit view of cutblocks along Baldy trail north. "Midnight Peak" at centre and to its right Baldy Pass.

From the parking lot, climb up the south ridge of the hill at a place of your choosing. Wherever you start, the going is initially steep, but meadows offer incentives to stop and enjoy the fine views opening up behind you of Barrier Lake and the mountains surrounding it.

Arrive at a flat, dark-forested saddle with a little deadfall to step over. Keeping left is best. That way you'll hit the Horton Hill trail at red flagging and yellow marker.

Follow this trail as it climbs the upper south ridge past Douglas firs and through a clearing to the summit ridge. Here, turn right and come to a clearing with cairn and ammunition box enclosing the register book. Settle down and peruse the view of the Fisher Range displaying its new checkerboard look from 2008 while you also read the register. For every kid who says "I am not coming back here again" there is another for whom the mountains are a revelation.

Return the same way or try going farther along the ridge.

View of Horton Hill and Mt. Baldy (left), Barrier Lake Reservoir and Yates Mountain (right) from the grassy section of 1A.

GOING FARTHER

1A Ridge 413572

Route
Distance 2.3 km one way
Height gain 192 m (630 ft.) one way
Height loss ~37 m (120 ft.) one way
High point 1830 m (6004 ft.)

While there is not much in the way of game trails, the going is easy along the ridgeline in open forest. Some views.

From the summit ridge of Horton, drop at least 30 vertical m (100 ft.) to the col to the northwest. Search for a trail that takes you down the steepest bit onto a more moderate slope of deadfall.

The climb up the southwest ridge to 413572 is easy, long ascents through open pine forest alternating with short flat stretches of denser forest. Go as far as you want; the section of grassy ridge is a logical turnaround place. Just know the summit is enclosed in pine forest and viewless. (Going farther to Sibbald Creek makes navigating the deadfall around the col seem like a walk in the park.)

2 BALDY PASS from the north — map 1

Half-day or long day hike
Official trail with red markers, sign-
posts and interpretive signs
Distance 1.9 km to viewpoint,
9.6 km to high point of pass,
10.3 km via the Old Mill Road
Height gain 107 m (350 ft.) to viewpoint,
564 m (1850 ft.) to pass
High point 1905 m (6250 ft.)
Maps 82 O/3 Canmore, 82 J/14 Spray
Lakes Reservoir

Access Hwy. 68 (Sibbald Creek Trail) at Lusk Creek day-use area.
Also accessible from Stoney Creek Group campground via the connecting trail. Also from #9 Baldy Pass from the south at the high point. Also from Lusk Pass trail via the Lower Cutoff (see Volume 2). Also from #6, the Forest Ecology Loop.

Relatively few people walk the Baldy Pass trail from one end to the other which requires two vehicles. This is the longer, northern half which traverses miles of forest and cutblocks on logging roads of various ages and one new trail. The pass between Midnight Peak and Mt. Baldy is usually reached by hikers from the south via the very much shorter trail #9.

More often this trail is used to access the south fork of Lusk Creek (#2) and the Lusk Pass trail (see Volume 2).

TRAIL NOTE Since the third edition, a new trail built in 2009 has superseded the lower, winding section of the Old Mill Road. The first section of it masquerades as the "Kananaskis Integrated Forest Interpretive Trail" and is bound to become a popular walk, past interpretive signs explaining forest management, to an end viewpoint with benches. (Brochures are available at information centres.) The old road is still open and can be used to make a 6.1-km loop with the new trail from the parking lot.

HISTORY NOTE The route still follows in its middle part the Old Mill Road, initially bulldozed in 1951 by the Olorenshaw Logging company lusting after 300

Baldy Pass trail just after it was built in 2009. In the background is Mt. Baldy, the south summit to left.

acres of spruce at the head of Lusk Creek's south fork. Around the same time, the Forest Experiment Station (later the Forestry School for field employees, now the University of Calgary's Kananaskis Field Stations Barrier Lake Station) began a research project on the northern slope of Mt. Baldy above Lusk Creek and for a while in the road's history it became part of a driving loop to look at cutblocks called the "Lusk Creek Tour of Logging and Reforestation Areas"—similar to today's loop in the Jumpingpound. As the trees grew up the old signs fell down and the roads were closed to vehicles.

After becoming part of Kananaskis Country in 1979, the Old Mill Road was conscripted into Baldy Pass trail and for a long period in its history hikers, bikers, skiers and researchers quietly went about their business on the old roads that were gradually reverting to trails.

This all changed in the winter of 2007/08 when Spray Lakes Sawmills moved in and, in anticipation of pine beetle attack, logged a large area of 80-year-old pines, in so doing dramatically changed the landscape into a temporary parkland (if it weren't for all the slash). The mid-portion of the Old Mill road was widened and a new access road—steep and straight—was pushed up the hillside to the east of the old one. Spur roads were

built, the upper cutoff to Lusk Pass trail disappeared in a cutblock, but the lower cutoff was spared and became the new Lusk Pass trail.

By the summer of 2009 the logging roads had been reclaimed and the lower section of the Old Mill Road reopened. Then, in the fall, with the building of a new interpretive trail, the old road was demoted and is destined to disappear from all K Country maps.

To Interpretive Trail turnoff 0.8 km

From the day-use area, either follow the access road or the trail out to Hwy. 68. Turn right, cross Lusk Creek on culvert, then follow the trail up the grassy bank to the flat above, which is the site of a gravel pit. Cross a grassy track, and pass between rocks onto the truncated end of an old road that leads to the Kananaskis Field Station. Immediately keep straight on the road past an interpretive map. (To left is the old Lusk Pass hiking trail.) Farther along, a trail from Stoney Creek group campground joins in from the right at an outdated signpost. In a few metres more a splinter trail comes in from the right, and opposite this, on the left side of the road, the Baldy Pass trail takes off up the hillside. You can hardly miss the interpretive sign.

starts to Baldy Pass trail from the north

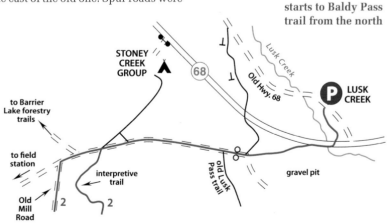

There are two ways to the junction of the trail and the Old Mill Road at 389538.

1. The Kananaskis Integrated Forest Interpretive Trail 1.9 km Initially the trail climbs through forest to a junction. Keep left. Up next is a lovely section of open ridge (new and old cutblocks, some natural meadow,) offering previously unknown views ranging from Mt. Baldy, Barrier Lake and Yates Mountain in the west across the Bow Valley to Horton Hill and Hunchback Ridge in the east. At 1.1 km the interpretive trail ends.

The Baldy Pass trail carries on climbing through more recent cutblocks, then levels off before reaching the Old Mill Road at a bend. Keep left.

2. The Old Mill Road 2.6 km Continue on the station road. Keep left at a Y- junction with a narrower track. (Right leads to the Forestry Ecology Loops #6.) At a T-junction turn left onto Old Mill Road. The road heads through aspen forest towards the precipitous north face of

Baldy Pass high point. In the background are the west and south peaks of Mt. Baldy.

Mt. Baldy. Beyond the reclaimed 2007 logging road, it steepens a little and winds up the right side of a huge cutblock. En route a researchers' trail from the field station joins in from the right. At the end of a long left-hander, you join the new trail at a right-hand bend where the gradient eases right off. Go right.

To Lusk Pass trail junction 1 km
Pass between alternating cutblocks and plantations dating back to 1972. The junction with Lusk Pass trail is marked by trail signs and notices. The Mountain Bike Alliance talks about RESPECT, which seems ironical given the surrounding devastation. Keep straight.

To South Fork of Lusk Creek 3.5 km
A minute's walk farther on keep left at a T-junction. (To right is a logging road overlying the old fire road that descends to the field station.)

A flat section of road winds between the uphill side slope and a small ridge on the left. Then it climb to a new 4-way junction in cutblocks where an old weather substation shack used to be. Go straight, then at a hiking sign turn right up a hill. You're back on the narrow old road.

The road climbs a little and turns left. As you descend to cross the south fork of Lusk Creek, you're motivated by a glimpse of the pass and Midnight Peak to its left. Climb a hill, recross the creek in a dip, then abandon the Old Mill Road, which turns left into the south fork (see #3). Keep straight on another logging road.

To Baldy Pass 2.4 km
The new road gains height quickly through mature spruce forest. From road's end, a trail traverses out left, then back right to the route's high point on the open north ridge of Midnight Peak. At a cairn you meet #9 come up from the other side.

Ahead are new views of Baldy's west peak, and the mountains of the Kananaskis Range. Looking north you can trace the trail up the south end of Baldy.

3 SOUTH FORK OF LUSK CREEK—map 1

Long day hike
Unofficial trails & route
Distance to meadows 2.5 km, 9.7 km from trailhead
Height gain 320 m (1050 ft.),
655 m (2150 ft.) from trailhead
High point 1996 m (6550 ft.)
Maps 82 J/14 Spray Lakes Reservoir, 82 J/15 Bragg Creek

Access Via #2 Baldy Pass from the north, just after the second crossing of South Lusk Creek. **Also accessible** from South Lusk Meadows in Volume 2.

The meadows of Lusk Creek's south fork are accessed via a trail with steep sections. Each point of interest builds on another: the millsite for a look around, the meadows for views, a pass leading over to Porcupine Creek, even a summit.

It's a long way in there, so it's worth considering a point to point with other trails. See Porcupine Creek (#12B), Belmore Browne Peak in Volume 2 and South Lusk Meadows in Volume 2.

View from the high point of the meadows of Boundary Ridge, showing the route onto the ridge and the route along it to peak 403471 at left.

To the mill site 1 km
Turn left and follow the last kilometre of Old Mill Road through old spruce forest to the sawmill site, a huge meadow with a confusing number of logging roads radiating out of it like the spokes in a wheel. In our exploratory wanderings we've found several artifacts, the largest a hoist with a donkey engine.

To the Meadows 1.5 km
The section with all the height gain.

The start is obscure. It's the middle of three roads heading up-valley from the sawmill site, starting neither uphill nor downhill but exactly opposite the road you came in on. It crosses the south fork at a flume and, narrowed to trail width, climbs up the left bank past a cabin and outhouse used by researchers from the Barrier Lake Field Station since 1983. Look for it in the 1984 CBC made-for-TV movie called *Ernest Thompson Seton: Keeper of the Wild*.

South fork hoist and donkey engine.

The researchers' cabin

The trail continues climbing into meadows about the watershed with a southwest fork of Jumpingpound Creek, then fades. By sheer fluke you may arrive in time to watch Martha's heli-yoga class, which, after exercising, proceeds to enjoy "a freshly prepared gourmet lunch." The whole scene has a touch of the surreal about it, not to mention a touch of "the envies" as you slump sweaty in the grass to eat your meagre offerings.

Continue up to the col, or, if not going onto Boundary Ridge and even farther afield, up to the high point of the meadows at left. Not exactly Drumheller, one would think. But amazingly enough, these innocent-looking meadows are designated a Protected Research Site by the Tyrrell Museum after Laure Maurel unearthed some petrified wood and dinosaur bones. As geological maps show, a thin band of Belly River Formation exists all along the eastern slope of the Fisher Range.

This is also where the government's Surveys & Mapping Branch made a major screw-up. Try fitting together map sheets J/14 and J/15. Just what IS the height of the col? Fortuitously, Gem Trek has it all on one map, so we'll go with their judgment.

GOING FARTHER

3A the Boundary Ridge

Scramble on unofficial trail
Distance 0.6 km
Height gain ~183 m (600 ft.) from col
High point at Boundary Ridge 2180 m (7150 ft.)

A steeper ascent up scree to Boundary Ridge puts you in position to descend into Porcupine Creek and to go for peak 403471. You may find yourselves rubbing shoulders with guided heli-hikers who for a cool half-thousand bucks get to do both of these things after departing their helicopter in the meadow.

From the col head up to the right in meadow to the base of a long wall of grey rock marking the spine of the Fisher Range. Hereabouts, the wall's only about 75 m at its low point and well broken up. Find the game trail that climbs from right to left past a tree island, and on past a solitary tree to gain the ridge at about 402482 (cairn).

Anyone going to Porcupine Creek (see # 12, 12B) should head north along the ridge a bit to where lower-angle slopes sweep down into the northeast fork.

3B Peak 403471

Scramble
Distance 1 km from ridge
Height gain from ridge 262 m (860 ft.)
High point 2441 m (8010 ft.)

Don't let the opportunity to bag an easy peak slip by, especially one that figures so prominently in views from Hwys. 1 and 68 and Powderface Trail the road. It is, therefore, odd that this is the only peak in the area to remain just a number.

From both north and south this big heap of a mountain is an easy climb that enables you to connect at the top with other easy peaks to the south. (Most often 403471 is climbed in combination with Belmore Browne Peak. See Volume 2.)

Simply head south along the Boundary Ridge and on scree and rubble walk up the broad and moderately inclined northeast ridge to the summit cairn. Easy!

Who would guess this peak looks so spectacular from the west? Check it out from trails #10, 11 and 12.

Boundary Ridge, looking north.

Boundary Ridge. Looking south towards peak 403471, climbed by the easy left-hand ridge. Peeking above the ridge is Belmore Browne Peak.

4 BARRIER LAKE FORESTRY TRAILS—map 1

Half day hike
Official trail
Distance 2.5 km of biggest loop
Height gain 40 m (130 ft.)
High point 1417 m (4650 ft.)
Map 82 O/3 Canmore

The eighth guard tower during its time as a fire lookout on what is now Prairie View trail.

Access Hwy. 40 (Kananaskis Trail). Just south of Barrier Dam Road turn onto James Cragg Road. Turn first left into the Veteran's Loop parking lot. If that is full, turn second left into the Colonel's Cabin parking lot.

Two interpretive loops—the Forestry Ecology Loop and the Forestry Loop—can be joined to make one enjoyable forest walk. There's plenty of interpretive signage to read. There are also 18 numbered signs that are explained in booklets produced by the University of Calgary's Barrier Lake Field Station and available May to November from the two kiosks and from the front of the Colonel's Cabin. The trails are open year-round, but the 76-year-old cabin is currently closed to the public.

Amazingly, the one trail is also part of the Trans Canada Trail (TCT), in that it connects the Baldy Pass trail to Barrier Dam and the ongoing Prairie View trail. But only for walkers.

HISTORY NOTE The Dominion's Forest Experiment Station opened in 1934 and was accessed by the fledgling Hwy. 40. (See #18 Stoney trail.) Shortly after, during the Second World War, it became POW Camp #130 for alien internees, Canadian conscientious objectors and prisoners of war. (See #44 Opal traverse.) After the war the bunkhouses were moved to serve as youth hostels up and down the Icefields Parkway and the eighth guard tower was taken onto McConnell Ridge, painted white and renamed Pigeon Lookout. (See #7 Prairie View.) After 1952 the station returned to its original purpose for the most part and today is used for research and educational purposes.

On the Forestry Ecology Loop.

ANTICLOCKWISE

From just beyond the Veteran's Loop parking lot a trail heads right past a kiosk to a T-junction of sorts. (To the right a trail leads to the History Loop, which includes the Colonel's Cabin and the eighth guard tower, now painted grey.)

Turn left. Pass another kiosk, then go straight at a 4-way junction marked with a TCT sign. Cross Barrier Creek by bridge to a T-junction, then turn immediately right.

The trail climbs through a mixed forest of lodgepole pine, white spruce, Douglas fir, aspen and Scots pine from Sweden. Interestingly, the pine were planted in the 1940s, and though thriving, their seeds don't ever germinate. Just after sign 09 turn right on a narrower trail that crosses a track (old road) onto the smaller loop.

Wander through a grove of Norway spruce to the shelter at the far end of the loop, where you can stop for a rest. Then continue on past the hole (soil exhibit), recross the track and climb up to the big loop. Turn right.

After an initial climb, pass the site of a viewing platform (the trees grew up) and meander along and downhill to a junction. Detour right to a viewpoint for McConnell Ridge and Yates Mountain, where you learn about what trees grow where. Return to the main trail and turn

right down a hill which deposits you back at the Barrier Creek T-junction. Cross the bridge and return the same way you came to the parking lot.

4A TCT Connector

EAST TO WEST

As mentioned, this is the route for walkers. (Bikers must use the station roads. It hasn't been determined yet where equestrians can go.).

Drop off Baldy Pass trail to the old road and turn left. After a few minutes of walking turn right onto a narrower track. At an intersecting trail (the connector between the two loops) turn left. At the following T-junction turn left and follow the south leg of the big loop out to the T-junction beside the bridge over Barrier Creek. Most people continue straight ahead on a trail, so missing out on the beautifully constructed stepping stones of the official route. The trail curves around right up a grassy draw below the high bank and up to Hwy. 40 beyond the guard rail. Walk left down the highway a short way, then turn right and follow Barrier Lake Road to the parking lot near Barrier Dam.

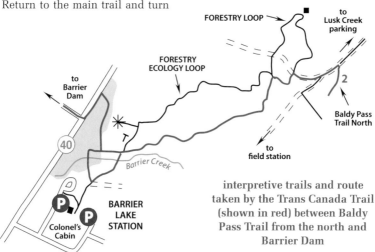

interpretive trails and route taken by the Trans Canada Trail (shown in red) between Baldy Pass Trail from the north and Barrier Dam

5 WIDOWMAKER TRAIL and on—map 1

Half day
Official and unofficial trails
Distance from Access 1 to 4, 4 km via banktop trail
Height gain N-S 46 m (150 ft.)
Map 82 O/3 Canmore

An interesting part of the trail barely above the slalom course.

Access Hwy. 40 (Kananaskis Trail)
1. Canoe Meadows day-use area.
2. Barrier Lake Information Centre. From the parking lots an access trail leads down towards the river.
3. Widowmaker day-use area opposite Hwy. 68.
4. Barrier Lake Dam parking lot via Barrier Lake Rd.

An easy riverside walk along the east bank of the Kananaskis River with lots of viewpoints and picnic tables. The walk is short enough that returning the same way is feasible. The official trail runs between accesses 1 and 3. An unofficial trail carries on to Access 4 at Barrier Dam.

The bed of the Kananaskis River below Barrier Dam has been almost completely reconstructed, first by TransAlta Utilities, and then by the Alberta Whitewater Association and members (i.e., the LKRUA and the ARSA, the Alberta government, and Lafarge Canada, who donated rocks) to create a playground for whitewater enthusiasts. Refashioning the bed is an ongoing activity, with enhancements to rapids and the creation of eddies, ledges and holes—all of which has to be done at low water. You thought building a trail was difficult?

So there's plenty to watch on a weekend: novice canoeists dumping in the water, kayakers and river surfers playing in the waves, rafters floating by—but ONLY when TransAlta turns on the tap. High water is guaranteed during slalom competitions held the last weekend in May and in the middle of September, although at such times the car park at Canoe Meadows is likely to be full. For competition dates see the web site of the Alberta Whitewater Association.

NORTH TO SOUTH

Access 1 to Access 2, ~1.2 km
The usual route follows the banktop, the more exciting route the 2009 trail alongside the river built for competition watching. Both starts can be combined to make a short loop. See the sketch map.

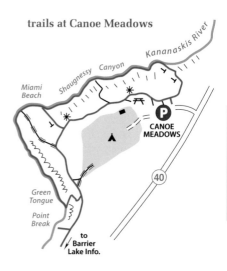

trails at Canoe Meadows

1. Banktop trail From the first parking stalls on the right side of the parking lot follow a short trail out to the banktop and turn left. Be sure to visit a couple of fenced viewpoints looking down on Shaugnessy Canyon and the slalom course. A trail from the end of the parking lot (rock) joins in from the left. Pass a trail heading down the bank. On your left is the camping area in a large meadow. On your right is another viewpoint and another trail down the bank. Keep straight.

In an opening with gravel pile and Atco trailer come to a 4-way-junction with a wide gravel track. Go straight on the trail that follows the fenceline above a crag. (The track to right leads down to Cartwheel Corner. The track to left leads to the camping meadow.)

Join a wider trail (an offshoot of the gravel track) and turn right down a slight hill. On your right a stepped trail leads down to the top of the slalom course. This is the way up from the riverside trail.

2. Riverside trail From the first parking stalls on the right side of the parking lot take the short trail out to the banktop and turn right. Descend into Shaugnessy Canyon at the end of the slalom course opposite Otter Slide. Turn left and follow a narrow twisting trail below a steep, sometimes craggy bank to Miami Beach, which is the shingle flat level with Miami Hole. En route pass a memorial plaque and two access trails climbing to the banktop trail.

A few metres on is Cartwheel Corner, where the river turns left and a gravel track comes in down the bank. Continue on the riverside trail as it edges below a crag past the well-named Green Tongue rapid and its wavy outflow Green Gullet. At the beginning of the slalom course, just downstream of Point Break surfing feature, climb steps up the bank to the bank-top trail. Turn right.

Green Tongue

The trail follows the banktop around the right-hand bend. (En route a side trail leads to the crag overlooking Point Break.) Then it moves a little inland for a longer stretch of damp forest with boardwalk. Come to a T-junction. Keep straight. (The rising trail to left leads to Barrier Lake Information Centre parking lots.)

Access 2 to Access 3 1.1 km

Shortly the trail descends, crosses a side creek and enters wolf willow alley on a flat alongside the river. The second picnic table to right is level with the tricky Santa Claus rapid.

At the next junction keep right and cross Lusk Creek on a footbridge. Shortly after is an acrobatic crossing of an overflow channel on one plank. Keep right on the far side and climb the bank. A little farther along is a slightly dicey overlook above a cliff for Hollywood Hole. Descend and keep straight (picnic area to right down steps) into Widowmaker day-use area parking lot, which was the site of Lusk Creek Cabin. The rapid a little upstream is Widowmaker.

Access 3 to Access 4 1.7 km

The route continues from the far side of the parking lot beyond a gate. Pass a put-in trail) below Widowmaker and continue on unofficial, unsigned track through flat forest. After passing a flow monitor cable strung across the river, the track turns left around a river bend and descends mounds of shale to an open flat. To your left rises a line of high crags; to your right the river is squeezed in a narrow, rocky channel with signs everywhere warning of fluctuating water levels. The track narrows to trail and you push through a stretch of willow bushes and cross a side creek below two waterfalls tumbling down wet, gravelly banks covered in mounds of yellow saxifrage. Come to Barrier substation 325, out of which spouts the Kananaskis River. Pass behind the fenced-off buildings and join the access road from Barrier Dam. Turn left.

On road, cross the spillway, then curve up left to reach the road (Prairie View trail) to the left of the dam. Turn left and follow it out past a gate into Barrier Dam day-use area.

Kananaskis River in a narrow channel below Barrier Dam. Mt. Baldy behind.

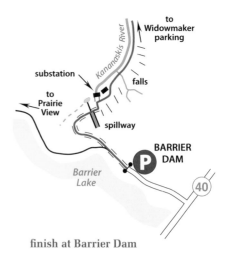

finish at Barrier Dam

#5. Trail in forest near Barrier Lake Information Centre.

#5. One of the waterfalls near Barrier substation 325.

#6. Barrier Lake Reservoir from the summit of the hill. Looking towards G8 Summits at left and Mary Barclay's Mountain at right.

6 BARRIER LAKE interpretive trail—map 1

Half day hike
Official trail
Distance 2.2 km
Height gain 61 m (200 ft.)
Height loss 122 m (400 ft.)
High point 1509 m (4950 ft.)
Map 82 O/3 Canmore

Access Hwy. 40 (Kananaskis Trail) at Barrier Lake day-use area. After leaving Hwy. 40, keep straight at a T-junction and drive to the interpretive trail parking lot located in a gap between your hill and a slightly higher hill to the northwest.

This trail has two parts to it. A short climb to a craggy hilltop and a descent to Barrier Lake. Unless you retrace your steps or walk along paved access roads there is no good way to get back to your starting point. Best to get non-hiking friends whose idea of a good day is a loll on the beach to drop you off and say you'll join them later.

map showing final section of
trail to Barrier Lake beach

Up the Hill 1 km return
The trail starts from the far end of the parking lot on the loop road. Climb steps to a view point above a grassy strip that was the site of old Hwy. 40.

From here the trail winds up the west side of the hill under a canopy of aspens, which the Barrier Lake info centre calls "the Bride's Arch." On reaching open slopes of kinnikinnick and juniper, the trail turns right and heads to the rocky top overlooking Hwy. 40.

Look across the highway to Mt. Baldy, née Barrier Mountain, née Sleeping Buffalo Mountain. Maybe they'll be climbers on Barrier Bluffs. To the north is Horton Hill in line with the highway. The calendar view, though, is southwards along Barrier Lake to "G8 Summits." Who would think that such a small hill would be such a good viewpoint?

Return to the parking lot.

To Barrier Lake Beach 1.2 km
The trail leaves the west side of the parking lot at the biffy. Immediately turn right (picnic area to left) and descend to Barrier Lake through a pleasant forest of pine and aspen. As you wind above the lake shore past picnic tables, keep straight twice. (Trails to right lead to parking lots.)

The trail then turns right into an inlet and splits. Turn left. (The trail ahead leads to another parking lot.) Walk down the boat launch ramp, then step off left onto a beach of pale yellow sand for a spot of R & R.

Across the lake you can see Barrier Dam and the route taken by Prairie View trail to McConnell Ridge. To the west look through the gap of Jewell Creek to Grant MacEwan Peak.

7 PRAIRIE VIEW TRAIL—map 1

Day hike
Official trail with signposts
Distance 7.7 km one way
Height gain E-W 500 m (1640 ft.)
Height loss E-W 240 m (790 ft.)
High point 1875 m (6150 ft.)
Map 82 O/3 Canmore

Access Hwy. 40 (Kananaskis Trail) at Barrier Dam day-use area reached via Barrier Lake Rd.
Also accessible from #8 Jewell Pass trail and #18 Stoney trail, and from Quaite Creek trail in Volume 3.

A very popular trail with one steep section that connects Barrier Dam day-use area to Jewell Pass via McConnell Ridge. Most obviously the trail can be part of a 14.5 km circuit from Barrier Dam incorporating #8, Jewell Pass trail. If you want to be surprised by the surprise view, hike the loop clockwise.

More popular than the loop is the foray from the trail's high point to Barrier Lake Lookout atop Yates Mountain—an irresistible objective from either Barrier Lake or Quaite Creek via Jewell Pass.

HISTORY NOTE The first part of the route is a fire road that once accessed Pigeon Lookout (see #4). Perhaps many of you remember the white fire tower, even sat on its steps to eat lunch. In 1984, made redundant a year earlier by Barrier Lake Lookout, it was taken down to the Colonel's Cabin, painted grey and stocked with artifacts. The lookout that first saw service as guard tower 8 at POW Camp 130 in the early 1940s had returned to its birthplace. The name caused an immense amount of confusion with hikers during its 24 years—Pigeon Lookout is *not* on Pigeon Mountain. Ruthie believes the name alluded to stool pigeons.

The last lap to McConnell Ridge.
To right is Yates Mountain.

Barrier Dam to Stoney trail 1.9 km

Access the gravel road beyond the gate by a trail from the parking lot. Keep left (the descending road to right leads to Barrier substation) and cross Barrier Lake Dam.

At the far end, cross under a powerline, then in a reclaimed meadow follow either the road or a trail to its right up a hill. At the top is a intersecting powerline right-of-way with signpost. Go straight. (To left is Jewel Pass trail.)

Continue uphill for another 300 m to a T-junction with Stoney trail, which is a stony powerline access road. Turn right, then straightaway left on what used to be called the Pigeon Lookout fire road.

To McConnell Ridge 3.7 km

Closeted in trees, the fire road winds uphill in easy zigs with shortcuts not worth taking. At the end of the 11th and final zig turn left onto the northeast ridge. It's here, at the bend, where the unsigned Lookout trail from Camp Chief Hector joins in from the right (see Volume 3).

The road continues up the ridge and ends at a levelling above meadows sloping south, a popular rest spot with a view of Barrier Lake. The flat to your right, between the road and the trees, was the site

of Pigeon Lookout. Near the site and on the same side of the road are some Stoney prayer flags.

A trail carries on along the ridge, then makes a short, steep climb, zigging left, right and up a rocky step below a TransAlta repeater station. (Note shortcuts and deviations.) Keep left of the station to an arrow sign on McConnell Ridge—the trail's high point. Just beyond is the surprise viewpoint at the top of a cliff. Pose a friend on the edge and you have yourself a great pic with Barrier Lake and Mt. Baldy in the background.

McConnell Ridge to Jewell Pass 2.1 km

Another arrow points the way down a badly eroded ridge above the line of crags Watch for marmots doing sentry duty on the rocks. At a low point, the trail turns right into the trees and it's here where the very much better shortcut from the lookout trail joins in from the right.

Now heading northwest, you make a gradual descent into the pine forest of Jewell Pass. Come to a 5-way junction with signpost. Left is Jewell Pass trail, second right is Quaite Creek trail.

McConnell Ridge viewpoint. Looking southeast to Barrier Lake Reservoir and Mt. Baldy.

OPTION

Chip at the lookout.

7A Barrier Lake Lookout

Unofficial trail
Distance 1.2 km return to Prairie View
Height gain 125 m (410 ft.)
High point 1996 m (6550 ft.)

Who can resist a detour to the high point of McConnell Ridge (Yates Mountain) for the view of the prairies, finally, and for a chance to say hello to the lookout. A short, steep trail.

NAMING NOTE The Stoney name of Tokyapebi îpa, meaning "lookout point for Blackfeet," is very apt. Its English name of Yates Mountain comes from Emily Yates, who ran the Diamond Cross ranch located on the site of today's Camp Chief Hector, seen down below to the right of Chilver Lake.

After passing the repeater station turn right (northwest) on a faint trail, which becomes clear as you climb up the broad forested ridge. The first section is very steep, then the gradient eases right off. Go either way at a split: left on a scree trail, or right along the ridge-top above a deepening cliff. After they join, one uphill burst gains you the summit, a big open area of grass and rocks.

Since the last edition the summit has had several important additions and now sports a helipad, shed, private biffy, two wireless masts, a brightly coloured wind sock, a Stevenson screen, blobs of cement inscribed "pilot mistake #1," "pilot mistake #2" et al., and a pink flamingo.

To save asking, the fencing above the big north-facing cliff—the Diamond X Face—is not to stop people falling off, but to protect nesting prairie falcons from rocks being kicked off by the hordes straining for a bird's-eye view of the prairies.

In 2002 the summit offered a grandstand view of another kind: the arrival by helicopter of US president George W. Bush into the Kananaskis Valley for the G8 Summit, *were you allowed up there*. Lookout Chip McCullough was designated head of security on the summit and all known trails to the top had security forces stationed at the bottom to stop people from hiking up. It seems security never read the guidebook, though, because on this momentous day "the summit was crowded with gawking kids" come up the connector trail from Camp Chief Hector!

DESCENT NOTE Anyone bound for Jewel Pass can take the shortcut trail that leaves the right side of the lookout trail just above the repeater station.

35

8 JEWELL PASS — map 1

Day hike, paddle 'n' hike
Official trail with signposts
Distance 6.8 km one way
Height gain 259 m (850 ft.)
High point 1631 m (5350 ft.)
Map 82 O/3 Canmore

Access Hwy. 40 (Kananaskis Trail) at Barrier Dam day-use area on Barrier Lake Rd.
Also accessible from #7 Prairie View trail, #18 Stoney trail and from Quaite Creek trail in Volume 3.

As a destination, Jewell Pass isn't up to much, although the walking is pleasant enough. Most people use this trail in combination with Prairie View (#7) to make a 13.2 km loop. This trail also connects the Kananaskis Valley to the Bow Valley via the trail in Quaite Creek Valley.

It's a two-parter. The least interesting first section of under-the-powerlines walking can be avoided by a quick paddle across Barrier Lake from the boat launch at Barrier Lake day-use area. Aim for Jewell Bay, where a short stint right on Stoney trail sees you at section two in a few minutes. The second section is a forest walk alongside Jewell Creek with a few steepish hills.

See the sketch map under #18.

Barrier Dam to Stoney trail 3.9 km
The first part of the route is shared with Prairie View trail.

Access the gravel road beyond the gate by a trail from the parking lot. Keep left (the descending road to right leads to Barrier substation) and cross Barrier Lake Dam.

At the far end cross under a powerline, then in a reclaimed meadow follow either the road or a trail to its right up a hill. At the top is a signed 4-way intersection with a powerline right-of-way. Turn left on the track under the powerlines. (Ahead is Prairie View trail.)

The track, running parallel to the northwest shore of Barrier Lake reservoir, winds and undulates a little to a T-junction with signpost. Go straight on a fainter track. (The track to right leads to Stoney trail.)

Very shortly is another junction. Keep straight on a trail. (The track to left ends under the water of Driftwood Bay.)

The trail dipsy-doodles above the bay in meadows offering views of the lake and Mt. Baldy. At an unsigned trail junction keep right and walk under powerlines to a junction with Stoney trail (gravel powerline access road) at a hiking sign. Turn left.

The road rises through trees past the God is Love boulders, then descends a little to a signed junction at 347542. Turn right onto a trail. (The road continuing ahead is Stoney trail. Only 200 m distant across Jewell Creek bridge lies Jewell Bay backcountry campground.)

To Jewell Pass 2.9 km
The trail crosses the powerline right-of-way and follows a terrace above Jewell Creek a short way before dropping into the lodgepole pine forest of the valley bottom. Climb alongside the creek to the first bridge. Cross and continue more easily to a second bridge at the forks. Just before, a side trail on the left side leads to Jewell Falls up the left fork. Visit after rain or runoff; at other times it dries to a trickle.

Return to the main trail and cross the second bridge. Shortly the trail zigs steeply up the right bank, then settles in for a long, easy jaunt through pines to Jewell Pass. A 5-way junction with signpost indicates the spot in the trees.

Prairie View trail heads off to the immediate right. Quaite Creek trail is second left. The other two are logging roads. In this area Bud Jewell had the lease to log Douglas firs still standing after a fire.

#8. Jewell Falls after rain.

#8. Jewell Pass in the trees.

*#9. Looking up to the high point of Baldy Pass trail from the pass.
At upper right rises the north ridge of "Midnight Peak."*

9 BALDY PASS FROM THE SOUTH—map 1

Day hike
Official trail with signposts, red markers & posts
Distance 4.1 km to pass,
4.3 km to high point
Height gain 487 m (1600 ft.)
High point 1905 m (6250 ft.)
Map 82 J/14 Spray Lakes Reservoir

Usual Access Hwy. 40 (Kananaskis Trail). At 10.3 km south of the K Country boundary, turn right (west) into the signed Baldy Pass parking lot.
Also accessible from #2 Baldy Pass from the north and from #15 the Wasootch-Baldy connector.

This forest trail up an unnamed valley is the usual hiking route to Baldy Pass, which is located between Midnight Peak and the long southeast ridge of Mt. Baldy. It is considerably shorter than route #2 from the north, and leaves time for a little ridge wandering. (See also the next two entries, #10 and #11.) Carry water.

The trail starts from the opposite (east) side of the highway at the sign.

For the first 700 m head though trees to a 4-way junction with red markers and a sign. Turn left. (The logging road straight ahead is route #15 to Wasootch Creek parking lot. The logging road to right leads out to the highway south of the parking lot and is still available to hikers who wish to shave off 100 m.)

Your logging road, gradually dwindling to trail, leads into an unnamed valley confined between the west peak of Baldy and the west ridge of Midnight Peak. The going is flat at first and the valley bottom wide and stoney with poplars growing in the creek bed. At posts, cross the creekbed to the right bank.

In mossy spruce forest with rotting log piles the valley narrows to a V. After passing the scree slopes of West Baldy,

the trail steepens as you climb across the steep south slope of the valley to the pass. Through the trees are occasional glimpses of the South Peak of Baldy and its south ridge. Higher up you cross two avalanche slopes, the second occurring five minutes before the watershed is reached at a cairn. Barely rising above the trees, the pass offers only marginal views.

It pays to continue up the trail for another 200 m, climbing 40 vertical m up the open ridge to the south to another cairn marking the trail's high point where it slips over onto the north slope. This is a far superior viewpoint for the Mt. Baldy massif — you can trace the trail up the south end of Baldy described in #11, and look back through the V of the valley to Mary Barclay's mountain. Nearer at hand rises the grossly foreshortened north ridge of Midnight Peak described in the next entry.

Below the screes of West Baldy.

10 "MIDNIGHT PEAK" — map 1

Day scramble
Intermittent trails, routes
High point 2332 m (7650 ft.)
Map 82 J/14 Spray Lakes Reservoir

Midnight Peak from the south peak of Baldy. The photo shows almost the entire north ridge route at left, and the route to the upper north- west ridge (facing) via the vegetated strip of grass and small trees. The west ridge follows the right-hand skyline over the rock step.

Access Via #9 Baldy Pass from the south at the trail's high point.
Also accessible from #15 the Wasootch-Baldy connector.

This is the dark-coloured mountain to the south of Baldy Pass, at 380492. From the trail's high point there are two obvious routes to the summit: the very loose north ridge and the much more solid variation up the northwest ridge. Combine them to make a small loop, or a longer loop if you take the shortcut descent off #10B. My pref- erence is to descend the long west ridge, which prolongs the enjoyment of being up high and makes a loop of about 9.1 km.

Technically, all routes are about the same easy standard of scrambling: mod- erately steep slopes of scree and broken rock with no exposure. A GPS is useful for finding the correct way off the west ridge.

NAMING NOTE Its unofficial name comes courtesy of Art Davis, who led a group of Rocky Mountain Ramblers up to its top on October 21, 1973. Attempting to find another way down, they got hung up above cliffs and didn't get back to their cars until midnight.

10A North Ridge

Distance 0.9 km
Height gain 427 m (1400 ft.) from high point of pass, 914 m (3000 ft.) from trailhead

From the high point on Baldy Pass trail, continue up the broad north ridge of your mountain, navigating through trees and glades to the right of a rocky knoll. There's a bit of a trail.

At the steepening above treeline, climb the rather shapeless ridge separating the moderately inclined north face seamed with shallow gullies and the much scarier east face to left. Low down, unstable rocks in the dark grey zone are ankle breakers, but conditions improve once you start encountering broken-up rock bands fixed solidly to the ground. Sooner or later you'll reach the summit ridge, which is long and narrow. A cairn with a pole marks the high point.

The view is incredible in every direction. Standouts are the three peaks of Mt. Baldy to the north. Of more immediate interest to scramblers is the slightly higher summit to the southeast that is yoked to Midnight by a seductively curving ridge that takes half an hour to negotiate. Some wits call the peak "Half Past Midnight." For me it's more likely to be "Quarter to One."

10B Northwest Ridge

Distance 1.3 km
Height gain 427 m (1400 ft.) from high point of pass, 914 m (3000 ft.) from trailhead

Start off along the north ridge. When about level with the rocky knoll head right to the central gully that splits the seamed north face. Because it's steep-sided at this point, head up the left side of it and cross it ABOVE a slabby step.

Next, choosing whatever line appeals, climb out of the basin onto the northwest ridge via grassy ribs with outcrops to manoeuvre around.

The ridge is narrower than one might guess. Scree falls away from the right side, but the ridge itself is a solid staircase of grass and rock that is easy to plod up. You top out at the west end of the summit ridge and must walk left to reach the cairn.

Shortcut descent to Baldy Pass trail
Descend off the northwest ridge into the basin the same way you went up. Do not cross the central gully. Instead continue north. Ahead is a treed ridge. Wend left between the trees and the northwest ridge into a low-angled scree gully cum creekbed that is easy to follow down to its intersection with the Baldy Pass trail. Alternatively, stay in the trees on the right side of the creekbed.

The easy northwest ridge. Note people walking along the summit ridge.

The step on the West Ridge can be avoided by slipping through the gap to its left.

OPTIONAL RETURN

10C West Ridge

Distance 3 km to intersection with #9
Height loss 930 m (3050 ft.)

From the summit, walk west along the summit ridge past the northwest ridge turnoff and descend the rubbly west ridge. On the second, steeper drop, a few slabs near the top can be circumnavigated by a trail on the right side that winds all the way down to an orange shale col.

Ahead is the up step. When seen in profile from Baldy Pass trail in the valley below, this rockband appears to present a problem. But it's really an imposter, and while you can scramble safely over the top, you can also sneak around the left side.

A little farther along, the ridge bends left, then back right. Here a really good game trail leaves the crest and traverses the right flank down into trees at col no. 1.

Hike over a bump to col no. 2 with fire circle, then ascend to 369490. This is where you drop off the end and lose almost 610 m (2000 ft.) in one fell swoop. Whatever you do, don't follow the logical extension of the ridge to the left. Besides being boobytrapped with cliffs, the southwest ridge is not the direction you wish to

go. Your route is the northwest rib at the demarcation of the north and west slopes, which lower down curves more to the west. Looked at it from Hwy. 40, it's the partially grassy rib to the left of the gully.

After an easy start the going becomes progressively steeper and rockier, until a third of the way down you reach the white pinnacles at a narrowing. Thread together pieces of trail on the left side. Below this the gradient gradually eases and the rocks dwindle to small areas of talus on a predominantly grassy slope.

Where trees brush right across the rib there are two ways to reach official trails at the bottom of the slope:

1. Simply bash on down through open pine forest to intersect the Wasootch/Baldy connector. Turn right and some time later come to the 4-way junction with Baldy Pass trail. Go straight.

2. Follow a cutline at 2 o'clock down through open pine forest to Baldy Pass trail, which you meet a little way up from the 4-way junction. Turn left. NOTE Should you be going up this way, deadfall obscures the bottom end of the cutline.

Looking up at The Tower, which is climbed direct. To its left is the south end of Baldy.

Looking back down from the shoulder to the ridge extending to the south end of Baldy.

Crossing rocky humps en route to the steepening. A trail in scree climbs below the crest on the left side to the prominent shoulder.

11 SOUTH PEAK OF BALDY — map 1

Day scramble
Unofficial trail
Distance 2.1 km from pass,
6.2 km from trailhead
Height gain 344 m (1130 ft.) from pass,
771 m (2530 ft.) from trailhead
High point 2158 m (7080 ft.)
Maps 82 J/14 Spray Lakes Reservoir,
82 O/3 Canmore

Access Via #9 Baldy Pass from the south at the actual pass.

The south summit of the Mt. Baldy massif at 372519 is gained from Baldy Pass via its long south ridge—an enjoyable ridgewalk with one scramble step. Of course, there is the odd steep section and some scree, but a trail makes things easy. Nearly half-way along, the south end of Baldy is the perfect stopping place for those who want to call it a day.

Descending The Tower.

To the south end of Baldy. 0.9 km
Starting from the cairn at the pass, a good trail winds up the pine-sprinkled ridge to the north. At the top of the first and longest rise the ridge narrows. The trail stays right of the first rocky step. Next up is "The Tower" with orange screes leading up to its base. Arriving at the rock, DO NOT follow the trail that traverses right above a steep gully. DO scramble up diagonally left.

Descend the far side of the tower to a gap, then climb in zigs to the south end of Baldy at 2082 m (6830 ft.). Cairn.

Behind is Midnight Peak displaying its various ascent and descent routes, and ahead the South Peak of Baldy. Who can resist?

To the South Peak of Baldy 1.2 km
The ridge descends into trees (small hiatus at a low point), then rises slightly over a series of rocky humps which can be taken direct. After a flat section the ridge steep-ens, stacking up in great rocky steps that look a little imposing. Bypassing the rock is very easy. Just don't be lured onto the right side of the ridge by a trail. Follow the scree trail that runs below the crest ON THE LEFT SIDE. Higher up, it wriggles up a short scree slope to a shoulder on the skyline. Above it the ground lies back, and it's an easy walk up grass and stones to the summit cairn above eastern cliffs.

Into sight comes the rocky head of Mt. Baldy—only 34 m higher—and the whole of the scramble route in profile. For hikers, going for the main summit is easily resisted when you know it's a difficult scramble from this side. The same applies to the West Peak of Baldy off to the west.

Without doubt the most depressing view of the whole day is of cutblocks to the east, their vast extent finally revealed from this high vantage point.

Return the same way.

12 PORCUPINE CREEKS—map 1

The dry mid section of the southeast fork.

Long day hikes, backpack
Unofficial trails & routes, many creek
crossings
Maps 82 J/14 Spray Lakes Reservoir,
82 J/15 Bragg Creek

Access Hwy. 40 (Kananaskis Trail). Park at
Porcupine Creek bridge.
Also accessible from #15 the Wasootch/
Baldy connector. The north fork is accessible
from #3A South Fork of Lusk Creek at Bound-
ary Ridge.

Both forks of Porcupine Creek are popular
with adventurers wanting to get off the
beaten track. As a bonus, several ridges
and tops are available for scramblers,
including Porcupine Ridge (#13). For
mountains far back, take a tent; nothing is
as maddening as finding yourself within
150 m of an attainable summit when time
runs out. At runoff, creek crossings may
require a paddle.

To the Forks 1.3 km
Step out along a gravelly road on the
left (northeast) bank of Porcupine Creek.
Cross the Wasootch/Baldy connector,
and on trail continue along the left bank.
Shortly after scrambling around the bottom of two small crags (Hyperion and
Blind Man's Bluff), you reach the forks at
a fire circle. Through the gap of the northeast fork is a rare view of peak 403471
displaying its spectacular west ridge.

12A Southeast Fork

Distance 5.2 km from forks
Height gain 317+ m (1040+ ft.)
High point 1722+ m (5650+ ft.)

An easy walk between Porcupine and Wasootch ridges. For the most part the valley
floor is flat and wide, dead-ending in cul

de sacs below the main axis of the Fisher Range. Several scramble peaks are available as well as a high col over to Wasootch Creek at 384431.

Just above the forks, a trail crosses the northeast fork and gets you started along the left bank of the southeast fork.

The valley is typical of the eastern slopes: wide floors of arid dryas mats alternating with woody narrows with running water. Farther in, densely forested side slopes on the left give way to lighter sprinklings of trees and grass which lure you onto the unnamed summit east of Porcupine Ridge. But only if you have time...

It's here at the most scenic part of the valley at 384442 that 90% of people turn around and go back. If you've brought along a tent, it's good to know there's always water around this point.

The upper valley 1.7 km

Upstream of 384442 the main valley curves round to the left and narrows. Cross and recross the creek. After passing the stony side creek on the left at 396445, you hit an obstacle: a long and impenetrable canyon with waterfalls. To circumvent, get onto the left-hand bank just after the side creek and climb diagonally through trees to a forested notch about 130 vertical m higher up at 400444, where you can pick up ticks in September and the change fallen out of Tony's pocket. Don't all rush at once; it was only a dollar's worth.

From the notch it's a short, easy descent to the valley beyond the impasse. The valley definitely ends around the next bend, below peak 412443.

Incidentally, at the notch scramblers are in position to tackle **Tiara Peak** via its southwest ridge—a relentless bash up orange-coloured screes for 564 vertical m (1850 ft!). As you may have gathered, we didn't get too high up the ridge, having not camped! Nowadays it seems everyone climbs the peak from the Jumpingpound side in one day.

The southwest ridge of Tiara Peak. Trees at bottom right indicate the forested notch. The normal route from the Jumpingpound joins in at the bottom of the summit block on the right-hand skyline.

The canyon in the upper valley.

12B Northeast Fork

**Unofficial trail then route with many
creek crossings
Distance 5.7 km from forks
Height gain 783 m (2570 ft.)
High point 2180 m (7150 ft.)**

The northeast fork takes you through Red
Fox Canyon with its spectacular rock
scenery, to an unnamed pass on Boundary Ridge at 402482. Improbable as it
seems, this is one of only a handful of
routes crossing the Fisher Range to the

Lower Red Fox Canyon.

Jumpingpound and Elbow. It can be combined with trails #9, 2, 3, 3A and 12 to
make a 16.6-km loop, which works better
anti-clockwise.

Although the terrain is continuously
stoney, the gradient is never steep and
there's no scrambling. Unlike most canyons, there are no hidden horrors waiting
around the next bend.

To Boundary Ridge

From the forks, a trail heads left up the
east fork, following the left bank into the
first narrows. Like the south fork the valley floor alternately narrows and widens,
necessitating lots of back and forth creek
crossings. As you can see from the fixed
protection on a slab named "The Hedge-
hog," sport climbers are gradually working their way in from the road.

At 381471 the valley splits. Keep left
up the magnificent northeast fork. (The
waterless fork ahead ends in a box canyon
2.5 km distant.)

Straight off, enter lower Red Fox Canyon, where perpendicular walls topped
by wafer-thin ridges winging upwards to
unseen summits will have your mouth
hanging open. There are actually two parts
to the canyon separated by side slopes of
scree. Both are quite easy to walk through
aside from the creek crossings, the water
supplemented by springs bubbling out
of mossy banks. Above the canyon, the
slopes on either side fall back a little. At
a questionable fork at 394478, take the
right-hand fork.

The creekbed narrows as it approaches
Boundary Ridge. Head up the last forested
rib on the left, a very moderate slope despite converging contours shown on the
topo map. On shale near the top, traverse
right to a low point on the ridge at 402482,
which is marked by a cairn.

This is where you join the route come
up the other side from the south fork of
Lusk Creek. Bookending the long ridge
to the south is peak 403471, which is an
easy plod. Conversely, Half Past Midnight
at the north end is definitely a scramble.

13 "PORCUPINE RIDGE" — map 1

Day scramble
Unofficial trails, mostly route
Distance 4.6 km to high point
Height gain 713 m (2340 ft.)
High point 2118 m (6950 ft.)
Map 82 J/14 Spray Lakes Reservoir

Access Hwy. 40 (Kananaskis Trail) at Porcupine Creek bridge. Via #12 Porcupine Creeks to the forks.

The seemingly forested ridge between the two forks of Porcupine Creek is a fun trip for experienced off-trail hikers, who can expect some easy scrambling on a par with Wasootch Ridge.

As seen from Wasootch, Porcupine is a prickly ridge, characterized by staggered cliffs on one side or the other, and two massive pinnacled ribs stepping down the west slope from the ridge crest. The ridge itself is clear of obstacles until you reach the top at 377463, the usual turnaround point unless you're a proficient scrambler.

From the end of the rock ridge looking toward the first pinnacle rib.

Start off by following Porcupine Creek trail to the forks.

Just above the forks, a trail crosses the northeast fork and gets you started along the left bank of the southeast fork. When past the end of your ridge with its north-facing cliffs, climb up left on vegetated scree to the ridge crest, which is higher and farther away than it looks.

The going is then easy through trees and over a hump. A long stretch up grass leads to the rock ridge, which is mainly a walk above mini-ribs with gargoyles slanting off the right side. There are three scramble steps: the groove on the left side that gets you onto the ridge, a slab in the middle accessed from a broad ledge on the right side, and a crack leading down off the other end.

Continue down to a col. (At the col there's a break in the cliffs on the left side, making it possible to descend to the northeast fork of Porcupine Creek without too much trauma.)

Ascend through trees to turnip-shaped pinnacles marking the start of the first pinnacle rib. They're easily bypassed by a trail on the left flank. However, if you have time it's worth scrambling to the top of one of them for a spectacular view of the next pinnacle along the rib, which looms higher than the ridge itself.

To continue, either ascend the forested ridge or follow the trail below it to a top from where a second pinnacled ridge takes off down the west slope. From here to the high point a little way on, the ridge narrows above a cliff band on the left side. A clearing at 377463, in view of the impasse ahead, is a good place to end the trip.

From a comfortable couch of juniper there is much to look at that is familiar: the view across to Wasootch Ridge, up Red Fox Canyon to Boundary Ridge, the west ridge of Midnight Peak in profile, a large portion of the Fisher Range from Midnight Peak through peak 403471 and sundry bumps to Tiara Peak and on down past peak 409435 to Mt. McDougall.

Going farther
The topo maps indicate a very wide, treed ridge descending to the col at 383461. In reality this is where cliffs on both sides meet in a point. Well almost. The result is a very loose rock arête with considerable exposure. Because the slabs on the right sweep a long way down the hillside, there's no easy way to bypass this obstacle. Possibly a traverse on the left side from way back?

Below top: Looking down on the rock ridge.
Below bottom: Looking back to First Pinnacle Rib from farther along the ridge.

14 WASOOTCH CREEK—map 1

Half-day, day hike
Unofficial trail & route
Distance ~7.7 km to valley head
Height gain 472 m (1550 ft.) valley head
High point 1890 m (6200 ft.) valley head
Map 82 J/14 Spray Lakes Reservoir

Access Hwy. 40 (Kananaskis Trail) at Wasootch Creek parking lot.

While the walking to the forks is easy, it's debatable whether the upper valley is worth the tedium of the endless stoney flat to get there. Most people just go to Wasootch Slabs to watch the climbers.

NAMING NOTE The valley's most interesting aspect is its name, which derives from the Stoney word "wazi," denoting uniqueness and solitariness. Possibly it's connected with Wasootch Tower, a valley landmark that would have been seen from a prehistoric camp site now demolished by the highway.

The flats of Wasootch Creek. Wasootch Slabs to left, Wasootch Tower to right.

To the forks 6.3 km

A short trail leads to Wasootch Slabs on the left, a popular practice cliff for beginner rock climbers. The large white letters at the bottom of various slabs were painted on by the Canadian army, who used the slabs for training during the 1950s when the guidebook by Ben Gadd was still 30 years in the future. The spectacular rock outlier on the opposite side of the valley is Wasootch Tower.

From the slabs, pass through a comparative narrows onto a stoney flat, completely rewritten during the 1995 flood that tore up dryas mats (unfortunately for the walker), but spared the balsam poplars. Usually, water is intermittent, disappearing underground for long stretches at a time. On either side the slopes rise steeply: Wasootch Ridge on the left and a long stream of nameless summits on the right.

Upper valley ~1.4 km

At the forks overlooked by Mt. McDougall the scenario changes. The main left-hand valley narrows and the trees close in. A trail along the left bank leads to a small canyon with waterfall steps. To circumvent, scrabble up a gully to the left, then cut back right over a rib to the creekbed. A little farther on, cross a stony side creek at 378423. (This leads to the col separating Wasootch Ridge from the main axis of the Fisher Range. While it can be crossed to the southeast fork of Porcupine Creek at 384442, both sides of the col are very steep.)

From here on, stream hopping, awkward side hill traverses around small waterfalls and fights with willow bush are the norm. There seems no easy ways over the ridges to Upper Canyon Creek.

Upper Wasootch Creek.

15 WASOOTCH-BALDY CONNECTOR — map 1

One hour
Official trail
Distance 2.7 km
Height gain 46 m (150 ft.)
High point 1454 m (4770 ft.)
Map 82 J/14 Spray Lakes Reservoir

Access Hwy. 40 (Kananaskis Trail) at Wasootch Creek parking lot.
Also accessible from # 9 Baldy Pass from the south and #12 Porcupine Creeks.

This easy forest trail connects Wasootch Creek parking lot to Baldy Pass trail south. Officially it's called Baldy Pass trail and is another start to #9. But who wants to walk another 7.2 km when you don't have to?

Better uses: if you're doing a circuit with both Baldy Pass trails and Porcupine Creek over the Fisher Range, this is the connector. (See trails # 9, 2,3, 3A, 12.) It is also part of the Midnight Peak loop (#10B).

The trail starts from the trail sign on the left side of the parking lot. After rounding the end of Wasootch Ridge, you join a logging road. Turn right and follow it over a pine ridge into Porcupine Creek Valley.

Leave the road and on trail cross Porcupine Creek via a bridge. On the far side is a T-junction with a newer logging road. Go right, then almost immediately left. (Straight on is the trail up Porcupine Creek to the forks).

Follow the road as it heads north, staying right at the next three junctions. The hillside to right is the west ridge of Midnight Peak.

Reach a 4-way junction blazoned with red markers. Turn right for Baldy Pass; keep straight for Baldy Pass parking lot.

Opposite: #16 Wasootch Ridge. The view of the summit from near the rock shelter. The normal route descends the orange rocks to right just before the start of the rock ridge.

16 WASOOTCH RIDGE — map 1

Day hike, Long day scramble
Unofficial trail, route with cairns
Distance 6.9 km to summit
Height gain ~975 m (3200 ft.) to top
High point 2332 m (7650 ft.)
Map 82 J/14 Spray Lakes Reservoir

Wasootch Ridge, the undulating forest section. The summit at top left still looks a long way distant. To its right you can see the two open tops, which is where most people stop.

Access Hwy. 40 (Kananaskis Trail) at Wasootch Creek parking lot.

The long ridge dividing Wasootch Creek from the south fork of Porcupine Creek has evolved into one of K Country's classic ridgewalks with a delectable little summit at the end of it. It may be almost as straight as a ruler, but in profile it's as wavy as a rough sea with many tops. Unfortunately, maps, especially metric maps with contour lines at 40-m intervals, show none of this. Regardless, all this up and down hiking puts Wasootch Ridge in the strenuous category, especially when you factor in all the uphills of the return trip.

In terms of technical difficulty, it depends how far you go. Most people wander along to wherever it suits them, then sunbathe for the rest of the day. Others

end the trip on the open top with cairn at 365447. Thus far you have been on a really good trail.

To go for the summit at 375438 is more difficult. Expect one pitch of easy scrambling and lots of rock rubble and some route-finding difficulties eased here and there by an intermittent trail and occasional cairn. But no exposure. That's reserved for serious scramblers who on the final approach climb the rock ridge. Because of the odd dicey move, a rope is advised for novice scramblers tagging along in a group.

To top 365447, 5.3 km
The trail starts from the parking lot behind a picnic table and without preamble winds very steeply up the gable end of the ridge, forest alternating with a few slabby sections out in the open. A long flat follows. The second rise is higher and just as steep: scree and slab, then forest. It's good to know that when you reach the

top you've put the worst of the climbing behind you.

The ridge makes a brief jog to the left, then turns right and resumes its straight line progress. A shorter climb gains you what might be called top no. 1, which is broad and fairly open, offering views across Porcupine Creek to prickly Porcupine Ridge on the left and down to Wasootch Creek on the right, its stoney bed presided over by the twinned "G8 Summits" and Wasootch Tower. Ahead, the highest summit of your ridge looks far, far away.

The view changes little as you progress along the ridge, climbing up and down the numerous tops. Expect three longish descents and a brief moment of excitement where the trail traverses a narrow ledge above a small cliff. Care is needed here.

Ultimately, the ridge rises gracefully out of the trees to an open top with cliffs plummeting down the Wasootch Creek side. Continue easily to the next top with cairn—a very fine viewpoint for the final section of ridge to the summit. After about 762 m (2500 ft.) of height gain this is the end of the road for most people. The ridge beyond is for scramblers.

To the summit 1.6 km

Continue on trail to the foot of the rock fin. This obstacle is bypassed to the left by a scramble down a rockband. Use either a slab or a crack a little farther on. Either way, you end up on a black shale trail near the base of the rockband. Turn right and follow it up onto the ridge crest again, then down to the col between the fin and the rocky top at 369444, which is where another percentage of hikers call it a day.

Climb a little, then traverse below the rocky top to another col on the far side. From here a good trail climbs up over another small top and down to a man-made wind shelter—a fabulous viewpoint for the summit, which looks terrifying or interesting depending on your point of view. Be assured that the route up the southwest face gets you to the summit without turning you into a gibbering jellyfish begging for a rope.

Walk a little farther along the ridge, then descend right, following the base of slabs. (Scramblers who continue along the ridge crest at this point nearly always come unglued at the notch.)

The usual finish at top 365447. Looking over sundry rocky tops to the summit.

At a gap in the slabs continue on the same line and pick up a good trail descending scree. Then continue as before below slabs to a cairn. This marks the notch up left. There are actually two notches divided by a pinnacle. Ridge scramblers should head for the right-hand one.

Everyone else, continue along the trail below the slabs. Shortly the trail traverses right, then heads uphill to round the base of a rock buttress. When the buttress is outflanked, scrabble the broken slope

up left to cairns—an exceptional photo viewpoint for the airy, scary-looking ridge crest, especially if you can catch someone climbing up it. Continue up on easier ground, then, just below the crest, traverse right below slabs to gain the ridge above all difficulties.

All that remains—and this section takes longer than you might think—is to pick your way among large rocks on the right side of the crest to the summit. At a protruding wall en route, it's easier to stay on the crest.

Apart from revealing the long length of the ridge you've just come up, the summit view is not substantially different from before. You are, however, much closer to the myriad of unnamed peaks at the head of Wasootch and Porcupine creeks, which are more easily reached from Upper Canyon Creek. (See Volume 2.)

Return the same way.

Left: Summit block, showing the approximate route. The dashed line indicates route hidden by the buttress.

On the last stretch to the summit.

17 PEAK 336454 "THE G8 SUMMITS"—map 2

Day scramble
Unofficial trail
Distance 5.1 km return
Height gain 902 m (2960 ft.)
High point 2353 m (7720 ft.)
Map 82 J/14 Spray Lakes Reservoir

Access Hwy. 40 (Kananaskis Trail). About 200 m north of the Kananaskis Village/Nakiska Ski Area junction, park at the side of the hwy.

The twin-headed mountain overlooking Kananaskis Village at 336454 "is named in honour of the G8 Summit held at Kananaskis Village in June of 2002," suggested scrambler Sonny Bou, who came up with a lot of equally wacky names. Over the last few years, the names "Wasootch" and "Winnipeg Peak" have appeared in the summit register, the latter after it was climbed by two bus loads of high school students from Winnipeg. Eagle counters in the valley below call it "Patrick." Who knows what name it will end up with: Eagle Mountain? Mt. Sherrington after the chief eagle counter?—But for now we can have some fun with the name.

Looking up the south ridge from the top of the rock ridge.

The mountain presents a bold front to the west, so it's all the more remarkable that there is a trail to the higher south summit via the southwest and south ridges. Nevertheless, there is still scree to contend with and the odd bit of easy scrambling. All in all, a very enjoyable route you'll want to do more than once. For die-hard scramblers it's a mere stepping stone to more difficult peaks to the southeast. Often in condition by May.

On the east side of the highway is a stony bed of an unnamed creek. Head up-creek on the rocks, then transfer to a trail on the left bank. Keep left. A few uphill zigs leads into a traverse above a steep bank below which is Six Flags bouldering area. A longer, twisty climb sees you to the edge of a perpendicular cliff where the trail has nowhere to go but up. This steep section ends at a fabulous viewpoint for the Kananaskis Valley and Kananaskis Village—an obvious halting place before tackling the rocky southwest ridge. Do a tick check before you leave.

The trail dips into a few trees before starting a wandering climb up the ridge to avoid small crags. On reaching the base of a cliff, traverse right on scree, scrabble over a few rocks, then climb up behind the cliff to a bit of a saddle. After this the trail continues much as before, keeping left of the crest, the many wonderful situations calling out for photos. At last trees the ridge butts against the west-facing slope of the south ridge.

Zig up pale-orange scree, gradually bearing left up the south ridge. High up, the trail stays close to a mane of rock on the ridge crest. A cairn signals both an easing of the gradient and the place where you cross the rock to the east side of the ridge via an obvious gap with easy scrambling

both sides. The far slope drops away very much more steeply but the trail is good and after a couple of minutes you're walking a short, rubbly ridge to the summit cairn. (Register.)

Suddenly revealed is the lower north summit and a view down onto Wasootch Tower. Close by and yoked to your summit is a string of nameless tops heading southeastwards and known collectively to eagle counters as "The Bumps."

NOTE Getting to the lower summit is not as easy as it looks. Expect loose, awkward scrambling down to the saddle.

Below top: Looking down the screes of the south ridge to the rocky southwest ascent ridge.

Below bottom: The trail has crossed the gap in the rock crest to the east side of the ridge.

18 STONEY TRAIL — maps 1 & 2

Day hike
Bike, equestrian
Official trail with signposts &
red markers, possible creek crossing
Distance 22.2 km
Height gain ~80 m (260 ft.)
High point 1470 m (4820 ft.)
Map 82 O/3 Canmore,
82 J/14 Spray Lakes Reservoir

Rock painting of a falling man from the Lorette site.

South access Hwy. 40 (Kananaskis Trail). Turn west onto Mt. Allan Drive (signed "Kananaskis Village, Nakiska Ski Area"). Keep straight at the first junction with Centennial Drive, then turn next right into Stoney Trail parking lot.

North access Hwy. 1 (Trans Canada Highway) at Bow Valley Provincial Park South. At the Seebe interchange (exit 114A) follow signs to Rafter Six Ranch Resort and the Rocky Mountain YMCA. At the T-junction go straight ahead into a parking lot.

Also accessible from Hwy. 40 (Kananaskis Trail) at Barrier Dam. Via #8 Jewel Pass and #7 Prairie View trail.

From Hwy. 1 (Trans-Canada Highway) at YMCA Camp Chief Hector. Via Hector trail.

From Hwy. 1 (Trans-Canada Highway) at Rafter Six Ranch Resort.

Walking a powerline access road and the old Hwy. 40 is tedious, though views are really good and you travel past a large number of unnamed valleys and ridges up and down the west side of the lower Kananaskis Valley. So use it as access to better things and don't grumble when overtaken by horses and bikes. Most people use the trail in conjunction with Prairie View and Jewel Pass trails. The south end is heavily used by birders accessing Powerline Beaver Ponds and by climbers and scramblers biking to Mt. Lorette. In this southern area keep an eye out for cougars.

En route is Jewel Bay backcountry campground, that can also be reached by a paddle from Barrier Lake day-use area.

TRAIL NOTE The northerly section in Bow Valley Provincial Park South passes through a network of trails which are described with sketch map in Volume 3 under "Bow Valley Provincial Park South."

REGULATORY NOTE The section between Evan-Thomas Recreation Area boundary just north of Lorette Creek and Jewel Pass trail junction is closed April 15–June 15 to protect the spring movement of elk. During this time, no random camping is allowed and the Jewel Bay campground is closed. After July 15, camping is only permitted at Jewel Bay.

SOUTH TO NORTH
To Powerline Beaver Ponds 2.3 km
Walk around the gate onto the powerline access road. Straightaway, Hay Meadow trail intersects the road, then follows a long straight, sloping slightly downhill into meadows, used as parking lots during the 15th Olympic Winter Games in 1988. (Up the hill is Nakiska ski area.) Here the road semi-circles to the left to a road junction. Turn left. (The better road ahead leads to a pumphouse.) On the way up a slight incline (alluvial fan), recross Hay Meadow trail.

On top of the fan, cross Marmot Creek by culvert. The powerline winging up the slope to left is the optional descent route from Hummingbird Plume Hill. Descend past the Mt. Allan substation into an undulating stretch that begins with an uphill.

Eventually the track descends below the craggy east face of Hummingbird Plume Hill to Powerline Beaver Ponds, and undulates along the west shore of the biggest pond. Reflected in the water is the precipitous west face of "G8 Summits" across the valley. Who could guess a trail leads up to its summit.

There are many more ponds worth getting off the beaten track for. According to local birders, you might find here such rarities as Cassin's finch and black swifts. In early spring look for a heronry of about seven birds.

To Mt. Lorette 1.9 km

Shortly after the road leaves the ponds, a faint trail heading left through the aspens is the climber's access to the south ridge of Mt. Lorette and the hiker's access into Lorette Creek Canyon.

Climb another vegetated alluvial fan and on top cross Lorette Creek which is sometimes dry by this point. Continuing on, the road avoids a steep descent by looping down right into the forest, then back left onto the powerline right-of-way directly under K Country's killer mountain, Mt. Lorette, which throws down two spectacular rock ridges towards the road. The left-hand ridge, a classic 5.6 climb famous for its hand traverse, has been the scene of several fatalities, all to inexperienced young men climbing solo who believed the ridge to be a doddle. The gully between the ridges is the climber's descent/scrambler's ascent route. Note the small cairn.

To Jewell Pass trail 7.5 km

As you cross the creek north of Lorette you finally get a close up view of a mountain much admired for its beautiful orange and grey colouring by Mary Barclay, co-founder with sister Catherine of the Canadian Youth Hostel movement. The moderately difficult scramble up Mary Barclay's Mountain starts up the south ridge from the road.

Typical powerline access road. Mary Barclay's Mountain ahead.

Powerline Beaver Ponds, looking south to Mt. Kidd.

The powerline north of Mt. Lorette. Across the Kananaskis Valley rises Pk. 336454.

Then follows a long, uneventful stretch below the mountain's steep eastern slopes, boring if it weren't for continuing good views across the Kananaskis Valley to the twin valleys of Porcupine and Wasootch, divided by Wasootch Ridge, and of Mt. Baldy, showing some of the scrambling route to its summit.

The road makes a big detour to the left to avoid a boggy valley bottom, then on regaining the right-of-way climbs to a first viewpoint for Barrier Lake Reservoir, a depressing scene at low water when a vast expanse of mud flats is revealed. A picnic shelter roof on an island indicates the line of Hwy. 40 in pre-reservoir days.

Undulate high above the reservoir to a side creek crossing at 344524. If you're into geological structures, this valley is worth a day trip to view excellent examples of horses and duplexes (a mass of rock completely boxed in by thrust faults). Apparently, this structure is something every prospector dreams of finding... should it occur in oil-bearing rock. Which is not the case here.

After another boring stretch, you pass Jewell Bay backcountry campground to your right. Then cross Jewell Creek bridge at the head of Jewell Bay. In only another 200 m near the top of a hill, Jewell Pass trail turns off to the left at a signed T-junction, bound for Jewell Pass. Keep straight on the road, which is also Jewel Pass trail at this point.

To Prairie View trail 2.5 km
Shortly, the road descends past the "God is Love" boulders strewn upslope in the trees and enters meadows above the reservoir. Where you cross the powerline right-of-way, the Jewell Pass trail turns off to the right at a hiking sign.

The road continues north below McConnell Ridge's long line of cliffs, which were once popular for mountain rescue practice. Keep straight at a T-junction with another road. (The road to right connects with the Jewell Pass trail.) The next T-junction is with a road from Barrier Dam, which is Prairie View trail come up the hill from the right. In a few metres Prairie View trail heads left up the hillside. Keep straight both times.

To Rafter Six Access 5.9 km
Continue north below McConnell Ridge. After the road bends to the left, watch for a meadow on the right side that is the Powerline Route. At last visit it had picnic tables. At this point there are two ways on:

1. The Official Trail Stay on the road, which in 1.8 km descends to a Y-junction on a bend and turns right. (The track straight ahead leads to Camp Chief Hector.)

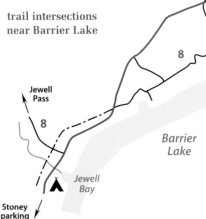

trail intersections near Barrier Lake

Head wrong way southeast. Note a track coming in from the right just before you cross the N-S powerline right-of-way. This is the Powerline Route joining back in. Go straight.

2. The Powerline Route If you can't bring yourself to head south when you're supposed to be heading north, try this option used by equestrians. It's slightly shorter.

Turn right into the meadow that connects to the powerline right-of-way, where you turn left. (Right leads to the 4-way junction with Prairie View and Jewel Pass trails.) Follow the grassy track down a hill to a V split in powerline right-of-ways. Keep left. Then, before the meadow becomes bog, wend left across the right-of-way into the trees. On reaching Stoney trail turn right.

Broken Bridges. All that's left of the 1934 highway bridge over the Kananaskis River that led to the Forest Experiment Station.

Round about here you enter Bow Valley Provincial Park South. The road swings left up a hill, then makes a long gradual descent past a spate of trails peeling off to right and left as you approach the Kananaskis River. At a Y-junction of roads keep left. (The road to right is the original Hwy. 40, built in 1934 between Seebe and Kananaskis Field Stations, which was a camp for the unemployed. It's worth a short detour to look at Broken Bridges.)

Walk the old hwy. to another Y-junction where you keep left. The following section along the shady river bank is known to some as the River Road. Again, ignore side trails en route to where the road climbs the bank to a gate in a fence. On the far side keep straight on the road. (The trails to right lead over a ridge to Rafter Six Ranch Resort.)

To North Access 2.1 km
The old highway travels through meadow between an esker on the right and an array of Sundance Lodges in various states of disintegration on the left. A loop road on the left farther on is the old Soapy Smith trailhead, which you could once drive to.

The road bends right around the esker and passes under the powerline. Ahead is a vast grassy flat criss-crossed by a large number of tracks and trails—the site of Canadian and World Scout Jamborees in 1981, '83 and '93. Imagine the whole area filled with tents and flagpoles with flags flying in a stiff west wind.

Walk the 1-km-long straight to the main entrance for Bow Valley Provincial Park South, passing between strategically placed boulders into the parking lot. (If heading in the opposite direction, a hiking sign points you in the right direction.)

NOTE If curious about all these side trails you've been passing in Bow Valley Park South, refer to the description and map in Volume 3 of the series.

Two tiers of cliffs in Lorette Creek Canyon.

OPTION

18A Lorette Creek Canyon

Distance to falls 3 km, 5.6 km from trailhead

Occasionally I get asked what Lorette Creek is like because it looks so alluring from Stoney trail. In two words: hard going. However, people actually exist like Alf who love pushing through willow and deadfall, risking rockfall from overhanging cliffs, thrutching up a horribly steep slope to get around the waterfall step and side-hilling for hours above a clogged V-shaped valley bottom. Oh and there's lots of mandatory paddling.

The start is easy enough. From the end of the beaver ponds follow the climber's access trail towards Mt. Lorette. Then on hitting Lorette Creek, head off left up the northeast bank.

Progress slows, and for most people little Lorette Falls and back is more than enough. The rock scenery is amazing, though, especially the undercut cliffs lining the creekbed.

19 TROLL FALLS LOOP—map 2

Half day hike
Official trails
Distance 3.7 km loop
Height gain 30 m (100 ft.)
Map 82 J/14 Spray Lakes Reservoir

Troll Falls from the ledge.
You can walk around it to behind the falls.

Access Hwy. 40 (Kananaskis Trail). Turn west onto Mt. Allan Drive (signed "Kananaskis Village, Nakiska Ski Area"). Keep straight at the first junction, then before the bend turn right into Stoney trail parking lot.
Also accessible from #18 Stoney trail, #21, Skogan Pass from the south, and from Nakiska Ski Area via Hidden trail and Ruthie's.

"If you haven't been to Troll Falls, you haven't been to Ribbon Creek" goes the saying. Luckily, it's easily reached by trails winding through forest and meadow.

BIRDING NOTE You also take in the valley's premier eagle-counting site at Hay Meadow during spring and fall migrations. Incredibly, it takes birds zooming up the Highwood and Opal Ranges only half an hour to get from Highwood Junction to "G8 Summits." Because this is the narrowest part of the Kananaskis Valley, most birds cross to Mt. Lorette before continuing northward. 'Most' means 800 or so out of a thousand plus counted *per day* during the peak times at the end of March and the beginning of October.

WARNING Cougars have been spotted a few times on the Hay Meadow section (it's believed they den on the lower slopes of Lorette), so don't let your youngsters run on ahead.

CLOCKWISE

Troll Falls trail section 1.7 km
From the parking lot, pass through the gate onto the pumphouse access road, which is also Stoney trail. Almost at once turn left into the trees on Hay Meadow trail. Turn next right onto Troll Falls trail. Stay left, then keep right. (To left is a connector to Skogan Pass trail.) A longer undulating

stretch through pines and aspens, widened despite much outcry in 1982, ends at the 4-way intersection with Hay Meadow trail (right) and Ruthie's trail (left), named after Ruth Oltmann, author and hostel house parent in the days when hostellers were avidly exploring the trails left behind after mining and logging.

Go straight on a much narrower trail that follows the left bank of Marmot Creek into a gloomy recess filled with spray. Plunging over a cliff is Troll Falls. And keeping an eye on the falls through huge empty eye sockets is the troll himself. To get a better view of the falls, grub up a trail to a ledge below the undercut cliff. And while there, have your photo taken besides the troll's head.

Hay Meadow trail section 2 km
Return to the 4-way intersection and turn left onto Hay Meadow trail. Cross Stoney trail (gravel track), wind downhill through aspen forest, then cross the pumphouse road between the primary and secondary pumphouses.

Eagle counting at the Mount Lorette Site. Mt. Lorette in the background.

Walk the dike between the Kananaskis River and a ditch. On the right is Hay Meadow with a meteorological station as centrepiece. To left at dike's end is a small meadow on the bank of the river called "The Mount Lorette Site." It was here in 1992 that Des Allen and Peter Sherrington demonstrated to the world that the Kananaskis corridor is a major eagle migratory route between the sunny south and breeding grounds in Canada's far north. Though unlikely to see Peter these days (he's counting down in the Crowsnest), you are bound to encounter locals like Cliff who have their telescopes trained on mountains they call "Patrick" and "The Bumps." There's always binoculars to spare for passing hikers, so be careful! It could be hours before you get back to your car.

Shortly the trail heads back into trees for a long straight stretch, then curves right to emerge on the pumphouse road near the gate. Turn left into the parking lot.

Tony and the Troll of Troll Falls.

63

Marmot Falls.

Double Falls.

Hiking the canyon edge.

20 MARMOT CREEK WATERFALLS — map 2

Half day hike
Unofficial trail
Distance 1 km
Height gain ~130 m (426 ft.)
Map 82 J/14 Spray Lakes Reservoir

Bottom Access Via #19 Troll Falls loop at Troll Falls.
Top Access Via #21 Skogan Pass trail at Marmot Basin Road.

Between Marmot Basin Road and Troll Falls trail, Marmot Creek skips and plunges its way down the hillside to its ultimate drop-off at Troll Falls. It's a gorgeous piece of water to be savoured by all waterfall lovers, at its best during snowmelt or after a week's rain.

The trail running down its northeast bank in pine forest is reserved for the more adventurous: it is sometimes steep and has rougher variations that are easy to stray onto when hiking the trail in the downward direction. This is my preferred direction of travel, but for a first visit the main trail is MUCH easier to locate going up.

Combine with Skogan Pass trail and Ruthie's to make a 5.5 km loop back to Stoney trail parking lot.

BOTTOM TO TOP

Take #19 to Troll Falls.

Backtrack a short way and cross Marmot Creek on a log. The crossing place is identified by flagging on the far bank. Straightaway the trail climbs very steeply up left, levelling off above Troll Falls (which can't be seen without risking life and limb).

At a split keep right, uphill. Higher up, a side trail to left descends to the bottom of "Lower Canyon Falls." Shortly after, keep left on the main trail which veers left and nears the top of the falls, then swings away up right to a 4-way junction. The side trail to left leads down to "Marmot Falls"

(a Troll Falls lookalike you can stand behind). Continue uphill at the 4-way onto flatter terrain near the forks.

The trail follows a calmer piece of water until you hit "Boulder Falls," where the river, dashing itself against a large boulder, is forced to make a right-angle turn. Above is a series of picturesque falls culminating in "Double Falls." Climb a little more steeply to another right-angled bend in the creek. Don't cross the creek via a crude branch bridge. Stay on the good trail that heads way out right to a T-junction on a grassy hillside. Turn left. (Right leads to a bluff with view of the Kananaskis Valley.)

The trail climbs through increasingly stoney pine forest back to the creek, here encased in a deep canyon. En route, you'll see "trails" plunging down the hillside which are made by downhillers bent on staying as close to the creek as possible. Take it from me, you're not missing too much by sticking to the main trail.

The canyon is featured in the long-running German TV series *Forsthaus Falkenau (Ranger Station Falconfield)*, this segment made in 2006. An Indiana Jones bridge with missing slats was slung across the narrowest part and for a while provided hikers with a dizzying view of "Upper Canyon Falls."

Hike carefully along the canyon edge to its end where the valley opens out a bit at a Water Survey of Canada groundwater site measuring water flow. Continue upstream, cross a metal bridge and climb the bank to the start of a grassy track. Follow the track out past a groundwater well to Marmot Basin Road (Skogan Pass trail).

Return

Turn left on the road, then left again down Skogan Pass ski trail. At a 4-way junction, turn left and descend Ruthie's to the 4-way junction with Troll Falls trail. Return the same way you came, or follow Hay Meadow back to the parking lot.

21 SKOGAN PASS from the south — map 2

Looking northwest to Mt. Collembola.

Day hike, bike 'n' hike
Official trails with signposts
Distance 10.1 km via Access 1,
8.8 km via Access 2
Height gain 625 m (2050 ft.) from Access 1, 585 m (1919 ft.) from Access 2
Height loss 49 m (160 ft.)
High point 2073 m (6800 ft.)
Map 82 J/14 Spray Lakes Reservoir

Access Hwy. 40 (Kananaskis Trail). Turn west onto Mt. Allan Drive signed "Kananaskis Village, Nakiska Ski Area."
1. Ribbon Creek parking lot. Turn first left onto Centennial Drive. Turn next right onto Ribbon Creek Road and drive past Kananaskis Wilderness Hostel to the parking lots at the end of the road.
2. Continue to follow Mt. Allan Drive past intersections with Centennial Drive and Stoney trail parking lot to Nakiska ski area. Park just before the summer gate. The whole ski area is closed in summer, including the day lodge.
Also accessible from #19 Troll Falls loop, and from Skogan Pass from the north in Volume 3. An easy uphill walk following 4-m-wide

ski trails, then a powerline access road to the watershed between Lorette and Pigeon creeks. Even more so than its northern half, it's closeted in forest, offering just brief glimpses of surrounding mountains over the treetops. You can of course follow it right through to Hwy. 1 (see Volume 3), but aside from mountain bikers, most people use it to access Hummingbird Plume Lookout, Marmot Basin and Marmot Creek Waterfalls.

HISTORY NOTE Just over a hundred years ago Pigeon Pass, as it was called then, was a quiet place crossed by an Indian trail shown on George Dawson's map from 1886. Likely it was the same trail, by then called the Kananaskis Pack Trail, which was widened in 1936 by the Forest Service to carry the telephone line linking Dead Man Flat ranger cabin to Boundary ranger cabin near the mouth of Ribbon Creek. Henceforth it was known as the Canmore Boundary Telephone Line trail over Dead Man Pass.

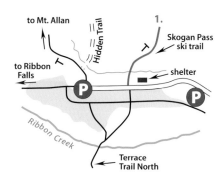

Access 1
Ribbon Creek parking lot

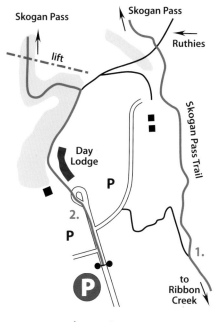

Access 2
Nakiska Ski Area.

Since then, the trail, and the whole hillside on the south side of the pass has been carved up by the powerline right-of-way and its access road, and by a proliferation of logging roads and cutblocks, coal mine access roads, Marmot Basin project roads, and more recently by ski area access roads, ski runs, and cross-country ski trails.

In fact it was skier Don Gardner who named the pass "Skogan" in 1973, the old names having never caught on. Skogan is a Norse word meaning "Magic forest with elves and trolls" and though it's come into general use, the name remains unofficial.

Starts

There are two starts that join at the junction of Marmot Basin Road with the Skogan Pass ski trail. While starting from Nakiska reduces both distance and height gain, walking a road is much less pleasing than walking a forest trail.

Access 1 via Skogan Pass ski trail, 2.5 km Start from the trail sign at the west end of the picnic shelter located between the two parking lots. Heading north, cross the bridge over a tiny creek and climb a hill to Mt. Allan Drive. Cross. Continue along the trail, which, in an effort to be interesting for skiers, undulates all around the perimeter of Nakiska ski area. Keep left twice, then right twice. Go straight at a 4-way junction with Hidden and Ruthie's. Then climb the long hill to Marmot Basin Road, en route crossing a fork of Marmot Creek. Turn right.

Access 2 via Marmot Basin Road, 1.2 km Continue up the road beyond the gate, passing the south parking lot on your left, and the north parking lot on your right. At the loop, head under the arch and walk between Nakiska day lodge on your right and an administration building on your left. On reaching a gravel track, turn right and walk in front of the day lodge. The flat meadow to the left was the original setting for Calgary Philharmonic's wildly popular "Mozart on the Mountain" that

ran here for a few years before being transferred to the Stewart Creek Golf Course
in Canmore, then to Rafter Six Ranch on
Hwy. 1 before being scrapped altogether.
Interestingly, the idea escalated and there
is now "Beethoven in the Badlands" at
Drumheller and "Music on the Mountain"
in the Crowsnest.

But back to the track. At the 4-way track
junction at the end of the lodge turn left.
(Should you go straight, Hidden ski trail
joins with start no. 1—but much father
down the slope.) Pass under the Olympic chairlift, then head right on a rising
traverse that crosses ski runs. Pass under
the Bronze chair. After you leave the lifts
and ski runs behind, the track widens,
reverting to its original status as Marmot
Basin Road.

Stay on the road as it winds around
an S bend. Cross a culvert over a fork of
Marmot Creek, then watch for the Skogan
Pass ski trail joining in from the right at a
sign. Keep straight.

To Marmot Creek Road 0.3 km
Shortly the road levels and within a short
distance are several junctions. First, make
a mental note of a grassy track to the right.
(This leads to a groundwater well and is
the route taken by #20 to look at the waterfalls of Marmot Creek.)

At a junction of roads shortly after, go
straight through a gate onto what is the
narrower Marmot Creek Road. (To left
the upper Marmot Basin Road climbs to
Mid-Mountain lodge and Marmot Basin.
See #23).

Around a few bends is another junction.
Keep right on the Skogan Pass powerline
access road that crosses Marmot Creek
on Two Ton Culvert, nee bridge. (Marmot
Creek Road to left follows the left bank of
Marmot Creek and is the optional return
route from Marmot Basin #23.)

To Sunburst trail 1.7 km
The powerline access road winds uphill
past a groundwater well—a relic of the
Marmot Basin Project era now maintained

by Alberta Environment—to touch briefly
the powerline right-of-way. This is where
Sunburst trail turns off to the right to Hummingbird Plume Hill.

To High Level trail 1 km
Swing back left and then right to a signed
junction with High Level trail (which also
leads to Hummingbird Plume Hill).

To Skogan Loop upper junction 2.7 km
Again you swing left, then gradually turn
right and climb a long straight through a
pine plantation. You're about 10 years too
late to view the view and over 30 years too
late to view a string of historic wooden
tripods running down the left side of
the road, holding up the telephone line
between ranger stations.

At the top of the hill pass the lower junction of Skogan Loop ski trail at a sign. Keep
straight and descend "Spruce Avenue" to
the powerline right-of-way. Here the road
turns sharp left and climbs, twining about
the right-of-way. At the top of the hill is the
upper junction with Skogan Loop ski trail,
which is also the road to a meteorological
station. This is a confusing place for many
people who think they've reached the pass.
It is *almost* the same height.

To Skogan Pass 1.9 km
The access road leaves the powerline
right-of-way and descends to a gate
signifying the northern boundary of the
Marmot Basin Project. Keeping left, you
swing around the heads of Lorette Creek
and cross the powerline right-of-way, the
opening giving you a chance to examine
the crux pitch on Collembola. The road
then turns left and paralleling the right-
of-way climbs to its high point, an inde-
terminate place in the pines just beyond
where the old pack trail turns off to the
right. (Look for telephone wire trailing
on the ground.)

From the road's high point it's worth
detouring left onto the right-of-way for a
view through the powerlines to Old Baldy
and the peaks around Mt. McDougall.

22 HUMMINGBIRD PLUME LOOKOUT—map 2

G8 Summits from the viewpoint. The snow-covered mountain to right is peak 356417.

Day hike
Official trails with signposts
Distance 1.7 km from Access 2
Height gain 143 m (470 ft.);
326 m (1070 ft.) from Access 2
High point 1865 m (6120 ft.)
Map 82 J/14 Spray Lakes Reservoir

Access Via #21 Skogan Pass from the south from Access 2. Follow to Sunburst trail.

Mostly a forest walk following 4-m-wide ski trails to an historic lookout atop Hummingbird Plume Hill. It was named in 1973 by Don Gardner, but dates back well before that, possibly to the mid-1930s.

Via Sunburst trail to High Level trail
1.2 km
Turn right onto Sunburst trail, which crosses the powerline right-of-way, then climb ever more steeply to the junction with High Level trail.

To Hummingbird Plume Hill 0.5 km.
Turn right and on level ground walk to the small meadow atop Hummingbird Plume Hill.

You missed the lookout in the rush to get seats at the picnic table? The "lookout" is the tar-papered shack on the right that doesn't appear to be worth a second glance unless there's an imminent thunderstorm, and then it pays to know the shack is grounded. But take a closer look inside. On the walls are inscribed the names and initials of German POWs from Camp 130: Erich Petrinski POW 17.11.1939, JQ 1941, PW July 6/41.

At the time the POWs were salvaging burnt timber from the 1936 fire there really *was* a view from the lookout. Since then the pines have grown high, so what you do now is follow a two-minute trail to the other end of the meadow and through a few trees to an overlook above the craggy east slope of the hill. Before you is the same view of the Kananaskis Valley, Mt. Lorette to the left, the Fisher Range opposite and to the right a clutch of ridges rising to "G8 Summits."

Return the same way, or try the optional descent route down the powerline right-of-way to Stoney trail.

The lookout, now surrounded by pine forest.

A POW inscription inside the lookout.

OPTIONAL RETURN

22A Balam

Distance 4 km to Access 1, 3.8 km to Access 2

A fast way down to Stoney trail where there is the option of taking in Troll Falls on your way back to the trailheads.

Backtrack to Skogan Pass trail. But this time follow the trail down the powerline. Back in early hostel days, it was a downhill ski run called Balam and even on foot it's a fast way down to Stoney trail reached near the Mt. Allan substation.

Turn right. Cross Marmot Creek. At the 4-way junction turn right on Hay Meadow trail. Come to 4-way junction with Troll Falls trail and Ruthie's. Turn left. (To visit Troll Falls turn right.)

The trail climbs through aspen and pine forest to a T-junction. Turn right and climb to a T-junction with Skogan Pass trail.

For Access 1 turn left and follow Skogan Pass trail back you way you came to Ribbon Creek parking lot.

For Access 2 turn right, then shortly keep left at a split. At the top of the hill (sign) turn left and wind up to a maintenance road reached opposite Nakiska's north parking lot. Turn left. At the T-junction with Mt. Allan Drive turn left. Pass the entrance to south parking lot and arrive at the gate.

23 MARMOT BASIN—map 2

Long day hikes
Official & unofficial trails, route, creek crossings
Distance 6 km to spring
Height gain ~762 m (2500 ft.)
High point ~2286 m (7500 ft.) at spring
Map 82 J/14 Spray Lakes Reservoir

Access Hwy. 40 (Kananaskis Trail). Turn off onto Mt. Allan Drive (signed "Kananaskis Village, Nakiska Ski Area"). Keep straight, following signs to Nakiska ski area. Park at the side of the road just before the locked summer gate. **Also accessible** from Collembola traverse in Volume 3.

A mishmash of old trails and logging roads through the Marmot Basin Project area give access to the cirque between Mt. Allan and the lower Collembola. You can, if you want, climb both these peaks from Marmot Basin, or make a loop with the Centennial trail or a point to point with the Collembolas. All trails stop at treeline but the open terrain above the larch belt is straightforward. It's the climb up through

Marmot Basin. In the background game trails climb onto Fisera Ridge. Photo Alf Skrastins

the forest that's so strenuous, with lots of height gain and navigational problems due to the surplus of original trails overlain by logging roads.

NOTE In spring be alert for guided grizzly hunts, and carry bear spray.

HISTORY NOTE So what WAS the Marmot Basin Project? Basically, it was a hydraulic study of the whole watershed by the Forest Experiment Station that began in the mid-1950s and lasted almost 30 years. The forest was logged in various ways to see what the effect would be on snow pack depth, snow melt and water flow. Since 2004, the studies, now part of the Improved Processes and Parameterization for Prediction in Cold Regions research network, have been revived by the University of Saskatchewan and Environment Canada working out of the University of Calgary's Kananaskis Field Station. Nearly all the instruments you see now as you wander around are recent, the old trails being kept open by researchers.

The forest has pretty well grown back, but a new threat lies on the horizon: the possible expansion of the Nakiska ski area, that was allowed for in the Evan-Thomas Management Plan of 2002. The one thing holding it back, apparently, is the basin's ongoing value as a scientific site.

NAMING NOTE And how DID the cirque come by its name? Even his friends might be surprised to learn the basin and creek were named by Gordon Scruggs, who as a young university student, assisted M.B.B. Crockford during the geological survey of 1947 prior to the opening of the Ribbon Creek coal mine. According to Gordon, their camp was overrun by marmots looking for easy pickings. In mountaineering circles, Gordon was best known as a member of the Grizzly Group who specialized in first ascents in remote areas of the Rockies.

Lower Marmot Basin Road 1.3 km
For navigation around Nakiska ski area see the sketch map on page 67.

In words: continue up the road beyond the gate, passing the south parking lot on your left, and the north parking lot on your right. At the loop, head under the arch and walk between Nakiska day lodge on your right and an administration building on your left. On reaching a gravel track, turn right and walk in front of the day lodge. At the 4-way track junction at the end of the lodge turn left.

Pass under the Olympic chairlift, then head right on a rising traverse that crosses ski runs. Pass under the Bronze chair. After you leave the lifts and ski runs behind, the track widens, reverting to Marmot Basin Road.

Stay on the road as it winds around an S bend. Cross a culvert over a fork of Marmot Creek, then watch for the Skogan Pass ski trail joining in from the right at a sign. Keep straight.

Shortly the road levels and you come to a T-junction of roads. Turn left onto upper Marmot Basin Road. (Ahead is Skogan Pass trail/Marmot Creek Road.)

Upper Marmot Basin Road 2.7 km
This section of road is a snowmobile access road to Nakiska's mid-mountain lodge that serves beer and burgers to skiers. En route stay right, then keep left four times as you climb around two sweeping bends. The uphill grind is relentless, calling for a collapse next to a fuel tank where a new piece of road turns left towards the lodge (unfortunately closed in summer).

Keep straight on the old road that descends and turns right to cross South Twin Creek, in the process becoming a X-C ski trail called Marmot Basin trail (returning down Marmot Creek to the Marmot Creek Road).

Cross bridges over South and North Twin Creeks. (The trail up South Twin Creek takes off left between the two creek crossings.)

To Marmot Basin spring ~2 km
After the second crossing, leave the ski trail and turn left on original trail, which follows the north bank of North Twin Creek. Ignore a logging road to right, and continue on the trail, which shortly bends right uphill and intersects a logging road that has arisen from the ski trail.

Turn left onto the road. In a few metres, turn left at a T-junction and climb to another T-junction. Again keep left and climb a steeper hill. At the apex, marked by a fallen tree, turn left at a T-junction. (The main road ahead winds downhill and eventually joins the ski trail.)

Your new road, in slightly worse shape, zigs left, right, left. Just before it peters out above North Twin Creek, head right, up the original trail in a flurry of flagging.

What joy to follow an easy-angled trail winding through spruce forest and patchworks of mini-cutblocks. Look for the first larch. High up you cross a straight-up shortcut trail three times. After the last intersection a long traverse right leads into willowy Marmot Creek at the site of instruments measuring stream flow.

Here leave the main trail, which zigs back left up Fisera Ridge, and follow a less distinct trail up the left (south) bank to the spring where Marmot Creek emerges in boisterous flight. Ahead are meadows dotted with boulders, rocky outcrops and spruce thickets.

People with spare energy can navigate to the Allan/Collembola col, climb Mt. Allan via its east ridge or more easily take in the lower summit of Mt. Collembola, which is just a grassy walk. See also options A and B.

Instrument near the junction of Marmot Creek and Fisera Ridge trails.

OPTIONAL DESCENT

23A Marmot Creek Road

3.1 km to Marmot Basin Road

A less steep but slightly longer option that returns you to Lower Marmot Basin Road via Marmot Basin (ski) trail.

Descend the up trail to the ski trail, perhaps taking in the afore mentioned shortcuts below the Fisera Ridge junction.

Turn left and follow the ski trail downhill through spruce forest, turning right where another logging road joins in from the left. Cross Marmot Creek to the left bank. A little farther along, your road joins Marmot Creek (logging) Road, that has come in from the left from cutblocks about Cabin Creek. Keep straight.

On Marmot Creek Road descend a long hill, then recross the creek to the right (south) bank. The gradient eases right off and you enjoy a pleasant riverside walk across from a line of sandstone crags.

Intersect Skogan Pass trail at the T-junction of roads at Two Ton Culvert. Turn right and walk to the next T-junction with Marmot Basin Road. Go straight and return the same way you came up.

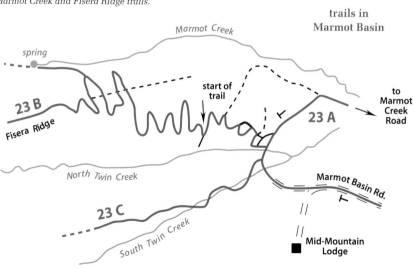

OPTIONS

23B Fisera Ridge

Distance ~1 km from Marmot Basin trail in Marmot Creek
Height gain ~120 m (394 ft.)
High point ~2286 m (7500 ft.)

This is a continuation of the main trail into the basin. At Marmot Creek, the better-used trail swings back left past a metal sign reassuringly stamped "Fisera Ridge."

Recross the straight-up shortcut trail and wind up the backbone of the ridge through larches (always a thrill) where in ages past Zdenek "Denny" Fisera tended to his instruments. Nowadays, researchers still hike up the trail to three hydrometeorological stations measuring everything from soil temperature to snow depth and wind speed, i.e., blowing snow-storms. Not for nothing did FES employees call Mt. Allan "Storm Mountain."

Continue to where the ridge levels in a meadow with views all around of Olympic Summit through to Mt. Allan and the lower summit of Collembola.

23C South Twin Creek

Distance ~1.3 km from Marmot Basin Road
Height gain ~228 m (750 ft.) from Marmot Basin Road
High point ~2133 m (7000 ft.)

A direct route to open slopes on the south side of the cirque.

Start from Marmot Basin ski trail between South and North Twin Creeks. Turn left up what was once a grassy logging road that crosses South Twin Creek twice before ending in a tangle of deadfall. A trail continues and crosses the creek another two times.

Then follows a long stretch along the north bank to a V-shaped valley bottom where the trail is forced into a steeply rising traverse to gain the rib between the twin creeks. Ends at an instrument site in the larches about 60 m below treeline.

This puts you in a good position to cut across to Fisera Ridge, which is one ridge to the north, and return that way.

Fisera Ridge. Behind is Mount Allan.

24 MOUNT ALLAN via CENTENNIAL RIDGE—map 2

Long day hike, scramble
Official trail with signposts, cairns &
red paint splodges on rocks
Distance 7.8 km to summit,
18.6 km to north trailhead
Height gain 1356 m (4450 ft.)
High point 2819 m (9,250 ft.)
Map 82 J/14 Spray Lakes Reservoir

Access Hwy. 40 (Kananaskis Trail). Turn west onto Mt. Allan Drive signed "Kananaskis Village, Nakiska Ski Area." Turn first left onto Centennial Drive, then next right onto Ribbon Creek Road. Drive past Kananaskis Wilderness Hostel to the upper Ribbon Creek parking lot at the end of the road.
Also accessible from "Mount Allan from the north" in Volume 3.

It was 1966. The next year was Canada's centennial and to mark this momentous occasion the Rocky Mountain Ramblers, spearheaded by Wally Drew, decided to build a trail up the long southeast ridge

Mt. Allan from Olympic Summit. To left rise the higher summits of Mt. Lougheed.

of Mt. Allan to the summit and down the even longer north ridge to Dead Man Flat. It would be the highest trail ever built in the Canadian Rockies, higher even than Jasper's celebrated Skyline trail. The work took three summers to complete and culminated in a champagne ceremony on the summit during a snow squall. A large wooden sign was erected but didn't stand for long. Within three months the picas had chewed away the supporting poles and in another two years the sign itself was fully digested. In 1983 an inedible bronze plaque was placed in the Mushroom Garden along the southeast ridge—or the Centennial Ridge as it is called nowadays.

Not many people do the whole traverse, because it requires two vehicles and a spare pair of feet, knees, hips etc. The vast majority of summiters prefer a there and back trip via the shorter Centennial Ridge, an entertaining ridgewalk with two

Looking up the second step with its rockband to Olympic Summit.

pitches of very easy scrambling. Bearing in mind the strenuous nature of the trip and the humongous height gain, start early from the parking lot.

REGULATORY NOTE Upwards of the Mine Scar the trail is closed for lambing April 1–June 21.

To Mine Scar 2.4 km
The initial climb is through woods in a maze of old coal mine roads narrowing to trails.

From the northeast corner of the parking lot at a kiosk, follow Hidden trail, which is signed and gated. Straight off, the trail curves up left. See the sketch map on page 67.

In about 300 m turn left onto the Mt. Allan Centennial trail, which is also Mt. Allan ski trail. Keep straight a little way in. At the next T-junction keep left up the hill (the ski trail traverses right, only delaying the inevitable), and cross the lowest of five roads leading to Mine Scar (going right returns you to the ski trail at a cabin). On reaching the second road, turn right a short way, then continue uphill. Cross the third road (Coal Mine ski trail). At the fourth turn left. Take the second "road" to the right and come to the sign about spring trail closures. Getting to this point takes about 30 minutes from the parking lot.

SIDE TRIP

24A Mine Scar

Mine Scar can be reached by following any of those intersecting roads to the left; they just lead to different levels of what was, over 50 years ago, a strip mine operated by the Kananaskis Exploration & Development Company, a subsidiary of Martin Nordegg's Brazeau Collieries. Appendix 1 of a brief released by the Energy Conservation Board in April 1975 recommended this mine be re-operational by 1982, but thankfully that never happened, although I wouldn't have said no to a parking lot at this level. Now 30 years reclaimed, the strip mine's a lush meadow with grass whose colour doesn't quite match that of the rest of the mountain.

The Claw. Photo Roy Millar

Centennial Ridge 5.4 km

Wind up to a not obvious fifth "road." Cross and head up right through last trees to open ground.

The sight of the trail crawling upwards, climbing 610 m in less than 2 km, is a real downer, but the grassy rib it follows has its compensations in the marvellous views that unfold, and summer's succession of flowers ending in late August with a purple colour scheme of asters and harebells. Take a breather on a shoulder, then zig some more up a shaley slope to the apex of three grass ribs—the start of Centennial Ridge proper.

Step no. 2 features a rock step that looks alarming but is easily turned on the right (north) side by a series of broad ledges and a gully that calls for hands in a few places. Under snow, however, this section can be awkward. When we were there one November, someone had rigged up a rope to the left of the gully.

Continue more easily to a grassy top pretentiously called Olympic Summit which is topped by a meteorology station. Having spent much energy in getting there it's discouraging to find the main summit looks as far away as ever and that immediately ahead is a dip that doesn't bode well for the return.

But the worst of the climbing is behind you and the most scenic part of the whole route is yet to come. This is where the trail winds through the Mushroom Garden (note the plaque), itself only a prelude to the passage between the rocky ridge crest and a row of 25-m-high conglomerate pinnacles. The most striking is called The Claw. Through the gaps look down on Memorial Lakes and across to mounts Sparrowhawk, Bogart and Ribbon Peak.

Some interesting down-scrambling follows and brings you to a section of scree ridge where you can either follow the crest or keep to the trail on the left slope. Tackle the final rise to the summit direct. (In case you're wondering, the trail traversing around the summit block to the north ridge is a sheep trail.)

The view from the top is little different from that seen on the way up. The greater height of Mt. Lougheed's four peaks effectively blocks the view to the west.

The easy upper section of the ridge leading to the summit. Photo Roy Millar

25 RIBBON FALLS — maps 2 & 4

Long day hike, backpack, bike 'n' hike
Official trail with signposts, minor
creek crossings
Distance 9. 2 km to Ribbon Falls
backcountry campground, 9.4 km to
Ribbon Falls
Height gain 311 m (1020 ft.) to
Ribbon Falls
High point 1814 m (5950 ft.)
Map 82 J/14 Spray Lakes Reservoir

Access Kananaskis Trail (Hwy. 40). Turn west onto Mt. Allan Drive signed "Kananaskis Village, Nakiska Ski Area." Turn first left onto Centennial Drive, then next right onto Ribbon Creek Road. Drive past Kananaskis Wilderness Hostel to the upper Ribbon Creek parking lot at the end of the road.
Also accessible from #77 Buller Pass.

Dipper Canyon.

This long and popular trail follows a spectacular valley hemmed in by cliffs to Ribbon Falls backcountry campground and Ribbon Falls. Your companion for the whole journey is the disgracefully behaved Ribbon Creek, its rapids and waterfalls at their very best after June rains and snow melt. Don't go for a first visit in late fall or you'll be disappointed.

Biking is allowed to the 4.3 km mark (end of logging road) where a bike rack is provided. This is a great boost, not only for hikers hoping to make Ribbon Lake and back in a day, but also for scramblers bound for Mt. Bogart.

REGULATORY NOTE The trail opens May 16.

To Link trail junction 2.4 km
From the end of the parking lot the trail crosses a meadow into the valley proper. Almost immediately stop to read the seat inscription commemorating Michael B. B. Crockford who wrote a geologic description of the Ribbon Creek area in 1949 prior to the opening of the strip mine. He also named Mt. Allan. To your right, the deep

Above Dipper Canyon.

79

Ribbon Falls.

grass hides a Rundle rock quarry opened by Elmer Smith in the 1960s.

Continue through the winding narrows, the way ahead seeming blocked by Ribbon Peak, which through many editions of the government topo map was incorrectly marked as Mt. Bogart. At 1 km cross the first bridge. Before K Country and bridges, hostellers were forced into a perilous shale traverse high above the river on the right bank. Back then Ribbon Creek was not the easy walk it is now.

In half a kilometre recross to the right bank. A longer stretch precedes the T-junction with Link trail. Keep straight. (Link turns off left down a hill, bridges the river and ultimately connects with Kovach trail, from where various trails can be followed to Kananaskis Village. (See #27, Kovach loops.)

To Memorial Lakes trail 0.9 km

Enjoy the stroll through "Toad Forest" as early hostellers called this section of spruce forest. En route is a pesky little side creek with plank bridge that forces most bikers to dismount, a picnic table on the left and an historic log loading ramp on the right. A cairn on the right side signals the trail up the north fork to Memorial Lakes.

To bike rack 1 km

In 300 m cross the north fork on a bridge. A meadow on the right side with picnic table, interpretive plaque and tastefully strewn pieces of metal was the site of an Eau Claire logging camp offering on-site accommodation. Eau Claire was busy in this valley and in the north fork at various times from 1886 to the beginning of the Second World War. A barn was still standing here in the late 1950s.

Shortly the road turns left (southwest) between the cliffs of Mt. Kidd on the left and the cliffs of Ribbon Peak on the right. Continue to its end at a bike rack. Actually the road crossed the river here. Back then logging took place in winter when the river was stilled and frozen.

To Ribbon Falls 5.1 km

A trail carries on, undulating between creek level and banktop viewpoints. On down sections, cross side creeks on assorted bridges. The trail then rises and traverses above a series of canyons with chutes and waterfalls. Allow extra time for forays to viewpoints. At 1.8 km from the bike rack, you pass the ruins of log cabins, their logs a popular place for a sitdown and snack.

After a second climb enter lower Dipper Canyon (named by early hostellers after "a chubby grey songbird with an amazing adaptability to rough water"), their progeny still bobbing about on mist-sprayed ledges. The trail descends to creek level, then makes a third climb above upper Dipper Canyon, which features more dippers and the highest waterfall below Ribbon Falls.

After this the creek calms down somewhat and apart from a slippery shale bank (bypass available) the going is uneventful below the avalanche slopes of Mt. Bogart. Pass by the big cirque between Mt. Kidd and its south summit. At snowmelt, waterfalls step plunging down the cliffs

The trail below the cliffs of Mt. Bogart.

of South Kidd are an arresting sight. A stoney side creek crossing with no bridge signals your imminent arrival at Ribbon Falls backcountry campground; #13 is the desired view lot if you can stand the increased decibel count of Ribbon Falls.

From the campground it's a short climb to Ribbon Falls viewpoint, identified by a bench and a memorial seat to 18-year-old Simon White. En route pass side trails leading to the bottom of the falls, a place to avoid when the falls are in spate unless equipped with full storm gear.

GOING FARTHER

25A Ribbon Lake

Scramble
Distance 1.9 km from campground
Height gain 277 m (910 ft.)
High point 2076 m (6810 ft.)

The cliff bands responsible for a spectacular series of waterfalls, cause much difficulty to the backpacker bound for Ribbon Lake. The trail beyond Ribbon Falls viewpoint is steeper, more difficult and even dangerous. There was a serious accident here in the 1970s before the chains went in. Backpackers with heavy packs, particularly women who generally have less arm strength than men, will have difficulty pulling themselves up the chains, stated Tony.

If hauling yourself plus pack up chains doesn't appeal, leave your camping gear at Ribbon Creek and make Ribbon Lake a side trip. If you must camp at Ribbon Lake take easier routes: Buller Pass (#77) or Guinn's Pass (#31). Lately, it's become the fad to make a one-day circuit using Galatea, Guinn's Pass and Ribbon Creek trails in that order. Why NOT let gravity work for you?

The headwall. Top: Kirsti near the top of the first chain. Photo Shelly Sochr

Bottom: Angélique descending the third-chain. Photo Allan Mandel

From the falls, the trail heads up right into dark forest, climbing quite steeply, then arcs back left below a scree slope and across the creek bounding down from the cirque southwest of Mt. Bogart (scrambler's ascent route). At runoff this creek may be impossible to cross.

Continue traversing, at the last crossing a scree slope to the bottom of the headwall.

With the help of chain no. 1, climb a moderately angled corner until level with a large ledge on the left, then traverse 3 m of intervening slick slab (handrail). Walk along the wide ledge to a third chain and heave yourself up 5 m of difficult rock, bulging in the middle, onto easier ground above. Wend right, then left onto a long horizontal ledge, again protected with a handrail. As you edge above the big drop, it's disquieting to know a fall from here would definitely kill you. Pass a caution sign for people coming the other way. This doesn't mean you can relax your vigilance; the upcoming step, easy, are greasy smooth and a sli, send you perhaps not over the edge the creek, but to the very brink, hang, on to a few bushes like the hero of a 192, Harold Lloyd movie. In the middle of all this trauma, the upper falls are well-worth a detour for a photo.

At the top, look back for a thrilling view of Ribbon Creek Valley hemmed in by the cliffs of mounts Bogart and Kidd. In the other direction is Ribbon Lake with its calendar backdrop of peak 217373.

The trail continues around the north shore to Ribbon Lake backcountry campground located at the far end in the shelter of trees. As you go look for springs bubbling out of circular depressions at the lake edge.

Ribbon Lake from the east shore. This is my favourite view of the lake with peak 217373 in the background. Photo Roy Millar

LAKES — map 2

crossings
second Lake,
...ird Lake from trailhead
Height gain 585 m (1920 ft.) to Second
Lake, 690 m (2264 ft.) to Third Lake
High point 2213 m (7260 ft.) above
Third Lake
Map 82 J/14 Spray Lakes Reservoir

Access: Via #25 Ribbon Creek trail. Turn right 300 m before the bridge over the north fork.

Waterfalls, tarns, cliffs. The head of Ribbon Creek's north fork is a magical place and reasonably easy to get to now the trail is well-trodden. Beyond First Lake, though, the way remains rough and steep in spots, particularly the slope below Third Lake, which is almost a scramble. Know also that by September Third Lake is reduced to two little puddles, so go early in the hiking season: mid-July is about right. For scramblers this trail doubles as the access route to Bogart Tower, Ribbon Peak and the fourth peak of Mt. Lougheed (NOT Wind Mountain — Gem Trek has it right on their maps).

HISTORY NOTE The three tarns were named Memorial Lakes on September 27, 1986, as a reminder of the tragic events of the previous June when 13 people died in three separate plane crashes, 11 of them searchers out looking for biologist Orval Pall and pilot Ken Wolff. Contrary to what some people believe, none of the crashes occurred in this beautiful valley. To learn more, read #31 Guinn's Pass, Cox Hill in Volume 2 and East Wind Pond in Volume 3.

REGULATORY NOTE The valley is closed Dec 1–Jun 15 and camping is by permit only.

To the Waterfalls 3.3 km

A pile of rocks marks the entrance to the north fork trail on the right at 272430.

Not far in is a warning sign with drawings of unexploded bombs. I thought at first this was a ploy to keep people like me on the straight and narrow trail, but discovered it's a precautionary measure taken by Nakiska's avalanche control. A sharp uphill precedes two skimpy traverses of shale banks. After a second uphill the trail divides; go either way. Then it's down to the creek. The second time you go down to the creek you're in for a long stint under 6-m-high willow bushes. Use the right-hand trail to cross a side creek.

Then a barely recognizable logging road comes in from across the creek and you follow it up to a small camping area. A few metres on is a junction. Turn right. (Straight on leads to the creek below the canyon.) Climb a few metres of steep ground, then detour left to enter the canyon between waterfalls — one of the day's highlights.

To First Lake 0.5 km

Retrace your steps to the main trail and continue grovelling up the slope to a junction. The main trail turns left into a traverse. (Continuing uphill is a climber's access trail to the valley between Sparrowhawk and Lougheed under "Nopasseron Col" as Pete calls it.)

Traverse above the canyon in which the river is behaving with reckless abandon. Note one long ribbon fall as you continue around a bend and up a small slab to flat ground where the water is calmly gliding along like nothing's going to happen. Past a confluence is another junction. Turn left and cross the tributary, (The trail ahead is another variation on the climber's access trail.)

Keep left and arrive shortly at First Lake about halfway along its north shore at a camping area. With its willowy surround and dish-water contents, this lake is in no way attractive, though the setting under Bogart Tower is undeniably grand.

Second Memorial Lake: The emerald. Rising behind is Bogart Tower.

Side trip to canyon waterfalls. Photo Alf Skrastins

Memorial cairn at Third Lake.

To the tower's left, Memorial Falls tumbles down the headwall from Third Lake. (Or to be scrupulously correct, the lake's water drains underground and bursts forth about a third of the way down the headwall.) To its right is the scrambler's descent from Third Lake: the top to toe scree gully immediately left of the tower.

To Second Lake—the Emerald 0.7 km
Coming up is a stiff climb of about 137 vertical m (450 ft.) up a headwall.

But first the trail continues along the north shore and crosses the inlet in a tangle of willow bushes to the south bank.

Turn right and head upstream between a rocky slope and the willowy bank. Where the creek angles right at a fall, climb a scree step (cairn). At the top, head left up more scree (cairns) to a bench below a belt of trees. Continue ahead to a cairn on a boulder.

There is the option here of zigging up the scree slope to your left, then traversing across to the lake.

Alternatively, climb the treed slope ahead. In detail: follow the bottom edge of the scree a way, then double back right, below a small rockband. When the way is clear the trail climbs straight up the slope and joins the scree option at the top. Turn right and descend slightly to Second Memorial Lake.

If, like me, you've looked down on this lake with great longing from the summits of Sparrowhawk or Allan, this is a special moment. The unusual clarity of the water and its brilliant emerald colour coupled with its setting are great inducements for idling away an hour or two on its shores.

To Third Lake 0.6 km
Out of sight in a cirque behind Bogart Tower, Third Lake is more difficult to access, despite the deceptively easy contour lines shown on the topo map.

From where you first saw the emerald lake, traverse on game trail to the west end of the lake. Pass below a rotten gully. You're going to be climbing the grass and rock slope to the right of the gully. (Farther to the right the whole hillside breaks down in screes.)

The trail follows the diagonal left to right grassy ramp between cliff bands. The ramp narrows sensationally, but luckily the top band ends at this point, enabling the trail to zig left. A couple more zigs, and a long easy traverse above the gully lead to a tiny hanging valley rimmed by steep slopes. The trail climbs the grassy rib up ahead. At the top (or before), head left, aiming for the lightly treed neck of land connecting Bogart Tower to Mt. Bogart—the day's high point.

From the neck descend into a cirque enclosed by the cliffs of Ribbon Peak and Mt. Bogart. At its outer edge lies Third Lake with its signature promontory of spruce trees. Hopefully by the time you get there the afternoon shadow cast by high rock walls will not yet have spread its pall over the scene, and equally hopefully the lake will be filled to the brim.

On a hummock at the edge of the drop-off is a memorial cairn and plaque. Read the first and last lines of the sonnet *High Flight,* written by 19-year-old fighter pilot John Magee. Strange how something scribbled on the back of a letter sent to his mother two months before he died during the Battle of Britain in 1941 has endured all this time. President Reagan quoted this very sonnet after the loss of the Challenger astronauts. It was also Brad Washburn's favourite recitation.

OPTIONAL DESCENT

This is a steep scrambler's route down to First Lake.

Starting immediately right of Bogart Tower as you look out is a scree gully. If uncomfortable at the top, wade through dense spruce thickets on the right side where it's hard to get any downward momentum going at all. Where the gully splits, follow the neck between the two, then continue easily down the right side of the left-hand gully, so bypassing a small rock band in the gully bed. Level with the bottom of Bogart Tower, cross to the left side to avoid a small cliff. Below the cliff wend back right (Memorial Falls view) and follow a dribble of scree into forest where game trails continue to the valley bottom. Likely, you'll have to step left a bit to locate the main valley trail this side of the creek crossing.

Third Lake. Photo Alf Skrastins

27 KOVACH LOOPS—map 2

Half-day hikes
Official signposted trails
Longest distance 7.5 km loop
Height gain ~150 m (492 ft.)
High point 1675 m (5495 ft.)
Map 82 J/14 Spray Lakes Reservoir

Access Hwy. 40 (Kananaskis Trail) at Kananaskis Village. Turn west on Mt. Allan Drive signed "Kananaskis Village, Nakiska Ski Area." Turn first left onto Centennial Drive and follow it up the hill to Kananaskis Village. At the top turn second right onto Terrace Drive and drive to a parking lot for Mount Kidd Manor.
Also accessible from #29 Terrace trail and #25 Ribbon Falls.

Easy, but hilly forest circuits with good views. Because you're following well-signed 4-m-wide ski trails, these loops are a good introduction to the area for novice tourists who have absolutely no chance of going astray.

The high point of Kovach. Mt. Sparrowhawk in the background, showing the final section of the scrambler's route to the summit.

Kovach 4.5–5 km
Start from the top end of the parking lot at a gated road with a hiking icon. At the 4-way junction a little way in, turn left on a paved trail. (The dirt road ahead is Terrace trail north.)

Follow the paved trail past a biffy and picnic tables to a signed junction on a left-hand bend. Turn right onto a wide track (former logging road), which is Kovach trail. In about 180 m go straight at a Y-junction. (To left is Terrace trail South.)

Kovach winds uphill, then heads right to a junction with Aspen trail in a damp meadow. Anyone resting at the picnic table will need to slather themselves in Muskol.

Keep left on Kovach and continue climbing. The next sweeping left-hand bend has a cairned shortcut trail. After the following right-hand bend, a large cairn on the left side indicates the unofficial trail to Mt. Kidd lookout site (see #28).

Continue on Kovach to a look-alike junction with Aspen Link trail and again stay left. As you climb the hill look back for a fine view of The Wedge before rounding a bend and disappearing into spruce forest indicating the upper limit of the 1936 fire. Come to the loop's high point with bench. Here join a logging road built to salvage timber after the fire.

On your way down, a fresh lot of mountains appears to the west across Ribbon Creek Valley: Ribbon Peak, Mt. Sparrowhawk and Mt. Allan. A picnic table marks the start of two long downhill zigs to the T-junction with Link trail. Should you go left here you'd link up with Ribbon Creek trail (another possible circuit that can be incorporated with Terrace trail north).

But for today turn right on Kovach and descend Buffalo-berry Alley.

Coming up are three different ways back to the parking lot.

ENDINGS

1. Aspen trail 3 km (7.5 km loop)
Turn first right on Aspen trail and climb to a junction with Aspen Link. Keep left onto the nicest stretch of trail in the area: aspens, of course, flowery meadows and two fine viewpoints, one with a picnic table. On rejoining Kovach, keep left and return the same way you came up.

2. Terrace Link 1.8 km (6.7 km loop)
Turn second right onto Terrace Link. The trail rolls across strips of damp willowy meadows before joining Terrace trail North. Turn right and in about 500 m reach Kananaskis Village.

3. Terrace trail North 1.8 km (6.8 km loop)
Follow Kovach all the way down the hill past the two signed junctions to a T-junction on a corner. Turn right and return on Terrace trail North to Kananaskis Village. Watch for Terrace Link joining in from the right about 500 m before the end.

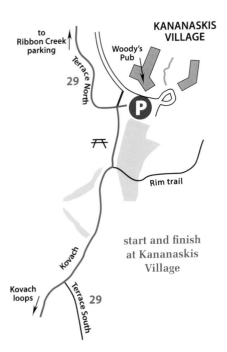

Aspen trail, looking toward the Mackay Hills and The Wedge.

28 MOUNT KIDD LOOKOUT SITE—map 2

Half-day, short day
Unofficial trail
Distance 3.1 km one way from village
Height gain 579 m (1900 ft.) from village
High point 2103 m (6900 ft.)
Map 82 J/14 Spray Lakes Reservoir

Access Hwy. 40 (Kananaskis Trail) at Kananaskis Village. Turn west on Mt. Allan Drive signed "Kananaskis Village, Nakiska Ski Area." Turn first left onto Centennial Drive and follow it up the hill to Kananaskis Village. At the top, turn second right onto Terrace Drive and drive to a parking lot for Mount Kidd Manor.

A lookout, even the site of one, is a magnet for view aficionados. The Mount Kidd Lookout, sited on the northeast shoulder of Mt. Kidd at 286418, was an unusually short-lived lookout that saw service between 1982 and 1992, then was removed in 1997.

At one time K Country had plans to access the lookout by a nice winding trail at the forest edge. That never happened and now a trail made by K Village staff goes straight up the steep east front on grass. Cruelly tiring it is, and not one to do when the temperature is hitting 30°C.

WARNING The meadows are a grizzly hotspot.

Kovach Access 1.9 km

First, you have to leave the environs of the village. See the sketch map under #27.

As follows: start from the top end of the parking lot at a gated road with hiking icon. At the 4-way junction a little way in, turn left. Follow the paved trail past a biffy and picnic tables to a signed junction on a left-hand bend. Turn right onto a wide track (ex-logging road), which is Kovach trail. In about 180 m keep straight at a Y-junction. (To left is Terrace trail.)

Kovach winds uphill, then heads right to a junction with Aspen trail in a damp, buggy meadow.

Keep left on Kovach and continue climbing. The next sweeping left-hand bend has a cairned shortcut trail. After the following right-hand bend, look for a large cairn on the left side and a dirt trail heading into the trees. (This is NOT the narrower trail heading left at the bend itself.)

To the Lookout Site 1.2 km

Shortly the trail steepens dramatically. At a division go either way and climb through a small rockband to gain the meadows. Then grovel (and I use that word deliberately) up steep grass to the right of a shallow, bushy gully. Arrive on the northeast ridge and follow it up left at the edge of trees to the shoulder. A concrete pad marks the lookout site.

As expected, the lookout site is a superior viewpoint. You look down on a large portion of the Kananaskis Valley, greatly changed since 1979. Rising above it all are heaps of familiar mountains: to the west mounts Bogart, Sparrowhawk, Lougheed and Allan displaying its Centennial Ridge in profile, and to the east the G8 Summits, Old Baldy, The Wedge and Fisher Peak up Evan-Thomas Creek.

The Lookout.

GOING FARTHER

Having done the vertical, who can resist wandering farther along the grassy northeast ridge to the foot of Mt. Kidd's northeast buttress?

#28. Climbing steep grass.

#28. The lookout site and the grassy ridge extending to the foot of Mt. Kidd's northeast buttress.

#29. Terrace trail south of Kananaskis Village runs below the east face of Mt. Kidd.

29 TERRACE TRAIL—maps 2, 3 & 4

Day hike
Official trail with signposts, creek
crossing
Distance 9.9 km whole trail
Height gain N-S 40 m (130 ft.)
High point 1590 m (5217 ft.)
Map 82 J/14 Spray Lakes Reservoir

North Accesses Hwy. 40 (Kananaskis Trail). Turn west onto Mt. Allan Drive signed "Kananaskis Village, Nakiska Ski Area."
1. Ribbon Creek parking lots. Turn first left onto Centennial Drive, then next right onto Ribbon Creek Road. Just past Kananaskis Wilderness Hostel, turn left into the lower parking lot. The trail starts at the picnic shelter between parking lots.
2. Usual start/finish at Kananaskis Village. Turn first left onto Centennial Drive and follow it up the hill to Kananaskis Village. At the top, turn second right onto Terrace Drive and drive to the parking lot for Mount Kidd Manor.
South Access Hwy. 40 (Kananaskis Trail) at Galatea Creek parking lot. Via #30 Galatea Creek trail just after the first crossing of Galatea Creek.
Also accessible from #27 Kovach loops.

Terrace is an easy but undulating trail that follows terraces of the Kananaskis River between Ribbon Creek and Galatea Creek. Most people start from either Access 2 or the south access and put a vehicle at each end, the plan being to end the walk in one of the village's numerous watering holes. The trail's intricacies around the village are shown on the sketch map under #27.

The southern part of the trail is also the scrambler's access to Mt. Kidd and the ice climber's access to Mt. Kidd Falls.

NOTES 1. Disregard all signs and trails pertaining to snowshoeing. 2. Mountain bikers are plentiful. 3. The annual spring closure of Galatea Creek trail does not apply to the section at the south end shared by both trails.

The gully between the two summits of Mt. Kidd is a popular tourist stop.

NORTH TO SOUTH

Terrace trail North
(Access 1 to Access 2) 2.4 km

This northern section is a 4-m-wide ski trail (logging road) that travels through forest within sound of cars revving up Centennial Drive to Kananaskis Village. In 2008 the section between Kovach and the village was widened further to accommodate horses and wagons.

From Ribbon Creek picnic shelter the trail crosses Ribbon Creek Road and heads for the bridge over Ribbon Creek. The same point can be reached by trail from the upper parking lot. See the sketch map on page 67.

On old road wind up the far bank for 800 m to a T-junction with Kovach trail on a terrace. Turn left on the very much wider Terrace trail, which undulates along to a Y-junction with Terrace Link trail coming in from the right. Again stay left. Reach a signed 4-way junction with a paved trail close to the parking lot for Mount Kidd Manor. Head straight for Woody's Pub patio for a burger and beer.

If you've brought your own lunch turn right on the paved trail.

Terrace trail South (Access 2 to South Access) 7.5 km

The southern section is a scenic forest trail with one unavoidable creek crossing.

Start from the top end of Access 2 parking lot at a gated road with hiking icon. At the 4-way junction a little way in, turn left on a paved trail. (The dirt road ahead is Terrace trail North.)

Follow the paved trail past a biffy and picnic tables to a signed T-junction on a left-hand bend. Turn right onto a wide track (logging road), which is Kovach trail. Follow for about 180 m to a signed Y-junction. Turn left onto Terrace trail South. (Kovach trail continues ahead.)

Head gradually downhill on an older, narrower track. Where the track turns left, go straight on a signed trail.

Finally free of junctions, though not yet of Japanese tourists, follow the trail to the start of the scenic section where the trail winds and undulates along the terrace rim, now and then offering great views up Evan-Thomas Creek to Fisher Peak. Down below you are chains of beaver ponds and the K Country golf course. I've spent an enjoyable 10 minutes at one of these viewpoints watching golfers putt into the largest pond, a small, and some might say petty revenge for being turfed off the golf course for wearing a Mo Zeegers T-shirt.

Thus far, the mighty east face of Mt. Kidd, which acts like a giant reflector, throwing the sun's heat back down onto a dry forest of pine, aspen and scrub, has always been in view. But then you enter a darker, cooler forest with deadfall where the trail flattens and you can see nothing at all. In spring listen for avalanches. At such time waterfalls leaping down gullies in the cliffs fill small streams crossing the trail.

Come to the one crossing possibly requiring a paddle. This is the wide, stony gully separating North and South Kidd—the scrambler's jumping-off point for Mt. Kidd's highest point which now sports Firenet's VHF repeater station #107 and two golf clubs in the cairn.

Continue through forest. Approaching the south end, you touch the Kananaskis River at a narrows where a rocky ridge slopes down to the water. Close by is a large algae-green beaver pond. Then you cross another stoney creekbed, which is Kidd Falls Creek (see SIDE TRIP).

Five minutes later you reach the T-junction with Galatea Creek trail on the north bank of Galatea Creek. Only another half kilometre to go.

Turn left and cross Galatea Creek on a bridge. Shortly cross the Kananaskis River via suspension bridge and stagger up the hill to Galatea Creek parking lot.

SIDE TRIP

29A Kidd Falls Creek

Unofficial trails
Distance ~600 m to first falls
Height gain 137+ m (450+ ft.)
High point 1676+ m (5500+ ft.)

The trail on the north bank of the creek has developed over the years as a climber's access to Kidd Falls, a IV WI 4 ice climb. No need to go that far; many lower falls in the creek make this a pleasant diversion. Just know that the trails are steeper and rougher than Terrace trail and they confuse with variations.

From up close you're treated to a view of the dramatic north end of the Lewis thrust fault—a perfect example of an anti-cline and syncline pair. Located on the syncline is the falls. More amazing are the wafer-thin folds of the anticline, which are not quite as ethereal as they look from Hwy. 40.

View from the first falls of the Spoon Needle. Some scramblers descend the facing ridge to the cliff, then head off into the valley to the west.

Leave Terrace trail one creekbed north of the Galatea Creek trail junction.

Follow the right (north) side of the stoney creekbed. After a trail develops, zig up a steep hill, then traverse left across a scree bank. At a fork, go left on stones. Climb a little to below the open bank. Again keep left (the much steeper right-hand trail is more often used as a descent route). At the right-hand bend in the creek the trail climbs the grassy ridge alongside to the base of the first fall. Contour right below a small rockband and meet the descent trail. Turn left along a ledge to the top of the rockband and waterfall. Already there is a fabulous view to the south of "Spoon Needle" ("Aiguille du Cuiller"), a scrambler's peak usually approached from the Fortress ski area access road.

Above here the trail degenerates. If inclined, climb past three more falls. The higher you go the steeper and stonier the terrain, but the better the view. Limber pines make an appearance and likely snow into June. Kidd Falls is not worth the final effort of grovelling up a whole lot of rubble and risking a rock on your head. Admire from afar.

30 GALATEA CREEK to LILLIAN LAKE—map 4

Lillian Lake. At the extreme right you can spot the optional descent route from Galatea Lakes.

Day hike, backpack
Official trail with signposts
Distance 6.2 km to Lillian Lake
Height gain 492 m (1614 ft.)
High point 2027 m (6650 ft.) at lake
Map 82 J/14 Spray Lakes Reservoir

Access Hwy. 40 (Kananaskis Trail) at Galatea Creek parking lot.
Also accessible from #29 Terrace trail and #31 Guinn's Pass.

Galatea Creek was once a place for adventurers, being fraught with difficulty and uncertainty. In the early morning, low water in the Kananaskis River would entice people to wade across to the "trail." On returning in the late afternoon, they would sometimes find the river a raging torrent and be forced to spend the night trapped on the west bank within sight of their cars.

Since then the trail has been rebuilt with umpteen bridges, including a suspension bridge across the Kananaskis River. Now every man and his dog goes to Lillian Lake, including part-time conser-

vation officers who pick up garbage and tick off anyone with a dog not on a leash. So the clientele has changed. Nevertheless, it's worth dodging the crowds up this moderately strenuous trail to view Lillian Lake and maybe stay at its backcountry campground. Lovers of the alpine can climb higher to Galatea Lakes. Scramblers also use this trail to access Mt. Kidd South.

NAMING NOTE The name of this disgracefully behaved piece of water is for once appropriate. It appears that Galatea, meaning "milk white," was a sea nymph who turned her beloved Acis (killed by Polyphemus with a rock), into a river that forever after bore his name. Okay, so it was named after a battleship named after the nymph.

REGULATORY NOTE Beyond the junction with Terrace trail South, the trail is closed until about July 1.

To Terrace trail 0.5 km
Descend to the suspension bridge over the Kananaskis River and cross. Shortly

Lower Galatea Lake. In the background is the ridge between the two lakes and The Tower.

the trail bridges Galatea Creek to a junction with Terrace trail on the north bank. Turn left.

To the forks 3.7 km
After an up-down, you cross to the south bank on bridge no. 2, then back again just before a side creek comes squeezing in between Spoon Needle and Fortress Ridge. The next two creek crossings come in quick succession under the precipitous gable end of the ridge. Between bridges 4 and 5 a chasm opened up during the spring floods of 1995 when the river was making a new bed for itself, forcing K Country to reroute the trail.

A long stretch follows on the north bank. You cross stoney avalanche paths, make another post-'95 detour, then climb high across more stoney paths to a grassy hillside above an impassible canyon. At the high point a side trail leads down to a dicey viewpoint for a waterfall. Nearby, a scrambler's access trail marked by cairns takes off up the hillside bound for South Kidd.

Descend and in a couple of minutes cross bridge no. 6 into spruce forest. Shortly come to a hard-to-spot T-junction at the forks. Turn right and cross bridge no. 7 into the northwest fork. (The lesser trail ahead is the unofficial trail to Guinn's Lost Lake #32.)

To Guinn's Pass turnoff 1.1 km
After wandering through the flowery glades of the right bank, you cross to the left bank and begin the stiff climb to Lillian Lake. Inevitably, it seems, some kind, concerned person on the way down will stop and tell you you're "almost there." Well not quite.

Almost a kilometre before your destination is a junction. Keep left. (Guinn's Pass trail takes off from the bottom of an avalanche slope to right.)

To Lillian Lake 0.9 km
After more climbing, arrive at Lillian Lake's east shore. Cross the outlet and follow the north shoreline, keeping left, to the backcountry campground at the west end. Every summer weekend, the environs of the lake takes on a festive atmosphere from the mingling of campers and day trippers who are fishing, socializing, even swimming in chartreuse-coloured waters shallow enough to retain a little of the sun's warmth.

Lillian Lake. Photo Alf Skrastins

GOING FARTHER

30A Galatea Lakes

Unofficial trails
Distance 4 km return to Lillian Lake
Added height gain 183 m (600 ft.)
High point 2210 m (7250 ft.)

While Lillian Lake is beautiful, the surroundings don't turn me on and I have to climb higher to that fascinating alpine country about Galatea Lakes that, incidentally, were known as Engadine Lakes when we first knocked around the area. Getting there requires a steep initial climb, but after that the going is fairly easy on rough trails marked by cairns.

The trail starts at the biffy and heads north. (DO NOT start from campsite #14 and head west!) Alternatively, reach the biffy by keeping right half-way along the north shore.

From the biffy the trail crosses a dry draw and climbs a steep, scrubby headwall to the left of it. Top out on scree and follow cairns veering left. In front is a small ridge. The latest version of trail climbs a scree slope and heads through the right-hand (northernmost) gap in the ridge. Beyond and below lies Lower Galatea Lake, a midnight-blue body of water filling a rock-girt bowl, A side trail leads down to the east shore.

The mountain backdrop is The Tower. To your right rise the south slopes of peak 217373, which is more readily climbed from Buller Pass if 396 m (1300 ft.) of scree appeals.

The trail continues west above the north shore. Ahead is another low ridge blocking the way to the upper lake. This time the trail descends to the lake's west end, then climbs through the left-hand gap of the ridge. In the gap is a 4-way junction. Go straight. (The trail joining in from the left is the optional descent. The trail to right heads out along the ridge top—a great viewpoint for the lower lake.)

The trail fast loses definition as it descends meadow to the brighter waters of Upper Galatea Lake, cradled in a hollow below The Tower. Along its west shoreline wild flower fanatics can search for a white version of creeping beardtongue.

OPTIONAL DESCENT

Because of its steepness, this trail only works as a descent route. Its only asset, apart from being a shortcut, is the view of Lillian Lake.

Return to the 4-way junction and keep right. The trail traverses scree above the south shore of Lower Galatea Lake, then passes through the southernmost gap in the small ridge. Descend a very steep strip of grass between scree and the forest edge to a brief levelling. Here you turn left and slither down a nasty, stony slope to campsite #14.

Upper Galatea Lake.

31 GUINN'S PASS — map 4

Long day, backpack
Official trail with signposts
Distance 2.6 km
Height gain 457 m (1500 ft.) from
Galatea Creek
Height loss 259 m (850 ft.)
to Ribbon Creek
High point 2423 m (7950 ft.)
Map 82 J/14 Spray Lakes Reservoir

South Access Via #30 Galatea Creek to Lillian Lake at the 5.3 km mark.
North Access Via #77 Buller Pass trail 1.3 km west of Ribbon Lake.

HISTORY NOTE FIRST Many years ago, Alvin Guinn took a string of 20 packhorses over the ridge from Galatea Creek to Ribbon Lake. Not by this route exactly. He went up the avalanche gully farther to the right. By the time he reached the ridge night was falling and in the need to hurry he led his horses straight down the scree slope to Ribbon Lake! Next morning he looked for a better route back and that's when he discovered Guinn's Pass.

Lest you think the pass is a pushover for those of us on foot, you're wrong. From both sides this is a steep, demanding climb exposed to bad weather. Wait until most of the snow has melted. For day trippers the pass is a worthwhile alternative to Lillian Lake, with the added pleasure of climbing a minor summit to look at Guinn's original route.

REGULATORY NOTE The southern half of the route usually opens up on July 1.

SOUTH TO NORTH

To the Pass 1.7 km

The trail leaves Galatea Creek trail about 800 m before Lillian Lake.

You cross the creek and start up a flowery avalanche gully that soon becomes a stony gully, a suffocating furnace at midday when the sun bounces off white

Alvin Guinn (1915-2006), father of Rick Guinn, who with his wife Karen runs Boundary Ranch in the Kananaskis Valley.

stones. In theory, backpackers should aim to put the gully behind them early in the day, but are usually found lying about in various states of heat exhaustion, greedily lapping up water from the gully bed. Higher up at treeline you transfer to a bit of scree on the right side, then (gully faded out), zig back and forth on close-cropped turf pungent with sheep droppings. A tremendous panoramic view opening up behind you is a good excuse to stop often. Ahead, the eye is caught by peak 217373, which only fully reveals its massive northeastern precipice when you reach the cairn at the pass.

Even if you are carrying on down the north side of the pass, it's worth dropping the packs for a walk up the easy peak to the east.

To Buller Pass trail 0.9 km

No greater contrast between the two sides of Guinn's Pass could be imagined. The north slope is grassless and treeless, just plenty of stones and lots of snow early in the season. Under the eye of the precipice make long, sweeping zigzags on easy-angled talus into a barren basin, all bumps and hollows, one of which holds a shallow tarn. On the bench an unofficial shortcut to Buller Pass heads left. The official trail descends the bench to the signposted junction with Buller Pass trail in upper Ribbon Creek. This occurs where Ribbon Spring gushes out of the hillside on mossy banks.

OPTION

31A Peak 237374

Route
Distance 0.9 km from pass
Height gain 180 m (590 ft.)
High point 2606 m (8550 ft.)

The little top immediately east of the pass is a simple walk up scree. What a viewpoint!

From the pass walk east up a wide, stoney ridge to the top, which is marked by a cairn and a pole.

To the south is a welter of peaks, Mt. Galatea and The Fortress among them, shadowy shapes among which Lillian Lake and Lower Galatea Lake glow like bright jewels. In the opposite direction you can inspect both Buller passes, Red Peak, Mt. Bogart showing the scrambler's route, and the long connecting ridge to Mt. Kidd South, which makes you yearn to carry on.

This insignificant summit is the scene of momentous happenings, from Guinn's adventurous crossing, to the tragic loss of Orval Pall and Ken Wolff, which started off K Country's largest search. The col to the east is where Guinn first crossed over the ridge with his packhorses. For variety, some people descend his ascent route to

The grassy south side of the pass, looking towards Mt. Galatea.

Galatea Creek, down the heathery hillside to the south and into the grassy avalanche gully that flows into Galatea Creek not far below Guinn's Pass junction.

Some friends and I once made the mistake of following the forested ridge to the left of the gully. Not only is it steep and rocky lower down, but we suddenly realized we were looking down the cliff where Wolff's Cessna crashed exactly a year ago to the day with tragic results. Some places are better left unvisited. (To read more, see #26 Memorial Lakes, Cox Hill in Volume 2 and East Wind Pond in Volume 3.)

Opposite top: The north side of Guinn's Pass, showing the zigzags on scree. At left is peak 237374, which is easily climbed from the pass.

Opposite bottom: Looking down on Guinn's Pass from peak 237374. The mountain 217373 is a scramble from Buller Pass.
Photo Ron Hunter

32 LOST LAKE—map 4

Alvin Guinn's cabin at the start of the trail.

Day hike
Unofficial trail with flagging, creek crossings
Distance 6.8 km from trailhead
Height gain 500 m (1640 ft.)
High point 2018 m (6620 ft.)
Map 82 J/14 Spray Lakes Reservoir

Access Hwy. 40 (Kananaskis Trail). Via #30 Galatea Creek to Lillian Lake at the forks.
Also accessible from #91A Rummel Pass.

Escape the crowds bound for Lillian Lake by taking a quiet forest walk to a lake in Galatea Creek's southwest fork. It's a much less strenuous alternative. However, this trap-line trail cut by Alvin Guinn is not a trail to be enjoyed by novices, there having been no deadfall removal for the last 50 years and more.

To peak 238342 turnoff 0.3 km
Just *before* you cross Galatea Creek for the seventh time, leave the official trail and head straight, then up the left bank to a trail that leads in a few minutes to the ruins of Guinn's cabin. From here you're set for an easy walk along the left (southeast) bank all the way to the lake.

Not too far along you come to a major side valley and trail junction. Keep straight and paddle across the side creek. (Trail to left is the route to peak 238342.)

To Lost Lake 2.3 km
After this the trail accumulates height gradually in a forest strangely bereft of shrubs, only occasionally making forays down to the creek. Two side creeks on, keep left up a hill (logs have been laid across the false right-hand, yellow-flagged trail). The only other recognizable landmark is a muddy side creek.

Not far beyond the muddy creek is another junction. Most people will go left up a hill into a glade and through a few willows to the northeast end of the lake. The colour? Olive green. I recommend you climb grassy bluffs above the south shoreline for the greatest view of the lake, backdropped by Rummel Pass and The Tower.

But back to the last junction. If bound for Rummel Pass (and 99% of people do this route in reverse) head right and read #91A backwards.

Lost Lake from the northwest shore.

Hill 238342, heading down the west ridge from the summit.
Down below is Lost lake. At far left you can just spot Rummel Pass under The Tower.

OPTION

32A Peak 238342

**Unofficial trail, mostly route, creek crossing
Distance 2.4 km to summit,
4.4 km to lake
Height gain 635 m (2080 ft.)
Height loss 466 m (1530 ft.)
High point 2493 m (8180 ft.)**

This is the big grassy hill that overlooks Lost Lake from the south. Most obviously it can be combined with trails #30 and 32 to make a 15.7 km loop. While not really a scramble despite a few rocks, this route does require you to be comfortable tramping about terrain with no trails.

To the summit 2.4 km

Leave Lost Lake trail at the first big side valley. Turn left (south) onto a trail that yo-yos along the left bank, then ends cold turkey in the creekbed. Cross. Continue up the V-shaped valley bottom between your hill on the right and a long, unnamed ridge to the left with grassy slopes. At the bend to the southwest stay on the right bank, using game trails through willowy meadows. Directly opposite is the low point in the ridge, which is treed; you can bet your last dollar there's a game trail crossing over it into Fortress Lake Valley.

Flower meadows at treeline.

Farther round the bend is the forks, both of them deeply incised. Climb the slope to the right of the right fork through a sub-alpine forest of spruce and larch with small meadows you can connect up. Either aim for the pink shale col at 238336, then turn right and follow the south ridge to the summit, or make directly for the summit through fields of purple fleabanes. Higher up, the gradient eases to short grass meadows with just a few rocks to scramble up below the summit.

While you've been ogling the Opals, and The Fortress all the way up, the summit view now adds in Guinn's Pass, the big grey peak at 217373, and Rummel Pass between The Tower and Mt. Galatea.

To Lost Lake 2 km

Descend the west ridge on grass and rocks. Because of a big drop on the right side overlooking Lost Lake, you have to keep going a long way west, even into trees and all the way down to the lip of a hanging valley. Only then can you descend to the flat forest floor at the west end of the lake. Even so, the way down is STEEP, but at least you have trees to hang on to.

Regain Lost Lake trail by going either way around the lake. Clockwise is easier and you can pick up a trail. Just past the lake the trail crosses the southwest fork via a beaver dam and joins the main valley trail. Turn left.

33 THE WEDGE CONNECTOR — map 3

From near the bridge is a view of Mt. Kidd.

Half-day hike, bike 'n' hike
Official trail with ski signs
Distance 2.8 km
Height gain W-E 24 m (80 ft.)
High point 1580 m (5184 ft.)
Map 82 J/14 Spray Lakes Reservoir

Access Hwy. 40 (Kananaskis Trail) at Wedge Pond parking lot (far end).
Also accessible from #35 Evan-Thomas Creek & Pass and #37 Mackay Hills.

A short forest trail (the Bill Milne biking trail, then a 1940s logging road) that connects Wedge Pond to Evan-Thomas Creek trail. While most often skied, it provides a way off the Mackay Hills back to Evan-Thomas Creek trailhead.

From the far end of the parking lot follow a paved bicycle trail (the Bill Milne trail) beyond the gate to a T-junction. Turn left on the bike path. (To right is the circuit trail around Wedge Pond.)

Where the bike trail turns left, continue ahead on a grassy track. Disregard a secondary track diving into the trees to left. The track then curves left to a T-junction with sign. Go right and begin a gradual climb to the trail's high point at a Y-junction. Keep left. (Logging road ahead is Finish no. 4 to the Mackay Hills.)

The track descends, then crosses flats to the bridge over Evan-Thomas Creek. Starting a half kilometre upstream are the great red cliffs of Evan-Thomas. The time to visit is winter when a trail is stamped out along the creekbed past Chantilly Falls to the very spectacular Moonlight Falls.

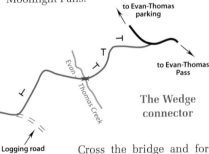

The Wedge connector

Cross the bridge and for 300 m wind up a steepish hill to the T-junction with Evan-Thomas Creek trail (exploration road).

Turn left for Evan-Thomas parking lot, which is 1.7 km distant.

34 THE WEDGE ACCESS TRAIL — map 3

Day hike
Unofficial trail
Distance 3.9 km to base of rock
Height gain 899 m (2950 ft.)
High point 2438 m (8000 ft.)
Map 82 J/14 Spray Lakes Reservoir

Access Hwy. 40 (Kananaskis Trail) at Wedge Pond parking lot (far end).

The climber's access to The Wedge (a difficult scramble) is via the north ridge. It's also used by hikers, not because there is a destination — there isn't — but because it' offers great views. But just because you're on a trail don't expect an easy time of it; the going is relentlessly uphill.

From the parking lot, pass through a gate onto the paved Bill Milne bike path. At the T-junction a little way in, turn right on a gravel road. There are two ways on.

1. In a few metres turn left into a little clearing that sometimes has a picnic table. A trail leaves the end of it and joins a logging road. Turn right. After the deadfall, turn right off the road onto a trail that descends to a glade where it meets the other access at a Y-junction. Keep left.

2. Continue down the gravel road to the trail circumventing the pond and turn left. In a few metres turn left onto a trail that starts *before* you cross a culvert. Faint at first, it soon becomes obvious as it heads through forest into the glade. Meet the other trail at Y-junction and keep right.

Initially the going is easy. Suddenly a creek appears on your right and you begin an ever steepening climb up its left bank. Come to a flat section. Here the trail turns left and climbs diagonally up grass onto the north ridge.

Turn right and follow the ridge, open sections alternating with steeper steps in spruces and larches. You'll be stopping often up this forever ridge to admire the views of Mt. Kidd and the Kananaskis Valley. As you get higher the Mackay Hills and Fisher Peak come into view.

Call it a day when you hit the scree. (The ongoing "trail" leads onto the rubbly northeast face, up which various lines can be followed to the lower summit.)

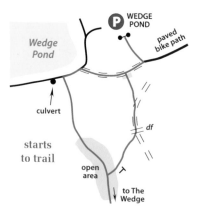

Climbing the north ridge. Looking back to Mt. Kidd and Wedge Pond.

35 EVAN-THOMAS CREEK & PASS—map 3

Environs of Evan-Thomas Pass.
Photo Alf Skrastins

Long day hike, bike 'n' hike, backpack
Unofficial trail, creek crossings
Distance 14.3 km to pass
Height gain 760 m (2493 ft.)
High point 2180 m (7150 ft.)
Map 82 J/14 Spray Lakes Reservoir

Access Hwy. 40 (Kananaskis Trail) at Evan-Thomas Creek parking lot.
Also accessible from North Fork of the Little Elbow in Volume 2.

Evan-Thomas Creek to Evan-Thomas Pass is one half of a route through to the Little Elbow. The other half is described in Volume 2 under "North Fork of the Little Elbow."

The route (exploration road, cutline) is a long, boring trudge best done by ski or horse or bike to the Rocky Creek Pass turnoff. Additionally, it's heavily used by trail riders and hunters on horseback who have made a muddy mess of the cutline section. It's debatable whether the pass is worth the trauma unless you're backpacking over to the Little Elbow or heading up to the tarn under Mt. Potts, or crossing the delectable Paradise Pass into the west fork of the Little Elbow.

Use this trail as a jumping off point for more interesting options such as Camp Creek (#36), the Mackay Hills (#37), Old Baldy (#38), and for Fisher Peak and exploratory scrambles in the Fisher Range.

HISTORY NOTE The valley was called Porcupine Creek when George Pocaterra and his co-prospectors built the road section to coal prospects in Camp Creek. The Stoney called it Îthorhan Odabi Waptan, meaning "Abundance of porcupines valley." In 1922 it suffered a name change and the old name was moved to another, far less appropriate valley.

WARNING In the off season, Cougars frequent the lower part of the trail.

To The Wedge connector trail 1.7 km
From the parking lot walk through to Shatto's exploration road, turn left and follow it up-valley through pine forest once slated to be axed for a golf course. Shortly, pass a horse trail to left, then another to right.

Come to a T-junction where The Wedge connector trail (signed "no horses") takes off to the right. Turn left.

To Old Baldy trail 0.3 km
Two trails leave the left side just before the side creek crossing of McDougall Creek. The first connects with the Boundary Ranch trail system. The second, marked with cairns, is the trail to Old Baldy (#38).

To Camp Creek turnoff 9.1 km
Twice the road climbs high and twice it descends, finally reaching valley bottom upstream of the unseen canyon. (You can just spot the tops of the cliffs.) The side creek to left is the jumping-off point for a peak, unmarked on any topo map, that was first climbed by John Martin back in 1979. Rob Eastick, who brought the anomaly to everyone's attention in 2009, probably made the second ascent 30 years later.

At 7.2 km, cross a much larger side stream hopefully bridged by a log. This is the departure point for backpackers bound for Upper Canyon Creek. (See Volume 2.) Just upstream of the confluence, look for three falls in Evan-Thomas Creek.

In another kilometre the road crosses to the right (west) bank and passes a camping spot, which is a possible departure point for Fisher Peak. Not long after, the road turns uphill to a T-junction with a cutline. Your route is the cutline ahead, which dips to cross Evan-Thomas Creek. (Shatto's Road to right climbs to Rocky Creek Pass and Camp Creek, which is the next entry.)

To Evan-Thomas Pass 5.2 km
This cutline has all the foibles of its kind. After crossing the creek at the confluence with Camp Creek to the east bank, it climbs high, undulates awhile (bypass trails available), then plummets back to creek level. Coming up is the flat, wet section, a muddy jaunt through willow brush below the runout zone of large avalanche slopes with seven river crossings, discounting paddling as opposed to fording. This comes to an end on the east bank at the point where the main tributary comes in from the southwest from under Mt. Denny. In the angle is a grassy meadow with a fabulous view of

Crossing side creek. Photo Alf Skrastins

the mountain in the angle of the west and north forks of the Little Elbow, its east ridge built like a ripsaw.

In front are two low gaps in the watershed ridge. The ugly black mess leads towards the left-hand gap. Higher up, where the surface reverts to hard pack, watch for a junction offering a choice of routes.

1. Cutline The cutline straight ahead climbs steeply, passing 50 vertical m above the gap in open forest, the reward for extra climbing being a clear view of the northern Opals. From the high point, the cutline descends the south slope to another junction with the gap trail, then carries on down the north fork of the Little Elbow.

2. Gap trail The trail to right dekes neatly through the gap in the forested ridge—the true pass—into the head of Little Elbow's north fork. In a meadow is a junction. Turn right for North Fork Tarn, keep straight for the Little Elbow, Boundary Ranch's "Happy Valley Camp" and Paradise Pass. See Volume 2 for ongoing routes.

36 CAMP CREEK—map 3

Long day hike, bike 'n' hike, backpack
Unofficial trail, creek crossing
Distance 2.5 km to Camp Creek,
11.6 km to Camp Creek from trailhead
Height gain 207 m (680 ft.),
579 m (1900 ft.) from trailhead
High point 2103 m (6900 ft.) at Camp
Creek crossing
Map 82 J/14 Spray Lakes Reservoir

Access Via #35 Evan-Thomas Creek & Pass at the Camp Creek turnoff.

Shatto's old exploration road (continuation of the road up Evan-Thomas Creek), leads to Rocky Creek Pass and on into Camp Creek. You can take a bike with you and have a grand run back down.

Camp Creek has meadows and larches and the option of doing a short ridge walk over Prospect Ridge into the bargain. Be aware it's a hunter hot spot, so at such times wear fluorescent pink and swear blind you haven't seen any elk.

HISTORY NOTE This is the place for George Pocaterra aficionados to come and look at his coal claims. Pocaterra spent much of his life trying to develop this site. Despite the coal testing superior to coal from Drumheller and Crowsnest, and interest expressed by the Brits, the Germans and the Japanese, access was a huge problem. That and trying to find backers, plus the interruption caused by two world wars. Finally the waning market sounded the death knell for his grand dream. I still wonder how he intended to get a railway to the site...

To Rocky Creek Pass 1 km,
First off is the climb to the pass at 343323 at an elevation of 1844 m (6050 ft.).

So, at the junction turn right, continuing up the Shatto coal exploration road. Alvin Guinn remembered as a youth persuading Pocaterra to build the track up the dry north bank of Camp Creek and not up the muddy south bank where it was likely to be washed out. So, thanking Guinn, you climb past an Edwards Coffee can hanging off a branch, note coal spoil down in the forks and game trails heading off to the right, tantalizing for those of us intent on connecting up trails along the west bank of Evan-Thomas Creek.

The meadows and larch forest of Upper Camp Creek.

The road levels off in a soggy longitudinal meadow on the watershed between Evan-Thomas and Rocky creeks. In the last edition I called the pass "Cloudburst" after the Cloudburst Coal Company, which did some prospecting under contract to Pocaterra in the early 1950s. Ruthie Oltmann says it was also known as Moose Wallow, likely referring to the black pool in the middle of the meadow. Most people seem to refer to it as Rocky Creek Pass.

To Camp Creek 1.5 km
After leaving the meadow, the road doubles back left, rounding the edge of a ridge and turning south into the main fork of Camp Creek. This is where you run into the first of the hunter's camps and garbage dumps. Wait a hundred years

and the dumps will become historic. I can imagine future hikers sifting excitedly through nose tags, bottles of Palm Breeze light rum and assorted plastic containers.

A little farther on, the road crosses the creek and splits into two grassy tracks. Possibly this was the site of Pocaterra's cabin. Where to go next?

The track to right heads up-valley into meadows where a trail carries on to the valley head below the northernmost peaks of the Opals. Alternatively, turn left and keeping left, climb a meadow on the diagonal to Pocaterra's coal claims on the north end of Prospect Ridge.

Below top: Prospect Ridge, showing the track to the coal prospects at lower left. The loop follows the skyline ridge from left to right.

Below bottom: On the summit of Prospect Ridge. Photo Alf-Skrastins

OPTION

36A "Prospect Ridge" Loop

Unofficial trails, route
Distance 4.2 km loop from Camp Creek
Height gain 488 m (1600 ft.) from Camp
Creek
High point 2454 m (8050 ft.)

A thoroughly enjoyable trip that incorporates the grassy ridge to the southeast at 348304 and the valley trail.

Set off towards Pocaterra's coal prospects, but at the far junction turn right up another track. Near track's end a trail heads left, gaining the north ridge much higher up.

The trail continues up the ridge to further prospects, then fades away at last trees. Clamber up rocks, prelude to a smooth grass slope interrupted at mid-height by a short horizontal ridge of tilted sandstone blocks. The actual summit (at km 1.6) is as broad as a soccer field and striped by rock bands you can step over.

You can now see over Evan-Thomas Pass to mounts Glasgow, Cornwall and Outlaw in the Elbow. To their right is the familiar profile of the ripsaw peak, and farther to the right Mt. Evan-Thomas, with Paradise Pass slung in between them. In the opposite direction the The Wedge and the Mackay Hills are naturally of most interest should you be headed that way.

Descend easily to the pass at 347296. An elk trail runs across it and down to Camp Creek, then up an equally scrumptious ridge to the west.

Before descending to Camp Creek, look southwards into the true head of Evan-Thomas Creek below Mt. Denny. This really is an elk's heaven, a mix of meadow, last trees, talus, and gullies criss-crossed with countless game trails, some of which emanate from this ridge. Nevertheless, heading cross-country to Evan-Thomas Pass or to the North Fork (of the Little Elbow) Tarn is no simple matter, despite the elk trail luring you on.

From the col turn right and descend the elk trail into Camp Creek at the flat. Leave it here and turn right, down-valley, shortly picking up a grassy track which conveniently joins with your outgoing track near the creek crossing.

OPTIONAL DESCENT

36B Rocky Creek

Distance 6.6+ km
Height loss ~442 m (1450 ft.)

Descending Rocky Creek from Rocky Creek Pass to Hwy. 40 is not popular. In 1995 it took a mountain biker two days to get down to the highway; the bike was abandoned on a hillside and later picked up by helicopter. The problem is the section downstream of the forks where the valley narrows and is steep sided. There are two ways through: the creek and the hillside below The Wedge. Both routes are rough and demand that hikers be experienced. No. 1 route has route-finding problems.

Descending this way requires another vehicle to be parked at Hwy. 40. Just south of the highway bridge over Rocky Creek is a pullout on the west side.

Because I have not done either of these routes for decades, the following write-ups lean heavily on Alf Skrastins's up-to-date descriptions. Thanks, Alf!

1. Via the hillside
Back in the 1970s, we found a traversing game trail high on the southwest-facing slopes of The Wedge. As of 2009, Alf found the trail in good condition still, but getting off remains unsatisfactory.

A trail starting from the other (north) side of the pass heads west through the longitudinal meadow, then, keeping right of the west fork, follows the uppermost bench below the steeper grassy slopes of the Mackay Hills. Cross a northeast fork, then climb across a small rib to the north fork, which is crossed lower down at the 1800-m contour at 320332.

To avoid a rock band, the trail climbs through trees, then up scree to a high point at about 313333 on the south ridge of The Wedge. From here it makes a long gradually descending traverse of steep hillside, crossing the odd rocky gully and avalanche slope. On the way are great views of The Fortress ahead, looking its sharpest. Across the valley the eye is drawn to a textbook syncline valley off the north end of Opal Ridge with waterfalls.

At 1700 m in elevation, the trail divides, both forks gradually fading. Which way? The obvious thing to do is to drop 100 vertical m down the right side of the avalanche slope to the creek and put up with a few creek crossings.

Alternatively, continue traversing, heading a little uphill to get above a diagonal cliff. On the other side pick up an intermittently flagged on/off trail on its way up Limestone Mountain (as we found out) and turn left. After the initial rocky step, the gradient eases off in the trees and it's a good trail that deposits you in the meadow at the mouth of the valley. Turn right and walk out to Hwy. 40. Cross the bridge to the parking area.

36B 1. The traversing trail. Photo Alf Skrastins

2. Via the creek

Basically a bush walk with many creek crossings. If you must try it, wait until the creek calms down and take Tevas.

Because there's a trail, it's best to follow the same route as no. 1 to the north fork. (Read the second paragraph.)

Descend the creek to the main fork and turn right. Straightaway you're into the narrows between The Wedge and North Opal Ridge. The creek swings from side to side between canyon walls, so there is much unavoidable paddling.

The lower half of the route only seems endless: a narrow forested valley with many more creek crossings. At the mouth of the valley, under a diagonal rock band, you cross the creek one last time to the right bank and follow meadow out to Hwy. 40. Cross the bridge to the parking area.

36B 2. Rocky Creek narrows. Photo Alf Skrastins

37 MACKAY HILLS — map 3

Long day hike, backpack
Unofficial trails & route
Distance 8.4 km from Rocky Creek
Pass, 21.2 km loop from trailhead
Height gain 701 m (2300 ft.)
High point 2454 m (8050 ft.)
Map 82 J/14 Spray Lakes Reservoir

Access Via #36 Camp Creek at Rocky Creek Pass.
Also accessible from #33 Wedge connector.

A beautiful ridge walk over three grassy summits. The penalty for enjoying yourself is an ending so horrible only experienced bushwhackers with a talent for routefinding need think about doing the whole loop. Of course, you can always just climb a couple of tops and return via the traversing sheep trails to the pass.

ROUTE NOTE Since the last edition the ending has changed.

BRIEF HISTORY NOTE According to James Ashworth's 1917 report of the coalfield, the northernmost top is called

The northwest ridge of the centre peak
from the centre-north col.

Mt. Mackay or Mackay's Mountain after claimant Walter Grant Mackay.

Start from Rocky Creek Pass.

The climb up the south ridge to the South Peak starts from behind the little black pond. A game trail zigs left, then right. At a division, go right and follow the trail all the way up steeply angled forest to open slopes. Sensible sheep; they traverse around to the left, to the col between South and Centre peaks. Not so hikers, who must grovel up even steeper grass to gain the summit. Fortunately, there are flowers to identify and views to look at. The lowest of the three summits is a smooth, grassy dome where you can spend a happy half hour identifying peaks in all directions.

Walk down to the south/centre col. The sheep trail reappears from the left and gets you started up the centre peak before heading off on another traverse. Rather disappointingly, this summit doesn't look up to much. On gaining the top, though, you discover that the northwest ridge, dropping 183 vertical m to the next col, is definitely interesting. In fact, it's hard to leave the summit. Detour to the right, then traverse back left below a rock band to gain the ridge. As I've said, it's an interesting descent and I was fascinated by its fragmented red cliffs and shiny sheets of black coal against which clumps of alpine cinquefoil dazzled.

From the centre/north col regain the 183 vertical metres in the simple climb up Mackay's Mountain, which is yoked by a saddle to The Wedge. On topping out, you're greeted by a fabulous aerial view of the Kananaskis Valley.

GETTING OFF

There is no good ending to this ridgewalk. Just four different routes, each with pluses and minuses and their own advocates. All routes end on or near The Wedge connector trail. See #33 and 34.

View from centre peak to Mackay's Mountain. To left is The Wedge. This photo shows some of finish no. 1, which descends to the col, then climbs up to the base of the rock of The Wedge, then traverses right to gain the north ridge.

1. The Wedge traverse – high

While Alf and I usually see eye to eye on routes, I'm not fond of this particular one for a number of reasons: it's exposed to rockfall and requires extra climbing and kilometrage. Add to that, snow on the traverse early and late in the season.

From the third summit descend the west ridge to the col at 32034, then climb 152 vertical m (500 ft.) up the grassy east ridge of The Wedge to rockline. Turn right and follow a skimpy trail that traverses immediately below the rock of the east face. Watch for rocks bounding off the summit ridge from scramblers. Emerge at the top of the north ridge, where you pick up the scrambler's access trail. Descend via #34 to Wedge Pond, then hike The Wedge connector to Evan-Thomas trail.

2. The Wedge traverse – low

Mike's suggestion to descend to the col at 32034, then traverse across to the north ridge of The Wedge to trail #34 would have some merit if only there was a trail. There are lots of awful gullies to cross and should you try to circumvent them lower down you run into horrendous deadfall.

We tried this route back in the 1970s when we were young and fit and have never gone back. Additionally, there is the hike back from Wedge Pond.

3. North Ridge

Another time when we traversed the Mackay Hills we decided to be purists and follow the north ridge all the way down, a grade 7 bushwhack that none of us has ever been able to forget.

In the steep upper part you squeeze between matchstick lodgepoles, grovel under alders and whiplash willows and climb over trees collapsed in heaps. Low down in willowy clearings you wallow along waterlogged moose trenches. If you're lucky like me you'll stumble over an ancient 7-Up bottle, then hit the end of a logging road square on. If you're not so lucky, you'll undoubtedly hit The Wedge connector at some point along its length.

4. East Slope

Despite the shortcomings of wet meadows and the fact that you need a GPS to find the logging road, this is still my descent of choice. All sensible animals, it seems, leave the north ridge before the trees start and follow trails along the west side of Evan-Thomas Creek Valley.

Drop onto the east slope at the demarcation of white and green shading as shown on the topo map. Head down one side or the other of the big, deeply incised gully to about 328358, where you intersect the old trail travelled by Pocaterra, Amos and Mackay to stake their coal claims in 1910. You can intersect this trail anywhere between this gully and the next big gully to the south, at 335350; just look for blazes and faded flagging. Wherever you hit the trail, turn left and follow it out of the forest into a series of wet meadows which confuse with their multitude of game trails.

Know that the finish described in the last edition has been decimated by deadfall. Instead aim for point 322373, a blazed tree with flagging near the end of a long meadow. From here a trail (new and old

On The Wedge traverse–high. Photo Alf Skrastins

flagging, trimmed branches) delves into trees and descends past a glade into a small meadow which is crossed to an intersection with a logging road in the trees. Turn right. (The road to left is chockablock with saplings.)

Descend this road, alias creek, to a junction and turn left. The going instantly improves and it's an enjoyable walk down to the Y-junction with The Wedge connector at 315381. Turn right and in 700 m reach Evan-Thomas Creek bridge, which makes a good seat for pouring the water out of your boots.

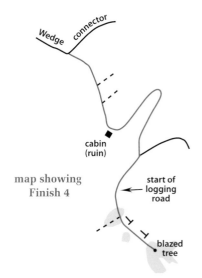

map showing
Finish 4

38 OLD BALDY—map 3

Old Baldy from the back. Shows the route up
from the tarn. Photo Peter Irwin

Day hike
Unofficial trail & route, creek crossings
Distance 5.3 km to summit from
trailhead
Height gain 862 m (2830 ft.)
High point 2386 m (7830 ft.)
Map 82 J/14 Spray Lakes Reservoir

Access Hwy. 40 (Kananaskis Trail) at Evan-
Thomas Creek parking lot. Via #35 Evan-
Thomas Creek & Pass.

This popular outing has a few tricky bits
in the valley section, after which it's a
straightforward plod up meadows to the
high grassy ridge at 344410. Who would
think this insignificant summit would be
such a fine viewpoint!

The present route is by far the easiest
and most scenic. Before K Country, people
staggered up Old Baldy (its unofficial
name for 50 years now) via the northwest
ridge, or the southwest ridge or up the
front (west flank). The giant-sized scree
made the ridge routes pretty horrible,
The west flank route, however, is still
used today, but mainly as an optional
descent route. I note that Andrew uses it
to access peak 356417, but then hardcore
scramblers are a fit bunch.

This route also accesses Mt. McDougall by
two different routes.

To the Forks 2.9 km
Follow Evan-Thomas Creek trail for 2 km
to the first side creek crossing, where a
narrow trail turns off to the left between
cairns. Be sure it's not the horse trail passed
a few minutes earlier that has no cairn.
The correct trail follows the left bank of
the creek arising from the west slope of
Mt. McDougall. Most people seem to call
it McDougall Creek.

The trail is initially easy. In the V-
shaped section of the valley, however, it
traverses four steep banks, which could be
intimidating to beginner hikers, though if
I've managed it in pouring rain holding an
umbrella with one hand it can't be all that
bad. Easier-angled grass and talus signal
your imminent arrival at the forks. Ahead
rises the lower southwest slope of peak
357404—see Option A.

To the tarn 1.1 km
The right-hand fork empties into the confluence in a chain of picturesque waterfalls and pools. After the obligatory photo

stop continue to follow the trail into the narrower left-hand fork. There is little surface water (though the grasses and flowers are luxuriant) and the five creek crossings are trouble-free. After the fifth crossing the trail climbs steeply up the east bank into a clump of spruce, then levels. At the point where you emerge from the trees, look up to the right at the optional descent route from peak 358405.

From here it's a flat stroll around the corner to a seasonal tarn (not marked on government maps) occupying a depression in the scree. The valley ends not too much farther on, surrounded by a slew of unnamed peaks.

To Old Baldy 1.3 km
From the near end of the tarn, climb steeply angled grass, gradually easing, to the col at 353412 between Old Baldy and peak 356417. Turn left.

I love the next part, because as you stroll west, then south along the ridge towards your objective, the mountains rise up one by one until finally, from the sum-

mit, a breathtaking panorama is revealed extending from Mt. Joffre—the white fang in the south—all the way north to Mt. Aylmer and the mountains of The Ghost. Naturally, the mountains about Ribbon Creek are pre-eminent.

It's easiest to return the same way.

Above: The tarn at full water.
Photo Peter Irwin

Below: Walking along the ridge to the summit. In the background are mounts Kidd and Bogart. Photo Alf Skrastins

The west flank. The down route follows the gully from right to left.

OPTIONAL RETURN

38A via the west flank

Distance 6.5 km to trailhead

A steep and direct route to Boundary Ranch lands that takes in a restaurant stop. Very slippery when the long grasses are wet or partially snow-covered.

To Boundary Ranch

From the summit stride down the relatively narrow northwest ridge to about 340419. Your objective is the top-to-bottom, fan-shaped gully below you on the west flank. You can either drop straight down from the ridge (very steep grass) or come in from the side from lower down the ridge (steep grass). Where the gully narrows and is shrubby, a trail develops on the right bank and takes you down through the alarming-looking contours shown on the topo map, which are pure fallacy. Pass two cairns and emerge in a small clearing with teepees. A good track leads out to a T-junction with an old dirt road.

You are now in the mess of old logging roads and trails used by Boundary Ranch for one-day trail rides. If you're going to get lost anywhere it's here, should you choose to cut across country.

Back to Evan-Thomas parking lot

While you can choose from a variety of trails, who wants to do MORE climbing and risk spooking the horses and upsetting clients who have never even seen a horse before let alone ridden one? Also you don't want to be yelled at by Steve.

So turn right, descend to a T-junction with a better road, turn right and descend the hill to a paved loop just before the Boundary Ranch parking lot. Turn left into Rick's Steakhouse for a burger and beer and corn on the cob. The restaurant and patio are open in July and August until 6 p.m. on weekdays, 7 p.m. on weekends.

Return to the parking lot and follow Guinns Road out to Hwy. 40. Turn left along the roadside ditch and join a trail that comes in from the left just beyond the blue road sign for Boundary Ranch.

In a few metres the trail splits at a grassed-over borrow pit. While you can follow the trail in the roadside ditch all the way back to Evan-Thomas parking lot access road, I much prefer the quiet forest trail that parallels it a little way in. It starts off by following the top edge of the pit. The trail touches the ditch trail in a couple of places, utilizes one section of old logging road, and finally joins the ditch trail for the last stretch into the parking lot.

OPTION

38B Peak 357404

Day scramble, route
Creek crossings
Distance 1.7 km from forks
Height gain 487 m (1600 ft.) from forks, 991 m (3250 ft.) from trailhead
High point 2515 m (8250 ft.)

A more challenging trip incorporates the two forks of McDougall Creek and the mountain in between at 358403. Although it doesn't appear on the topo map at a separate peak, it most assuredly is, with a definite col between it and peak 362405. Expect steep grass and some scree.

Follow Old Baldy trail to the forks.

Take the right fork. Unless you want to potter about between waterfalls, follow a faint trail along a bench on the left bank. When the bench peters out transfer to the valley bottom. Around the bend barge through willows to the right bank and follow it to the valley head under Mt. McDougall, from down below a foreshortened mess of scree and slabs.

On the west side of the valley is an enticing grass slope, not too steep, leading all the way up to your objective. Scattered crags high up are easily avoided by heading straight up the draw, then leftish towards the top. From high up it appears less tiring to traverse right below the summit crags, then cut left *behind them*, only there is no behind and the jagged right-hand skyline is the northeast ridge rising up from a col. Oops! My excuse to a friend faithfully following along behind was that the resulting scramble made for a more sporting finish.

The summit is mainly turf, a perfect grandstand seat for Old Baldy down below, showing the normal route up from the tarn. To its right is peak 356417, a moderate scramble up the left skyline from Old Baldy.

Your summit is connected to a ridge circling around to Mt. McDougall. According to Rienk, it's a moderate scramble with the crux—an exposed step—occurring between the col and peak 362405.

Option return to the left-hand fork

A more difficult descent route down the northwest flank requires some precise routefinding. However, it opens up a 3.6 km loop from the forks.

Initially the easy, grassy slope lures you down to a squared-off plateau above a drop-off. Now what? Any idea of descending directly to the tarn on the right side is forestalled by cliffs. The left side is similarly cliffy. Ahead, though, at about 352404, are boulder slopes set at a reasonable angle. Nevertheless, pussyfooting from one tippy rock to another is extremely tedious when you have to concentrate every inch of the way. We ended up in the left fork at last trees mentally knackered, vowing to resist temptation the next time.

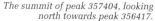

The summit of peak 357404, looking north towards peak 356417.

39 EAU CLAIRE interpretive trail—map 3

Hour hike
Official trail
Distance 1.5 km loop
Map 82 J/14 Spray Lakes Reservoir

Access Hwy. 40 (Kananaskis Trail) at Eau Claire campground. The trailhead is located on the left side of the access road between campsites 48 and 49.

A flat and easy forest loop alongside the Kananaskis River.

In only a short distance keep right where the trail loops.

Straight off, from the willowy bed of an old river channel you get a much photographed view of Mt. Kidd south, or Istimabi Iyarhe as the Stoneys call it, meaning "where one slept mountain." From this direction it displays some terrific examples of anticline-syncline pairs—folds to you and me—which are the northern termination of the Lewis Thrust, according to Ben. From the low point in the syncline plummets Mt. Kidd Falls.

Moving on, you follow the bank of the Kananaskis River below the steep east face of "the Spoon Needle" or "Aiguille du Cuiller" as scramblers call it, though no-one person will take credit for what is actually an appropriate name. Along this stretch, crumbling banks, sweepers and trail realignments tell you the river is on its way back to the east side of the valley.

At interpretive sign no. 8, the trail turns away from the river and recrosses the old (soon to be new?) river channel. If you look to the north east at the crossing you'll spot Limestone Mountain and The Wedge.

Heading north now, you travel through pine forest with much deadfall and burnt timber dating back to the inferno of 1936. Trees in this part of the valley have always had a hard time of it, what with repeated wildfires and with logging by the Eau Claire Lumber Company, which in the 1880s established a camp a little farther up river of the Fortress ski area access road.

Arriving back at the T-junction, turn right for the trailhead.

Kananaskis River and Mt. Kidd from the trail.

40 OPAL RIDGE SOUTH—map 3

Day scramble
Unofficial trail & route
Distance 4 km to high point
11.3 km loop
Height gain 1012 m (3320 ft.)
High point 2597 m (8520 ft.)
Map 82 J/14 Spray Lakes Reservoir

Access Hwy. 40 (Kananaskis Trail) at Fortress Junction gas station.

Driving up Highway 40, I had often wondered if this route went. Could you get through the cliffs to the ridge top? So one day we climbed it and discovered the "gates." We also found out this was no new discovery, but a well-used route taken by paragliders who jump off the top. Nowadays it's the descent route for scramblers doing Opal Ridge North.

As you might deduce from the distance and height gain, it's a demanding trudge up a rough terrain of grass and scree to the ridge. But despite its spectacular appearance from the gas station, there's nothing to the ridge itself and no exposure to worry about. Consider the optional return down Grizzly Creek (11.3 km loop).

Above the apex of ascent ridges looking up to "The Gates." Photo Gillian Ford

To the ridge 2.5 km
From the parking lot hike up a small creek a way, then follow the left bank to the powerline access road. Turn left and walk along the road. Cross a side creek. On your right and facing the highway is an open, triangular-shaped slope bounded on either side by ridges that meet at the apex. Both ridges go. The left-hand ridge is grassier. But naturally, the nearer ridge is more commonly climbed, so turn first right onto the paragliders's trail.

This ridge is broad and loosely terraced with small rockbands. Initially the trail winds upward on grass. Half way up, the terrain changes to scree and the trail splits, the result of people searching for ways up between higher, wider rockbands. Take whichever route appeals and don't forget to look out for a geocache holding such handy things as nail clippers.

Arrive at the apex. Continue up the short scree slope behind to a grassy top with an airy feel of being far above the cares of the world.

Opal Ridge South, looking down to Rocky/ Grizzly watershed at left and across to the Opal Range. Photo Gillian Ford

From here a rounded ridge connects to the grass slope below huge freestanding cliffs, which some call pinnacles. Can you get through? A trail climbs the slope and in a magical bit of routefinding by sheep wends right and up through "gates" totally invisible from down below. You arrive at another meadow, separated from Opal Ridge by a small band of crags. This the trail avoids by traversing way out to the right on orange screes to the low point of the ridge at 315281.

Another surprise awaits. While the ridge facing Hwy. 40 is plated in vertical cliffs, the east side rolls in a friendly convex curve down to the meadows of upper Rocky Creek and is mainly grass.

Opal Ridge south 1.5 km

Turn right. The trail continues up the rounded ridge to the south, where I was ecstatic to find clumps of woolly flea-banes. The two highest tops are rocky and the sheep elect to traverse the east flank. It's much more fun, though, to walk the crest, which is easy and has a buffer zone between you and the plunging cliffs so you never have to look down.

Look back along Opal Ridge North towards The Wedge. To the south is a magnificent view of Kananaskis Lakes and the Opal Range, named erroneously by George Dawson in 1883 after he found quartzite crystals in the limestone coated with films of "opal." On our first visit to this summit it was a day of sun and storm, and across the dark range a constantly moving spotlight was fanning back and forth, illuminating each spectacular peak in turn. Entranced, we sat and watched the theatrics for an hour.

You can follow the ridge in its entirety to a much lower top at 322262, then drop easily onto the watershed between Rocky and Grizzly creeks for a spot of meadow wandering (1.3 km). But check for grizzlies first. The watershed puts you in position to descend Grizzly Creek.

OPTIONAL DESCENT

40A Grizzly Creek

Unofficial trail, then route, minor creek crossings
Distance 2.7+ km from watershed
Height loss 740 m (2428 ft.)

I knew I'd find a use for Grizzly Creek parking lot someday! Should you return this way, it requires two cars, stashed bikes or a 3.3-km walk along Hwy. 40 back to Fortress Junction.

This steep V-shaped valley is not for the vertigo-challenged. The willowy creek bed has an impassable canyon. The intermittent sheep trail of the north bank is for scramblers. The only reasonable route is "the grizzly trail" of the south bank.

From the watershed, head south down the luxuriant grassy slopes of Upper Grizzly Creek Valley. There's a trail, if you can find, it leading to a flat below small waterfalls. Cross the creek to the south bank and continue on trail, passing between two big boulders into forest.

The trail traverses a deepening, steepening side slope. Cross two side creeks and a bit of talus, with the canyon far below and out of sight.

Suddenly emerge near the top of the huge scree slope below the northern cliffs of "Grizzly Peak" (which is climbed from the other side via Ripple Rock Creek). The trail traverses the scree high up and it's here where you meet my nemesis: cement till with a sprinkling of ball bearings on top. The tread has gone and without crampons or claws it's easy to go for a bit of a skid. On the far side of this slope the trail descends steeply, zigs right, then traverses back left not far above the creek. (At this point a side trail descends into the creekbed.)

The much improved traversing trail heads back into spruce forest interspersed with narrow avalanche chutes. At the end of this section it turns left to get onto the west slope of "Grizzly Peak." This requires descending diagonally left between rockbands to the head of a tributary, then climbing up onto a bench. Here ends the trail, the game dispersing in all directions across a wide, grassy slope.

Turn right and find two cairns on the bench. From here it's an easy jaunt of 213 vertical m down a benched slope of grass and aspens. Low down keep right to avoid small rock bands and emerge on the powerline right-of-way. Turn left to reach the parking lot.

Grizzly Creek, showing the big scree slope below "Grizzly Peak."

41 FORTRESS MOUNTAIN SKI AREA TRAILS—maps 3 & 4

**Long day hikes, bike 'n' hikes,
backpack
Official trails (road, ski area trails),
unofficial trails and route
Map 82 J/14 Spray Lakes Reservoir**

Access Hwy. 40 (Kananaskis Trail). At Fortress Junction turn west onto the Fortress Mountain ski area access road and park at the barricade.

Since the last edition Fortress Mountain ski area has been closed and you can no longer drive up the access road. This means the two popular routes leaving the ski area have turned into long-day marathons. You have to ask yourself: can I hack another 16 km in distance and another 500 m (1640 ft.) in height gain? Consider biking the road or packing in a tent.

The initial paragraphs describes trails within the ski area boundary ending at or near the upper terminal of Farside double chair on Fortress Ridge. It's here where ongoing routes to Fortress Lake and Fortress Ridge take off.

*Route 1 to Fortress Ridge winds all around
the head of Aussie Creek. To right is an
unusual view of Fortress Mountain.*

For scramblers this road is also the access to Mt. Lawson.

ACCESS NOTE Enter Warner Bros. in 2009 to make a movie. As part of the agreement, they made some improvements to the road, while the owners of the assets made repairs to the bridge over the Kananaskis River for the benefit of the film crew. So, we can all drive up the road now that the bridge has been approved by Stantec? Nope! Until a new lease is issued, SRD is keeping the road closed.

Fortress Mountain Ski Area
**Distance 8 km
Height gain 500 m (1640 ft.)
High point 2088 m (6850 ft.)**

Cross the bridge over the Kananaskis River and follow the winding road (corner 7 being the most famous turn) to the ski area. You are in forest throughout and there is not a lot of interest on the way up apart from the impressive rock wall seen above the treetops extending from Mt. Lawson, through Mt. Inflexible to Mt. James Walker. Maybe the big waterfall will be flowing from the cirque just north of Lawson, not from a lake, but from melting snow.

Arriving at the ski area, follow the road to the uppermost parking lot beyond the lodge. If there is anything more unsightly than ski areas in summer, it is ski areas that have been neglected.

To Fortress Ridge
Distance 3.4 km
Height gain 273 m (896 ft.) via no. 1
Height loss 60 m (197 ft.) via no. 1
High point 2316 m (7600 ft.)
The next objective is to gain Fortress Ridge, which is two ridges away across Aussie Creek to the northwest.

First ridge 0.4 km
From the top of the parking lot walk up the cat track to the right of the T-bar. Turn first left, cross the T-bar and paralleling it, head to the ridge top. All the way, you pass below ski runs dropping off Canadian Ridge—the site of the tower thing in the $20-million sci-fi movie *Inception*. Apparently, it took four tries to blow it up so it would fall down the Canadian Run.

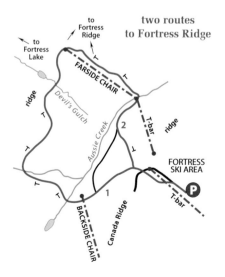

Cross the ridge at a low point and continue ahead (ignore a track up Canadian Ridge to left), then curve left and down to a T-junction.

To Fortress Ridge 3 km
At this point there are two ways to reach Fortress Ridge. No. 1 is the sensible route. No. 2 may be shorter but bear in mind the extra 68 m (223 ft.) in height loss and 113 m (370 ft.) in height gain ONE WAY!

1. Longer, easier Keep left on the cat track, making a very gradual descent across ski runs to the lower terminal of Backside double chair at the head of Aussie Creek. En route keep straight. (A track doubling back right leads to the lower terminal of Farside double chair.)

Still on the cat track, cross Aussie Creek downstream of a small tarn unmarked on any map. Then start the climb onto Fortress Ridge, keeping left through spruce and larch forest at the edge of ski runs scraped down to the ground. The whole hillside extending to Farside double chair must have been stunningly beautiful once, Glacier lilies filling every forest glade.

You reach the wide grassy ridge near its low point and are treated to a remarkable view of the Opal Range to the southeast. Stop here or continue on to the upper terminal of Farside double chair.

2. Shorter, steeper Turn right and plunge into Aussie Creek on cat track. Low down keep right and head past the reservoir and pumphouse to the lower terminal of Farside double chair in the valley bottom. It's hard to imagine this narrow valley was the setting for the 2000 movie *The Claim*, and was crammed with "houses" mimicking the 1840s Californian goldrush town of Kingdom Come.

Cross the creek on culvert. Don't follow the lift up No Mistake Gully, but toil up a horribly steep cat track to its right through Sherwood Forest. From the upper terminal, turn right for Fortress Ridge and left for Fortress Lake.

Fortress Ridge from Hwy. 40.

GOING FARTHER

In the following descriptions, distance, height loss and height gain are given from where you first reached Fortress Ridge. To get the full stats from the parking lot or from Hwy. 40, you'll need a calculator.

41A Fortress Ridge

Scramble
Unofficial trail & route
Distance 5.4 km return from upper terminal of Farside double chair
Height gain 244 m (800 ft.) one way,
Height loss 244 m (800 ft.) one way
High point 2365 m (7760 ft.)

The undulating ridge extending northeast from the upper terminal of Farside double chair ends at a superlative viewpoint overlooking the Kananaskis Valley at 264352. There is not much of a trail, nor is one needed, for the route over several tops is obvious and the going easy at first. Later, the ridge becomes steeper and rockier with the odd scramble step.

Follow either route 1 or route 2 to the upper terminal of Farside double chair. If taking route 2 you can shortcut right before reaching the terminal.

Heading northeast, walk along a broad grassy ridge to top no. 1 — the highest — which is striped with forget-me-nots and creamy androsace growing in moist runnels. The ski staff called it "Baldy." Already there is a fabulous view of The Fortress and Fortress Lake below it.

After the next grassy hump (top no. 2), a rocky descent of 120 m brings you to the lowest point of the ridge, which is identified by larches spilling over from the east slope.

Climb a long grass slope to top no. 3. Suddenly, the ridge narrows and the previously friendly slopes on either side steepen into cliff bands. A rock step immediately above the 3/4 col is avoided by a scramble down a grassy gully on the right (east) side. From the col a steep but straightforward climb up black-lichened rocks gains you the fourth and final top.

From your island in the sky the Kananaskis Country golf course is spread out below you like Google Earth. Look across to Mt. Kidd and up both forks of Galatea Creek. The trail climbing to Guinn's Pass is easily picked out. Of all the surrounding mountains none is more dramatic than The Fortress to the west. To the east and easily glossed over as you happily scan higher mountains is the little peak across the valley at 27934. When you drive north up Hwy. 40 from Fortress Junction, though, this little peak assumes an awesome needle-like shape. I have since learned that scramblers call it Spoon Needle, or Aiguille du Cuiller, and rate the traverse "moderate" with slightly exposed sections.

On the first top of Fortress Ridge, looking down on the low point of the ridge and Fortress Lake in the cirque below The Fortress and Gusty Peak.

Fortress Ridge. Looking back to top no. 2 from the 2/3 col. Photo Bob Spirko

Fortress Ridge. Top no. 3 from the 3/4 col. Photo Bob Spirko

41B Fortress Lake

Unofficial trail, minor creek crossings
Distance 3 km return
Height loss/gain 122 m (400 ft.)
High point 2301 m (7550 ft.) on Fortress Ridge

An easy downhill hike with one steep hill to a lake tucked under the northern cliffs of The Fortress.

Gain Fortress Ridge via route 1.

On reaching the ridge, don't continue along the track to the upper terminal of Farside double chairlift. Cut off left to the low point in the ridge, which is occupied by a tarn feeding Devil's Gulch.

Dropping into the valley to the north (a south fork of Galatea Creek) is straightforward via a trail that starts from the far end of the tarn.

Initially it follows the right bank of a west-bound creek to a fabulous viewpoint of your objective. Then, entering trees, it zigs right, then returns to the creek in one steep, shaley drop. The creek is crossed three times en route to valley bottom meadows where the trail turns left and in less than half a kilometre reaches a junction with creel box. Go either way; both trails lead to the lakeshore.

This inky-blue lake has a spectacular setting under the shadowy north cliffs of The Fortress. If you want to get both the mountain and the lake in the same pic, make sure you have wide angle. And bring binoculars to look for goats wandering the ledges.

The mountain to the right of Fortress is Gusty Peak and in between the two is a col guarded by a vertical cliff. In a bravura piece of climbing in 1957, guide Hans Gmoser and two clients climbed the cliff en route to the first ascent of The Fortress—a route unlikely to be repeated when the southwest ridge is available as a walk-up. They called their mountain The Tower, a name later transposed to the peak north of Rummel Pass.

Fortress Lake below The Fortress (out of sight at far left) and Gusty Peak.

42 KING CREEK CANYON — map 5

Half-day hike
Unofficial trail, creek crossings
Distance 1.6 km to forks, 2.1 km to
religious site
Height gain to forks 122 m (400 ft.),
to religious site 229 m (750 ft.)
High point at forks 1814 m (5950 ft.),
at religious site 1905 m (6250 ft.)
Map 82 J/11 Kananaskis Lakes

Access Hwy. 40 (Kananaskis Trail) at King
Creek day-use area.
Also accessible from #43 King Creek Ridge
via the north fork and from #44 Opal traverse.

Spectacular King Creek canyon leads to
the forks and the beautiful country of the
north fork hidden behind the outliers of
the Opal Range: the domain of grizzlies
and sheep. Part of the way is on old interpretive trail. When the bridges were demolished by the 1995 floods, the trail was
demoted and the final interpretive sign
about this trail being a grizzly highway
moved to Rawson Lake trail. Nevertheless,
the route is still incredibly popular with

*The canyon with backdrop of unnamed
Opal Range peaks.*

adventurous hikers who more often than
not are making the Stoney religious site
their destination.

Creek crossings have temporary log
bridges of the tightrope variety. By late
summer you can usually rock hop. Another good time to visit is winter when ice
climbers have beaten down a trail.

King Creek accesses climber's routes
in the Opals, the scrambler's route up Mt.
Hood and is the hiker's optional descent
route off King Creek Ridge (#43).

HISTORY NOTE "King's Creek" was
named after Millarville rancher Willie
King, who accompanied George Pocaterra
and party on their quest for coal in the
Pocaterra Creek area.

The Canyon to the Forks 1.6 km
The trail leaves the far end of the parking
lot in good shape, but gradually dete-
riorates after entering the canyon proper,
where it is forced back and forth across
the creek 10 times. The narrows is reached
after crossing no. 9. This entails an easy

Scrambling around the narrows.

scramble on polished rock along the left bank. One more crossing, then a longer stint along the right bank brings you to the forks. Thus far there have been tantalizing glimpses of Mt. Blane and The Blade. Now the Opal Range is more fully revealed from Mt. Hood to Mt. Jerram and is particularly spectacular at gaudy sunset.

To the Stoney religious site 0.5 km

Cross the south fork on logs to a junction. The trail to left is the valley route up the north fork (see King Creek Ridge #43A). Ahead is the trail to the Stoney religious site. Initially, it's a steep flog up the high grassy bank on eroded trail. This is where anyone who's worn flip-flops for the creek section will come a cropper.

At the top, turn left and climb a little more into the forest to the left of the grassy slope. In a few minutes come to many trees wrapped with cloth, ribbons and socks. Often called prayer flags, they can signify any number of religious events, be it a vision quest or the giving and receiving of a blessing.

The trail continuing on is the scrambler's access route to Mt. Hood.

Stoney prayer flags. They are never taken down, but are left to fade and rot in the elements. They should be shown "due respect... the same as any other religious object... and left inviolate."

Kananaskis Valley

and you enter flo...
zigzagging, and...
by game trail...
The trail t...
relief se...
Ent...
see...
h...

43 KING CREEK RIDGE — map 5

The open ridge below the main summit.

Day hike
Unofficial trail
Distance 3.5 km to summit
Height gain 731 m
High point 2423 m
Map 82 J/11 Kananaskis Lakes

Access Hwy. 40 (Kananaskis Trail) at King Creek day-use area.

The ridge north of King Creek, also called Kiska tha Iyarhe, or "Goat Mountain" by the Stoneys, is a strenuous climb on trail to a fantastic viewpoint.

TRAIL NOTE Since the last edition there's a new route onto the SSE ridge that misses out the steep south end of the ridge. Nevertheless, the new and improved trail up the west flank is still a sweaty grunt on a hot day. Watch for flagging and cairns.

West flank to SSE ridge 2 km
Start from the segment of old highway on the north bank of King Creek. This is most easily accomplished by returning to the present highway, crossing the bridge and climbing the bank. At survey mark-ers go straight (segment of old road to the left) and follow the grassy old road above King Creek. Very shortly, turn left on a trail that climbs into the trees. Keep left at the junction a little way in. (To right is the old route.) Now you're set.

The new trail makes a long traverse to the north. Finally it decides to head up the west face and launches into a set of steep little zigs with stones underfoot. There's a brief respite after "the big step"

very meadows. Resume
where the trail is crossed
s go uphill at every option.
en heads up left to a second
tion in a few trees.

r a new meadow—the ridge crest
ingly as far away as ever. A few up-
ll zigs leads into a long, rising traverse
to the right. Then climb up left into trees.
At a junction with an ongoing game trail
the main trail (flagged) turns upslope and
twists its way uphill to the SSE ridge.
Near the top the trail peters out and you
navigate past two cairns to the ridge trail.
The"junction" is unmarked. Up ridge, an
"arrow" on the ground is something to
look for on the descent.

Turn left (north).

SSE ridge to summit 1.5 km
Now for the payoff! Follow the ridge trail,
keeping left at a split. Soon you're out of the
trees and enjoying a curving, grassy ridge
with cliffs down the left side. Look back
down the ridge and across the gulf of King
Creek canyon to the mountain shaped like
whipped ice cream or the Matterhorn—take
your pick. Mt. Wintour was named after the
captain of the ill-fated HMS *Tipperary* that
sank during the Battle of Jutland in 1916.
Strangely, the ship is commemorated miles
away across the other side of the Divide
in BC.

Reach a top with a few trees and cairn.
Descend slightly then climb a broader
grass ridge to the main summit cairn. Five
minutes on there's a second rocky summit
with drop-offs on three sides; not a place
to drop your apple.

All the way up you've been ogling the
Opals' hacksawed ridge. Virtually all the
first ascents were made during the 1950s,
one of the last to fall being The Blade,
that impressive gendarme on the south
ridge of Blane. The best view, though, is
reserved for the summits. Now you can
look without obstruction to the north and
southwest where an immense ocean of
conifers extends past Kananaskis Lakes
to the mountains of the Elk.

Returning the same way is much the
easier option.

*The main summit cairn. Looking back down the
ridge towards Wintour. To left is Mt. Blane and
through the gap of Opal-King Pass, Elpoca Mtn.*

The trail off the ridge follows a draw.

OPTIONAL DESCENT

43A to King Creek

Distance 4.1 km to trailhead

Returning via King Creek is a popular 7.6 km circuit for experienced hikers who want a change from the ascent route. But it's not for everyone: the drop off the ridge is steep with a little scrambling and route-finding to contend with. Later on, expect innumerable crossings of King Creek in the canyon.

Getting off the ridge 0.5 km

From just before the rocky nubbin of the second summit a sheep trail plummets down the right (east) side of the ridge into the north fork of King Creek. Initially the trail is runnable orange shale as it descends a grassy draw between cliffs. Where the draw curves to the left at "the narrows," scramble down easy rock ledges. Below, it's easier to keep on the right side below the cliff. Scramble down another set of ledges, this time exiting off to the left. Descend a little to a flat spot on the left edge of the draw.

DO NOT continue down the rocky gully below. Instead, traverse left using numerous bits of trails onto a very steep grass slope. Wherever you feel comfortable head down the slope, the gradient lessening as the vegetation grows higher.

Low down a trail materializes and takes you to the valley bottom of King Creek's north fork. At this point you're within visiting distance to the col at 342224 between the ridge and Mt. Hood.

North fork 2 km

Heading south, the trail gains strength as it follows the right bank of the north fork through long-grass meadows. Be alert for where it crosses to the left bank in a tangle of willow brush. To your left, meadows sweep down from the Opals and are interspersed with numerous gullies. One with cairns on both sides possibly signifies the route up Mt. Brock. To right, King Creek Ridge rises in tiers of crags and trees. All too soon you descend into trees (keep left at a split) and cross the creek.

Pass below a scree slope, then fight your way across avalanche debris to the trail beyond. Cross to the left bank. A stint through forest ends with a descent to a wide, stony side creek with cairn. Pass below a high, steep bank at the top of which is the Stoney religious site. Ignore two trails climbing up left. Stay close to the creek.

Arrive at the forks, which is unmistakable. Ahead is the darkly forested south fork of King Creek with no trail. The trail crosses it on fallen trees and heads right (west) into the canyon that leads to Hwy. 40. Now read #42 backwards.

44 OPAL TRAVERSE — map 5

*Resting on Pocaterra-Elpoca Col
below Gap Mtn.*

Long day hike
**Unofficial trails & route, as many as 40
creek crossings**
Distance 12.6 km
Height gain S-N 960 m (3150 ft.)
Height loss S-N 1219 m (4000 ft.)
**High point at Pocaterra-Elpoca Pass
2414 m (7920 ft.)**
Map 82 J/11 Kananaskis Lakes

Access Hwy. 40 (Kananaskis Trail).
South Little Highwood Pass parking lot at the
junction with Valleyview Trail the road.
North King Creek day-use area.
Middle Valleyview Trail the road at Elpoca
day-use area.
   NOTE Valleyview Trail the road and
Hwy. 40 south of Kananaskis Lakes Trail are
closed December 1–June 15.

That wild country of larches and meadows hidden behind the outliers of the Opal
Range is only for experienced wilderness
addicts who can navigate without trails
if necessary. In fall when the larches are
gaudy and the sky is blue, this is a hiker's

heaven. At such times take care not to lin-
ger overlong or like us you'll be navigating
King Creek canyon in the pitch black of
night. Take Tevas and headlamps. Getting
benighted is acceptable: camping is not.
   Basically the route runs from Little
Highwood Pass day-use area to King
Creek parking lot, so you will of course
require two vehicles or bikes. I have also
described an escape route down Opal
Creek Valley to Valleyview Trail the road.
You have to decide whether road bashing
is preferable to the awful slog down King
Creek with its umpteen creek crossings.
   A word on distance, height gain and
height loss: those given under the main
heading are the maximum and can be cut
down by taking one of the options I give
between cols. Even so, the whole outing is
quite strenuous, because you can't avoid
that first col, which is the scrambler's
route to Gap Mountain and is by far the
steepest pull of the day. You may decide
to go no farther!

ACCESS NOTE Since the last edition Valleyview Trail the road has been closed to vehicles between Elpoca day-use area and Little Highwood Pass parking lot. When road kill is dumped on this stretch of road, it is closed to ALL users. So before you set out it pays to check the K Country web site for road closures.

HISTORY NOTE For background on this fascinating area read "Kananaskis Ram," by Ernst Hanisch, a true story dating back to 1943 when the author was a POW at Camp 130 in the Kananaskis Valley. I am still waiting for this gut-wrenching story to be picked up by a film producer and set to the music of John Williams. The quieter section of The Cowboys Overture is perfect: you can easily imagine the progeny of Ernst's three-legged ram filing quietly along the old trails under the pale peaks of the Opals, the mist swirling about and ultimately hiding them from view just as the final credits roll. Just remember you read of it here first, okay?

SOUTH TO NORTH

Pocaterra-Elpoca Col (38413)
Distance 1.7 km
Height gain 488 m (1600 ft.),
High point 2414 m (7920 ft.)

Above the parking lot is a steep slope seamed by three major gullies and you're going up the middle one. This is the scrambler's direct route to the ridge connecting Gap and Elpoca mountains, which is Pocaterra-Elpoca Col, and the highest point on the traverse at 2414 m. In these gullies George Pocaterra mined for coal from his cabin down in Pocaterra Creek.

From the parking lot head west along Valleyview trail for about 200 m. Just past the road sign on the right turn right into the bush on a trail. Shortly the trail enters the middle gully that takes you all the way to the ridge. Keep right at a fork low down, then left higher up. Above the second fork the angle steepens to shale: great fun to run down but a pain in the calf muscles going up.

Just after passing the left fork there is the option of taking to the grass and tree rib on the right and following that up.

Top out on the west side of the pass under Gap Mountain—a moderate scramble with a summit register.

While climbing the mountain called 'Gap,'
A fellow once took a big crap,
he said, "Holy cripes!
I didn't bring wipes!"
He now has a brown topo map!

Scramblers will know who the limerick writer is, so enough said!

Turn your back on Gap and head over a hump to the east side of the col under Elpoca Mountain (cairn). A coal outcrop halfway along is a fabulous place from which to view Highwood Pass and Pocaterra Ridge! From here Pocaterra took a photo of this same view sans road. He called Gap Mountain "George" and Elpoca Mountain "Paul" after his Stoney blood brother Paul Amos, but nothing ever came of this self-indulgence.

A very foreshortened view up the ascent gully and the alternate ridge to right.

The larch ridge en-route to Elpoca-Opal Col.

To Elpoca-Opal Col (378159)
High point 2362 m (7750 ft.)

This section crosses the head of Elpoca Creek below the magnificent west face of Elpoca Mountain.

From the cairn, head northeast on a trail that descends very steeply for a short while on shale. Arrive on a little ridge at 384135 dividing the east and south forks of Elpoca Creek. There are two routes onward. (Kilometrage, height gain and height loss are given as between cols.)

1. Ridge route 3.5 km, height loss 381 m (1250 ft.), height gain 320 m (1050 ft.) You are most tempted to follow the trail along the little ridge in the larches. The trail eventually drops off the end to the east fork (water). Rather than join the main valley of Elpoca Creek, which is close by at this point, cross the east fork and using one of many game trails traverse to gain the valley farther upstream past the confluence with its wee north fork, which arises from the col at 370155.

Continue along the right bank. Later, transfer to the left bank below the big grassy hill at 376157; then, where the valley turns left return to the right bank. Not too far along, avalanche debris in the creekbed forces the trail up the right side of some scree to an intersection with a traversing trail—the east fork route. Turn left.

2. East Fork route 3 km, height loss 259 m (850 ft.), height gain 198 m (650 ft.) From where you gained the larch ridge at 384135, descend the right (northeast) side of it into the upper east fork, which is all meadow. Walk down valley. Where the east fork turns left through a gap, pick up the traversing trail heading straight for the col. Cross two narrow scree fans. Keep straight at the junction where the ridge route joins in.

Routes united, the trail crosses more scree to a flat meadow at the base of the final rise. En route look up right to the ridge line. Spot the window? A short climb up shale gains you the grassy col at 2362 m below the steep east face of hill 376157. Ahead lies the Kananaskis Ram country of Opal Creek.

Climbing to Elpoca-Opal Col.

To Opal-King Col (368170)
High point 2332 m (7650 ft.)
This section crosses the head of Opal Creek below Mt. Schlee to the col between Mt. Wintour and Cats Ears. There are two ways of tackling it: the direct and straightforward descent to Opal Creek Valley and ascent to the col; and the very much more convoluted traverse with its numerous game trails.

1. Direct route 1.6 km, height loss 183 m (600 ft.) height gain 152 m (500 ft.)
Descend the trail to the head of the valley. Cross Opal Creek (water) and simply climb up the other side through meadows and larches to the col.

2. The traverse 1.9 km, height loss ~15 m (50 ft.) height gain ~30 m (100 ft.)
Head right on a trail that traverses a gullied shale slope to the third, more deeply incised gully. Descend a little before crossing into larches. On the other side the trail starts heading uphill, so leave it and cross a scree fan. Come to the main fork with water.

Cross and climb uphill a little, then traverse left across meadow. In the trees pick up a trail leading across a shallow gully, then climbing steeply up the left side of it. Shortly it cuts back left on a traverse line. Before a final gully, climb a shaley slope a short way, then again cut left above the gully to reach the grass and larch ridge that is the col. Walk down to the lowest point. Look back for a superb view of Elpoca Mountain through the gap.

South Fork of King Creek
Distance 3.9 km
Height loss 509 m (1670 ft.) to forks, 655 m (2150 ft.) to trailhead
The miserable forest section with no trail and innumerable creek crossings.

Head north down open larch forest to the infant south fork of King Creek, which comes in from the right off Mt. Jerram. Beyond the shale slope, cross to the right bank and for some time after cross back and forth across the creek in a dark forest.

Progress worsens with the start of crags along the left bank. Added to the creek

On Opal-King Col, looking back to Elpoca-Opal Col and Elpoca Mountain. To right of the pass is hill 376157, climbed in #45.

crossings are avalanche debris, plain old deadfall, stones and willow bush. Conditions ease just before reaching the forks. Aim to be on the left bank because this puts you in position to hike the canyon section to King Creek parking lot. (See #42.) Only another 1.6 km and 10 creek crossings to go...

ESCAPE ROUTE

44A Opal Creek

Distance 3.5 km from Opal Creek

From Elpoca-Opal Col, use route 1 into the head of Opal Creek and turn left down valley, later using a trail on the right bank. What a beautiful place of meadows, larches and spruce. Lower down, though, a shadow falls over the valley. Not only is it narrowing, but avalanche chutes follow one after the other all the way down to the drop-off place above Whiteman (Opal) Falls. After the trail crosses the creek to the left bank, either traverse avalanche slopes about 30 m up or muddle through the valley bottom to the death place of the Kananaskis ram above the drop-off. Now what?

Trust the sheep, which have spent thousands of years perfecting routes around the impasse. Climb the sheep trail up the left (east) bank avalanche slope. The trail eventually cuts right to another avalanche slope, then descends low down, deking left through an unsuspected gap between cliffs into the head of a dry canyon—an awesome place of ruddy-hued cliffs thrust vertically into columns. Still the trail continues, climbing along the top edge of the left-hand cliff and around a slit to a tree blazed with a cross on the western rim.

This marks the spot where sheep and scramblers can slither down a stoney gully to Elpoca day-use area. If you don't feel comfortable doing this, follow the rim trail in a southerly direction and lose height gradually. Low down beyond residual cliffs, circle left around a bog, then turn right and perhaps on elk trail descend to Valleyview Trail the road, reached about 300 m north of Elpoca Creek at a place impossible to pinpoint.

Turn right and walk the road to Elpoca day-use area.

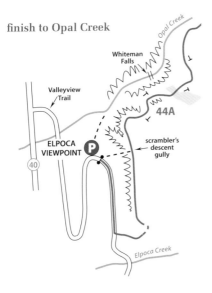

The fantastic rock scenery above the canyon,

45 ELPOCA CREEK HILL — map 5

Day hike
Unofficial trails & route
Distance 4.3 km to summit
Height gain ~670 m (2200 ft.)
High point 2493 m (8180 ft.)
Map 82 J/11 Kananaskis Lakes

Access Valleyview Trail the road off Hwy. 40. Drive to Elpoca day-use area at the gate. NOTE Valleyview Trail the road and Hwy. 40 south of Kananaskis Lakes Trail are closed December 1–June 15.

Rough terrain with intermittent game trails make this trip up Elpoca Creek one for experienced wilderness hikers. While linking up with route #44 would seem an obvious thing to do, the big grassy hill that rises west of Elpoca-Opal Pass at 376167 is a far finer objective. Climbing the hill AND making a loop with Opal Creek is another possibility.

ACCESS NOTE Since the last edition the road has been closed to vehicles between Elpoca day-use area and Little Highwood Pass parking lot. When road kill is dumped on this stretch of road, it is closed to ALL users. It is worrying that even when it is open, grizzlies will have become so conditioned to meals on wheels they will be hotfooting it down there just for a look-see.

Walk or bike south along Valleyview Trail the road for 1 km to Elpoca Creek (crossed by a bridge above a fine waterfall). The trail starts from a small parking area on the near left (north) side of the bridge.

The good north bank trail heads east into the valley confines between Gap Mountain and the grey rocky ridge to the north. All too soon it descends to creek level where you become mired in willow brush. Either struggle through the valley bottom or climb the steep, grassy bank to left and pick up traversing game trails, keeping right and down as you near the confluence with a wee north fork that arises from the col at 370155.

Cross the north fork and climb the hill's south ridge on grass to the saddle between the two tops. The east summit to right is narrow, a cairn balanced on top of a rockband overlooking Elpoca-Opal Pass. The west summit to left is the higher. From both vantage points Gap and Elpoca mountains are spectacular. Looking west between nearby heights, you spot Mt. Abruzzi with Pass in the Clouds to its right.

Returns
From the west summit descend to the col at 370155. Turn left and descend to your ascent route. Alternatively, turn right and descend a much steeper furrowed slope of larches to Opal Creek Valley.

The west top from near the saddle.

46 POCATERRA RIDGE—map 6

View of the larch belt and peak no. 2. Down right is Rockfall Valley showing a dried-up lake. Photo Maurice Gaucher.

Day hike
Unofficial trail & route,
possible creek crossing
Distance 5.7 km to peak no. 4
Height gain N-S 1036 m (3400 ft.) to
peak no. 4
High point 2667 m (8750 ft.)
Map 82 J/11 Kananaskis Lakes

Access Hwy. 40 (Kananaskis Trail) at Little Highwood Pass day-use area at the south entrance to Valleyview Trail the road. NOTE This section of Hwy. 40 is closed December 1–June 15.
Also accessible from #52 Little Highwood Pass in two places.

The "Kootenay Ridge," as geologist John Allan called it in 1947, is a heavenly ridge walk where it's possible to pick off four tops named even farther back in time, "the Pocaterra Peaks" by George Pocaterra. Scrambling is optional (except for the fourth top, the ridge is mainly grass), exposure is nil and you can escape from almost anywhere in the event of a thun-

derstorm. It is, though, a fairly strenuous flog with a substantial height gain. Making things easier since the last edition is a trail that has replaced the initial bushwhack to peak no. 1. In fact, there's a trail most of the way now!

The ridge is often hiked in combination with Little Highwood Pass and Rockfall Valley to make an 11.9-km loop back to the parking lot. Becoming more popular with groups is a one-way trip of 10.1 km to Highwood Pass using trails #52 and 49. Often it's hiked from south to north to take advantage of less height gain and easier-angled uphill slopes.

NORTH TO SOUTH

To Rockfall Valley trail junction 0.4 km
Walk through to Hwy. 40 and cross. Almost opposite, a narrow trail leads down into the trees and can be followed (scraps of faded flagging) to Pocaterra Creek. The creek was named by a Dominion land

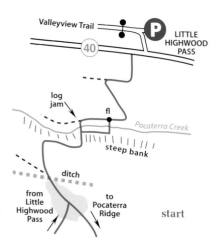

surveyor who found a mining stake with George Pocaterra's name written on it on behalf of the MacKay & Dippie Coal Syndicate. The Stoneys were of the same mind: Wasiju Wachi tusin ta Waptan Ze means "Crazy mischievous white man creek" or "where this Wasiju Wachi was taking a leak." What's left of Pocaterra's cabin lies downstream a way and is most easily reached by heading into the trees from Hwy. 40 to 1.1 km north of the fire road.

But I digress. At Pocaterra Creek the trail heads right. Either paddle across at flagging or fight your way across a small log jam a little farther downstream. On the far bank, midway between the two crossing places, a trail climbs the bank and heads right. Shortly it turns inland between willow bushes. Just before crossing a small ditch another trail comes in from the right. Then you enter a meadow. Keep an eye out for the unmarked fork at 383117. (Right is the return trail down Rockfall Valley.) Veer left past yellow flagging and in trees begin the climb up to peak no. 1.

The ridge 5.3 km

The trail is good and easy to follow as it twists uphill through menziesia bushes, which gradually thin out as you climb

higher into the coal belt. Emerge from trees onto a wide, grassy ridge with rocky outcrops bejewelled with clumps of alpine cinquefoil. Though beautiful and the sort of place one wishes could be transferred at the wave of a wand to the rock garden back home, it doesn't compare with the actual summit of peak no. 1 (cairn, surveyor's benchmark), whose west-facing slopes are packed with an incredible array of flowers. Now that I've said that, you'll probably hit a bad flower year and I'll lose credibility.

Descend to the low point on the ridge where larch trees spill over the gap. At this point an intersecting game trail offers an escape route into Rockfall Valley just down-valley of the lake. (Don't aim for the lake; a rockband gets in the way.)

After one brief sortie above treeline, the ridge shakes off the last of the larches and climbs a steepening, narrowing ridge to peak no. 2, which is capped with an elegant cairn.

Drop to 2–3 gap. Peak no. 3 is from either direction a very easy walk that one is tempted to miss out altogether by traversing to the 3–4 gap. Should you, as a ridge walker, be guilty of such unnatural behaviour, pretend to be looking for instruments that for a good many years measured creep along the traverse line.

Peak no. 4 looks more difficult. Start off by walking along the left (east) side of the horizontal section, then switch over to "the sidewalk." The cockscomb of rock can be bypassed on the left side by a trail along a grey shale bench that slants up to the ridge beyond the rock. Alternatively, enjoy an easy scramble along the crest.

An orange shale slope leads to the first of three tops. As you cross from one to another on shale, scree and a little rock it becomes apparent that the formidable-looking rock bands seen from down below and that may have caused you some apprehension are merely north face facades. The middle top is the one with a cairn.

Getting-off routes both start from the far third top.

*Looking from peak no. 2 across no. 3 to no. 4.
At right is Little Highwood Pass and Mt. Tyrwhitt. Photo Bernie Nemeth.*

*Looking back from top no. 4 to tops 3 and 2. In the background is Gap Mtn. and the Pocaterra/
Elpoca Pass (left), Elpoca Mtn. (centre) and the Elbow Valley and Tombstone Mtn. to right.*

GETTING OFF

1. Via Little Highwood Pass 6.2 km

The loop back to the trailhead via Little Highwood Pass and Rockfall Valley is the longer, harder option with scree, snow very often and tricky trail-finding. The hardest part is the 0.3 km-descent to Little Highwood Pass.

The west ridge route to the pass is a steep drop of 122 m (400 ft.). When snow-free, it's a fairly simple descent with the

1. The west ridge descent to Little Highwood Pass, seen at lower left.

benefit of a zigzagging trail on soft black shale near the bottom. When snow lingers on the ridge and northwest slope, though, and a cornice runs up and down the ridge, the descent transforms into something only an experienced scrambler should attempt. If necessary, head down the south ridge to the shoulder, then on game trail traverse back right to the pass.

Now follow the Rockfall Valley section of #52 back to your starting point, a distance of 5.9 km.

2. To Highwood Pass 4.4 km

The shorter, easier, more popular option uses trails #52 and 49.

Starting from the far top of peak no. 4, head down the broad south ridge on shale, then grass to a shoulder. Continue down more steeply to the north fork of Pocaterra Creek. Usually you can cross on rocks. On the far bank pick up Little Highwood Pass trail and turn left. Keep right, then turn left when you intersect Grizzly Col trail.

Alternatively, below the shoulder veer farther to the left down an even steeper grassy hillside, aiming for the flat meadow above Pocaterra Tarn. Unfortunately this shortcut has a minor glitch before you can access Grizzly Col trail on the far side of the meadow: a paddle across Pocaterra Creek.

2. The descent route from peak no. 4 to Pocaterra Creek follows the grassy south ridge at left. The steeper shortcut aims for the camera from the shoulder.

47 ELBOW LAKE — map 6

Half day, day hike
Official & unofficial trails
Distance 1.4 km to lake
Height gain 137 m (450 ft.) to lake
High point 2088 m (6850 ft.)
Maps 82 J/11 Kananaskis Lakes,
82 J/10 Mt. Rae

Access Hwy. 40 (Kananaskis Trail) at Elbow Pass day-use area. NOTE This section of Hwy. 40 is closed December 1–June 15.

This colourful lake and its backcountry campground are incredibly popular, in part because the access trail is so short. It is steep, though, and crowded. Be alert for such things as fishing rods, skis and poles, snowboards, picnic lunches in swinging Safeway bags, horses, llamas and descending mountain bikers.

Officially, the access is part of Big Elbow trail (see Volume 2), but most visitors just go as far as the lake. Lose the crowds by heading to Elbow Pass or the Rae Glacier or other destinations off Big Elbow trail described in Volume 2, such as Piper Creek and Tombstone Lakes, which

Elbow Lake. Looking from the south shore towards Elbow Pass and Tombstone Mtn.

are usually accessed from this trailhead as long day trips.

Straight from the parking lot it's a mostly uphill climb through forest and below talus slopes on a smoothly gravelled trail that was once a fire road. En route to the flat under an avalanche slope falling from Little Arethusa, pass caution signs and a well-placed bench.

Starting uphill again, the trail turns left, then right, crossing over a ridge — Elbow Pass proper — to the lake's southwest corner. (At the left-hand bend an unsigned trail with branches laid across the start heads straight for the campground.)

For the campground turn right. The high-tech Phoenix composting toilet is worth seeing and can shelter 10 people in a storm.

A circuit of the lake! Circling anticlockwise on trail, wind through campsites to the forested east shore. Pass the Rae Glacier turn-off (no sign) and in meadow arrive at the provincial park boundary. Look

145

back for a fabulous view of Mt. Rae. Turn left, cross the infant Elbow on planks and return along the west shore fire road to the T-junction on the southwest corner. My favourite piece of shoreline is where scree slopes shelve into translucent blue/green water. The lake's colour was described on a 1931 Belmore Browne family painting trip as "much finer than Lake O'Hara," but has turned a little greener in recent years.

GOING FARTHER

47A Rae Glacier

Unofficial trail & route
2.2 km from Elbow Lake
Height gain from lake 229 m (750 ft.)
High point 2316 m (7600 ft.)

Getting to the small glacier on the north side of Mt. Rae is a little more strenuous on unofficial trail, with scree at the end. The cirque is most often visited by skiers and boarders in late spring when the road is dry and you can bike in to the trailhead. At such time be alert for spring avalanches.

The only map the glacier is marked on is Gem Trek's map of Kananaskis Lakes.

Start out on the east shore trail. Abandon it about halfway along and turn right on a trail that heads northeast to the fledgling Elbow River issuing from Mt. Rae. Turn upstream. To avoid a mini-canyon, the trail climbs the rib on the right to a viewpoint for mounts Elpoca, Tombstone and Rae. Continue along the rib, then, crossing snow glades and tree ribbons, make a gradual descent to the creek. Walk up the right side on scree.

Where the creek turns left (the true source of the Elbow is névé in the twin cirque to the east), the trail climbs moraines straight ahead to the flat floor of the Rae Glacier.

Perhaps you'll bump into geology students from the University of Saskatchewan who, amongst others, have been gathering ice core and water samples from the Rae for nearly 20 years. I'm told that the glacier has shrunk by 50% over the last century. There's even differences to be noted between editions of this book.

Hardcore skiers and boarders will be making for the slopes at the back of the cirque, which steepen alarmingly just below the col between Rae and its southwest outlier. Not a good route up Mt. Rae for scramblers.

Rae Glacier.

48 PTARMIGAN CIRQUE interpretive trail—map 6

Entering Ptarmigan Cirque.
Fran's Rock at top of the grassy rise.

Half day
Official trail
Distance 3.6 km return
Height gain 229 m (750 ft.)
High point 2438 m (8000 ft.)
Map 82 J/10 Mt. Rae

Access Hwy. 40 (Kananaskis Trail) at Highwood Pass parking lot. NOTE this section of Hwy. 40 is closed December 1–June 15.

A short and popular trail from Canada's highest navigable pass into alpine meadows below Mt. Rae. With most of the height gain occurring within the first kilometre, this trail is no easy stroll; there's some uphill work to be done before you reap your reward.

Also the scrambler's access to Mt. Rae, the highest peak east of Hwy. 40.

WARNING Grizzly sightings close this trail on a regular basis.

Follow the trail over the bridge into the meadows. Keep right. (To left is the single track trail to Grizzly Col and Little Highwood Pass.) At the next T-junction fork right onto Ptarmigan Cirque trail. (To left is Highwood Meadows Interpretive trail that soon ends at an overlook.

The trail crosses the highway and starts a zigzagging climb through fir and spruce forest. High up at 1.1 km is a T-junction with the return loop. Keep straight.

Shortly the gradient eases and you enter the cirque. As you wander through flowery meadows, Mt. Rae comes into view ahead, not the summit but the lower summit or "the pinnacle" as some people call it. Where the trail turns right below a terminal moraine to cross the cirque, the scrambler's access trail to Mt. Rae continues up the valley and around to the left.

The main trail crosses the cirque creek above a small waterfall, then turns right, heading back down through a patchwork of scree and meadow below the cliffs of Little Arethusa. Ahead is a new view across Highwood Pass of Highwood Ridge, Grizzly Peak, Mt. Tyrwhitt and Pocaterra Ridge.

Recross the creek and traverse to the T-junction. Turn left and return the same way you came up.

147

Grizzly Col. Rising above it is Mt. Tyrwhitt, a moderate scramble up the facing east ridge. Note the people on the col.

49 "GRIZZLY COL" — map 6

Day hike
Unofficial trail
Distance 4 km
Height gain to col 518 m (1700 ft.)
High point at col 2606 m (8550 ft.)
Maps 82 J/10 Mt. Rae,
82 J/11 Kananaskis Lakes

Access Hwy. 40 (Kananaskis Trail) at Highwood Pass parking lot. NOTE this section of Hwy. 40 is closed December 1–June 15.
Also accessible from #52 Little Highwood Pass, #46 Pocaterra Ridge and from the west fork of Storm Creek described in Volume 5.

This is the col between Pocaterra Creek and the west fork of Storm Creek, which some call Tyrwhitt Col. Since the last edition the good trail to Pocaterra Tarn has been extended all the way to the col thanks to scramblers. I am happy to report that the horrible grovel up the scree below the col that once gave this route its strenuous rating is now a thing of the past. Nevertheless, the upper part of the route in Tyrwhitt Cirque is still fairly rough and rocky and until mid summer you can expect to cross steep tongues of snow.

This base trail gives access to Highwood Ridge (#51), Little Highwood Pass (#52), and Pocaterra Ridge (#46). It is the scrambler's access to Mt. Tyrwhitt for people doing the "Kanes."

To Highwood Ridge turnoff 1 km
Set off along Highwood Pass Meadows interpretive trail. Shortly turn left onto an unsigned single track trail running down the centre of a grassy meltwater channel—the original horse route over Highwood Pass. Reach a large rock at the bottleneck. Here the trail turns off left into the trees.

After crossing a tiny creek, the trail climbs muddily through open spruce forest. Around the first high point two smaller trails turn off to the left. The second trail at 419066 is the best route onto Highwood Ridge (#51).

To Pocaterra Tarn 1 km
The trail then descends slightly. At the bottom of the hill a third trail to Highwood Ridge turns off to the left. The main trail climbs briefly to a second high point below a rockband marking the ridgeline, then makes a long, twisty descent with occasional steep, shaley steps—something to look forward to on the return!

Finally it levels and crosses a lush avalanche slope of long-stemmed forget-me-nots, smelly cow parsley and large-leafed ragworts. The trail climbs a little, then descends in zigs to a fork of Pocaterra Creek. Climb up the left bank, then cross to the right bank shortly before the creek

Pocaterra Tarn and its backdrop of larches.

is concealed by rubble. In a few minutes reach tiny Pocaterra Tarn, located between scree slopes and larch meadows. In the height of summer the scree slopes are a riot of pink mountain fireweed.

To Little Highwood Pass trail 0.9 km
From Pocaterra Tarn the trail carries on at the demarcation of scree and larches, eventually turning right into a big flat meadow at the forks of Pocaterra Creek. Ahead rises the fourth summit of Pocaterra Ridge, from this direction a big grassy pudding of a hill. Come to a trail junction marked by a rock and turn left. (The trail continuing along the meadow edge is the messy old route to Little Highwood Pass that requires a creek crossing of the short-lived south fork.)

The trail leaves the meadow and climbs between larches, then traverses a grass slope to a T-junction below the high wall of the moraine. Turn left. (Right is the trail to Little Highwood Pass.)

All the way up from the meadow is a view of Mt. Tyrwhitt ahead, displaying its Wishbone Arch two-thirds up the left-hand skyline ridge.

To Grizzly Col 1.1 km
The trail hugs the bottom of the moraine as it gradually ascends a draw into Tyrwhitt Cirque. At a split keep right on the better trail that zigs into an upper draw. Part way along the draw, the trail climbs out the left side of it onto grass (cairn) and shortly peters out. Ahead rises Grizzly Col, a wall of scree and rock slung between Grizzly Peak and Mt. Tyrwhitt.

Where the trail peters out, head left across the flat to the scree slopes of Grizzly Peak. At a cairn, (a line of cairns to left indicates the left-hand split mentioned earlier), a trail materializes and climbs up the scree a way, then turns right and makes a slowly rising traverse to the col. The crossing of a broken rock rib near the top is easy.

As mentioned some call this col Tyrwhitt. "Grizzly" is the older name. While no one's yet met a griz face to face on the col, plenty of people have seen tracks in the snow.

To your right is the popular scrambler's route up Mt. Tyrwhitt, which is rated moderate (helmet recommended). To left is the southeast ridge of Grizzly Peak. Behind you is Little Highwood Pass, in front a blinkered view of Storm Creek's west fork squashed between the southeast ridge of Grizzly Peak and the mighty east wall of the Great Divide.

ONGOING OPTIONS

Anyone with energy to spare can tack on Grizzly Peak or at least the southeast ridge for the view. See #50 and 50A.

With two vehicles you can connect with the series of trails in Storm Creek via #50B. See also Storm Creek trails in Volume 5.

Almost at Grizzly Col.

This picture from Pocaterra Ridge shows most of the route from the avalanche slope at bottom left, past Pocaterra Tarn into Tyrwhitt Cirque (right) and up to Grizzly Col, located between Grizzly Peak (centre) and Mt. Tyrwhitt (right). Note the arch two-thirds up the left-hand ridge of Tyrwhitt. At left is Highwood Ridge, showing the ascent route up the left-hand ridge.

50 "GRIZZLY PEAK" — map 6

Day scramble
Unofficial trail & route
Distance 0.8 km from Grizzly Col
Height gain 165 m (540 ft.) from Grizzly
Col, 683 m (2240 ft.) from trailhead
High point 2770 m (9090 ft.)
Maps 82 J/10 Mt. Rae,
82 J/11 Kananaskis Lakes

Access Hwy. 40 (Kananaskis Trail) at Highwood Pass parking lot. Via #49 at Grizzly Col. NOTE this section of Hwy. 40 is closed December 1–June 15.

This is the orange-coloured mountain on the east side of Grizzly Col at 413055 — an easier and more enjoyable alternative to Mt. Tyrwhitt. Mostly it's a ridgewalk with one or two scrambly bits. Ongoing options enable you to make a loop or point to point.

You don't have to summit to do the options. By NOT summiting, deduct 1 km or more from both options.

On the southeast ridge of Grizzly Peak.
Note the orange tower along the ridge.

To the southeast ridge 0.3 km
On trail, head up the broad west ridge to the left (east), keeping an eye out for alpine poppies as you go. On rougher ground you zig right, back left, then head up steepish black-lichened boulders to the main south ridge. It's satisfying to look back to Mt. Tyrwhitt, where hardcore scramblers are having a much harder time of it labouring up high-angle scree and slabs.

To the summit 0.5 km
Turn left. Where the ridge turns northeast the black-lichened boulders give way to fine orange shales interspersed with a couple of rocky humps, the second of which has a slightly awkward descent on the right side. Farther on, turn the orange tower on the right side.

The ridge turns northwest and again changes character. The black lichen is back and you scrabble up broken rock on one side or the other of the ridge, finishing along the ridgeline to the summit.

There's a flat bit beyond the cairn where you can stretch out and look down on almost the entire route you came up from Pocaterra Creek, plus Little Highwood Pass, Pocaterra Ridge and Highwood Ridge. To the south, Paradise Valley is an amazing neon green colour. You can pick out the ramp leading down into it from lower down the southeast ridge.

Connecting you with Highwood Ridge is a serrated ridge, which poses a dilemma. Does it go? Not unless you're a proficient scrambler and can handle a tad of exposure and moderate scrambling on down-climbs. Everyone else should try Option A, the "ramp route."

OPTIONS

50A To Highwood Ridge

Route
Distance from Grizzly Peak ~3.5 km
Height loss 393 m (1290 ft.) from peak
Height gain 259 m (850 ft.) to ridge

A 10.5-km loop with Highwood Ridge (#51) is possible. Not the long, convoluted loop described in previous editions, but a tighter one that is no less strenuous on account of a substantial height gain coming late in the day. (Total height gain for loop is 942 m (3090 ft.)

The route dips into the head of Paradise Valley via the "ramp route," which is suitable for anyone who can handle moderately steep slopes with scree and can navigate around small rockbands.

From the summit, return down the south ridge to where you first gained it from Grizzly Col. Continue on down the ridge for about 250 m onto some orange scree before the ridge turns grassy.

Left: The summit.

Below: Paintbrush hillsides above Paradise Valley. Grizzly Peak in the background.

To Paradise Valley via the ramp 0.9 km

At about 413048 the steep slopes falling into Paradise Valley are replaced by a broad ramp of scree and grass offering a relatively straightforward descent on a slope only moderately steep. About half-way down, work your way between small, staggered rockbands, trending left. Lower down keep left of another rockband, then right of rocky bluffs below which a dozen springs burst forth. At this level the well-watered hillside is crammed with flowers, most notably magenta paintbrushes and long-stemmed forget-me-nots.

To Highwood Ridge 1.2 km

It's a simple walk across the valley floor below the serrations of the ridge connecting the two summits. Underfoot is short grass, also crammed with flowers, which makes me suspect that the name "Paradise," which was popular before 1947, was coined by amateur botanists. Farther on there's rivulets to cross.

Reach the base of Highwood Ridge and look up a 300-m-high slope of orange shale and broken rock rising to the summit. My recommendation is to traverse MUCH farther right to less-steep grassy slopes.

View of Paradise Valley from Grizzly Peak. To left is Highwood Ridge extending to the southeast summit in the middle of the picture. To right is the southeast ridge of Grizzly Peak, showing both the ascent route and the ramp.

After climbing about 200 m you arrive some way along the southeast ridge. Turn left and follow its broad back over a hump to the summit. Now read #51 backwards for the descent to Highwood Pass.

50B to Storm Creek

Route, unofficial trail
Distance 6.6 km to Hwy. 40, total distance between trailheads 11.4 km.
Height loss from summit to Hwy. 40, 835 m (2740 ft.)

A point to point between Grizzly Peak and Hwy. 40 south of Highwood Pass, via the entire southeast ridge. Apart from extending the ridge walk, the other good thing about this option is that you don't finish with a bushwhack but with a worry-free 3.5-km walk on a trail, which delivers you to Hwy. 40 some 750 m south of the Mt. Lipsett day-use area.

The southeast ridge 3.1 km

From the summit of Grizzly Peak return down the southeast ridge to where you first gained it from Grizzly Col.

Continue along the ridge, for another 2.6 km enjoying a slightly undulating ridgewalk with occasional rocky sections. On the right side the grass rolls tamely down into the west fork of Storm Creek. The left side is much steeper, offering no comfortable routes into Paradise Valley.

Descent 3.5 km

Drop off the gable end, a moderate slope of grass and first trees that lower down harbours some magnificent bushes of white rhododendron and bracted honeysuckle. Aim for the flat, treed ridge between the two forks of Storm Creek, specifically the point at 432024 where you can pick up the faint beginnings of the ridge trail.

Found it? Heading southeast all the way, follow the trail past a Y-junction (trail to right heads up Storm Creek) and on down to the promontory above the forks. Here the trail turns right and winds down to a hunter's camp. Continue to follow the trail alongside the west fork, to a junction. Keep straight. (The trail to right crossing the west fork is the west-side trail.)

On east-side trail, descend to the Paradise Valley fork just above the forks and wade across. The trail climbs up the opposite bank, then meanders (keep the faith) along the broad ridge and down to a T-junction. Turn left. The final stretch takes you out to Hwy. 40.

off Grizzly peak · to Grizzly Col · Paradise Valley fork · West fork · east-side · finish · to Storelk Cirque · Storm Creek · west-side · MOUNT LIPSETT · 40

51 "HIGHWOOD RIDGE" — map 6

Short day scramble
Unofficial trails, route
Distance 2.2 km to top from trailhead
Height gain 488 m (1600 ft.)
High point 2697 m (8850 ft.)
Map 82 J/10 Mt. Rae

Access Hwy. 40 (Kananaskis Trail) at Highwood Pass parking lot. Via #49 Grizzly Col. NOTE This section of Hwy. 40 is closed December 1–June 15.

Who can resist the summit looming over Highwood Pass parking lot? It's known that the Boundary Survey used this summit, the northernmost point of a long ridge, as a camera station called "Highwood Ridge North" in 1916. And it's known from an undated photo that George Pocaterra had been up there as well, though most likely just the southeast summit.

Expect a generally steep trudge on trail with a few scrabble sections. The scramble immediately below the top is optional.

The broad grassy section. Higher up, the trail takes to the crest and misses out the final tower by traversing left.

Most people return the same way, with a few electing to drop in on Highwood Pass before entering the trees. With two vehicles, you can carry on over the southeast summit and descend via trails in Storm Creek to Hwy. 40. See #51A.

To the open slopes 0.4 km
Follow Grizzly Col trail to the first high point on the forested ridge. There are two trails taking off to the left. The first makes a better descent route, while the second, at 419066, is the most heavily used for ascent. See the sketch map.

The trail climbs steadily through open forest. Keep left where fainter trails head right. After stepping over two fallen trees, come to a T-junction with the "descent trail" to left. Turn sharp right, making a beeline for a line of crags below the ridge-line (cairns). At the 4-way junction below the crags turn left. (Do NOT go straight.)

Work your way along a scree bench, keeping alert for where the trail zigs right then back left (flagging, cairns) up a more broken slope to gain the ridgeline through a little gap in the rocks. Turn left and follow the top edge of the rockband to red flagging at treeline. A little higher up the slope is a cairn.

To the north summit 0.8 km

Above looms a steep rise of shale and broken rockbands with multiple choice trails. Rather than take the steepest, blackest "main" trail to the far left, you'll have a happier time of it by getting onto the rock at the first opportunity at the far right and working your way up along ledges.

A brief, flat grass section leads into a second scramble up a shorter step. Above is a lovely stretch of broad grassy ridge. The trail continues along the right side of the ridge then divides below a steepening and narrowing. Left along the ridge-line is perhaps easier. The two trails join for a strenuous effort up black shale zigs to the base of the final tower. Scramble it direct, or bypass it entirely by traversing left on a trail that crosses easy-angled scree to the broad southeast ridge. Turn right and walk up grass to the summit cairn.

GOING FARTHER

51A Southeast Summit

Distance 5.8 km to Storm Creek
Extra height gain 152 m (500 ft.)
Height loss 850 m (2800 ft.)
High point at southeast summit
2555 m (8385 ft.)

The other end summit is 152 m (500 ft.) lower and reached by a 3.4-km-long grassy ridge. For this trip you need a second vehicle parked 750 m south of Mt. Lipsett day use area on Hwy. 40. See also Volume 5, Storm Creek trails.

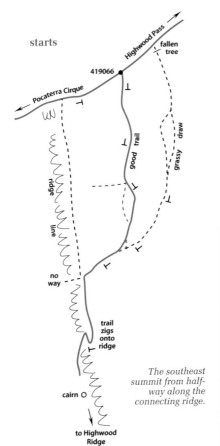

The southeast summit from half-way along the connecting ridge.

Head southeast along a remarkably wide, straight grassy ridge, ambling up and over two minor bumps. Because your attention is not constantly on where to put your feet, you're free to admire the views. To the east you're treated to a parade of cirques, including Ptarmigan (showing the route up Mt. Rae) and Arethusa (showing the route over to Burns Lake).

Farther on, the ridge tapers to an elegant crest. There's one narrow bit (avoidable on the right), then a cairn where you, too, can take a photo *almost* identical to the one taken by George Pocaterra, which archivists have inexplicably labelled "looking down the Elk Valley." A final climb gains you the southeast summit — a splendid viewpoint for Highwood Pass and the lovely country of the Highwood to the south.

From the top, Mt. Lipsett day-use area is in view below your feet. Dropping in from above is uncomfortably steep. Nowadays I prefer to descend the south ridge, which gives you the chance to

enjoy the myriad of alpines like roseroot that grow in the mix of grass and scree.

After you enter forest, the gradient begins to ease and likely you will be following one faint trail or another farther down the ridge to an intersection in a flat area with east-side trail in the Storm Creek network of trails. The trail is unmistakable and blazed. Turn left.

The trail meanders around a bit before descending to a T-junction with the west-side trail. Turn left and follow it out to Hwy. 40. (For anyone doing this trip in reverse direction, trail section is ~0.8 km.)

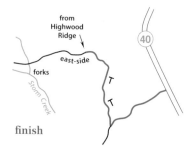

Looking back to the main summit. Highwood Pass down below.

52 LITTLE HIGHWOOD PASS — map 6

Little Highwood Pass from the south. To right is the fourth peak of Pocaterra Ridge.

Day hike
Unofficial trails & route,
possible creek crossings
Distance 7.2 km
Height gain S-N 229 m (750 ft.),
472 m, (1550 ft.) from trailhead
Height loss S-N 640 m (2100 ft.)
High point 2545 m (8350 ft.)

Access Hwy. 40 (Kananaskis Trail).
South at Highwood Pass. Via #49 Grizzly Col.
North Little Highwood Pass parking lot at the junction of Hwy. 40 and Valleyview Trail the road.
    NOTE This section of Hwy. 40 is closed December 1–June 15.
Also accessible from #46 Pocaterra Ridge

The official name is puzzling, because Little Highwood Pass lies neither within nor on the boundary of the Highwood River drainage, but between Pocaterra Creek and a south fork informally called Rockfall Valley.

The main thing to know about this pass is that it lies in the cold shadow of a great rock wall and is usually snowbound until mid summer. So take poles just in case.

The southern approach from Grizzly Col trail is straightforward with gentle gradients, though you could have a cornice to contend with at the end. The northern section in Rockfall Valley has complex terrain with lots of scree but is redeemed by a seasonal lake, larches and a fascinating "valleys of the rocks." Since the last edition a trail in the trees has cut out the bushwhacking. You just have to find it.

Most people climb up to the pass and back from Grizzly Col trail, or starting from north access combine the Rockfall Valley section with the ridgewalk along Pocaterra Ridge. Going right through requires two vehicles and isn't often done. Regardless, this south to north description should suit everyone.

SOUTH TO NORTH

To the pass 1.3 km

Follow Grizzly Col trail to the turnoff to Little Highwood Pass and turn right.

The trail leads into a sinuous, grassy draw below the moraine wall. Follow the draw to its very end, keeping left where the old route joins in from between boulders. The trail then climbs onto a rib above the north fork of Pocaterra Creek. When it seems you must stub your toes against the formidable wall of the Great Divide, descend easily to the creekbed. At this point the valley makes a right-angled turn to the north, disclosing a first view of the pass.

It's a simple walk up the enclosed valley on stones and patches of grass. Two-thirds of the way along, look up left to a cave at the bottom of an anticlinal fold. My neighbour Gord tells me its mouth makes a terrific frame for a picture of Grizzly Col and Mt. Tyrwhitt displaying its arch.

Cooling off in Rockfall Lake. Photo Alf Skrastins

As you draw closer to the pass, the gradient steepens and almost certainly you'll be tramping on snow and possibly kicking steps over a cornice. Often the cornice can be avoided by a detour up scree to the left.

The pass is a narrow one. To your right a zigzagging trail climbs the steep west ridge of Pocaterra Ridge's fourth summit. Starting from the bench just below the col another trail traverses over to the south ridge of the fourth. Ahead, little can be glimpsed of Rockfall Valley. As mentioned, the best view is backwards.

Rockfall Valley 5.9 km

Keeping right, descend into the south fork of Pocaterra Creek via the shallow gully at the demarcation of grey and brown rocks. Cross fans of névé/scree to the east bank of the emergent creek where a ribbon of meadow provides fast, easy going.

Half-way down the valley is Rockfall Lake, formed when a large portion of slope to the west slid and piled up in great mounds across the valley floor and halfway up Pocaterra Ridge opposite. In fall the lake dries, revealing the winding creek. Then you can hike across the lake bed. At other times pick your way along the left (west) shore. It's here where the water sinks and for nearly 2 km travels underground beneath the jumbled terrain.

From the end of the lake climb to the low point in the rubble pile. Descend stones at the base of the small ridge to the right, then round the end of the ridge to the east side of the valley. In larches pick up a trail that can be traced through a bumpy passageway of grass with boulders, which is the start of the east-side trough. (There is a parallel trough on the west side of the valley, a confusing number of cross-troughs, and a small tarn in the middle of it all.)

At the top of a small rise is a cairn. This signals the start of a much clearer trail that straightway descends a steep slope. The trail fades at the bottom. Look for a cairn and then head right into the trees where the trail picks up. Now you can either take

Rockfall Valley. Photo Alf Skrastins

the forest trail, or continue down the open trough that takes twice as long. On the forest trail follow cairns through a small area of rocks. Then look for a trail joining in from the left from trough's end.

Shortly after this junction the trail cuts across to the west-side trough at its last hurrah where rubble cascades into the old forest and the creek re-emerges for another brief fling in the daylight. In the rocks navigate from cairn to cairn, then follow the trail down the right bank into the trees.

The trail undulates along the right bank of the creek for some distance. A big rock on the right side is the wake-up call. A few metres on, the trail goes over a hump and down into a meadow where you have to be alert for the junction with Pocaterra Ridge trail at 383117. Go left.

Cross a ditch, keep straight (ignore trail to left) and head for Pocaterra Creek. The trail follows the banktop to the right a way, then descends the bank. There are two ways to cross. Either follow the trail

to right and wade opposite some flagging on the far bank. Or go a little left and cross at the log jam.

Either way, on the far bank turn right on a trail that winds its way through the forest to Hwy. 40. You emerge just slightly down road from the entrance to Little Highwood Pass parking lot.

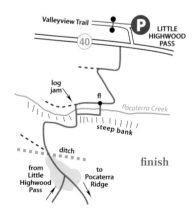

53 KANANASKIS CANYON interpretive trail—map 5

Hour hike
Official trail
Distance 1.2 km loop
Height gain N-S 18 m (60 ft.)
Map 82 J/11 Kananaskis Lakes

Access Kananaskis Lakes Trail (road) at Canyon campground. Driving into the campground, pass the entrances to loop A and loop B, then park on the right side of the road near the registration box.

A depressing walk through a little canyon to view the damage done to what was once the Kananaskis river bed. (Of course, some may say it's a tribute to man's ingenuity.) Trails #54 and 66 also show how harnessing the river and its two lakes for hydroelectric power has affected the landscape.

Walk a little farther along the campground access road to the trailhead on the left. A little way in is a T-junction. Turn right.

A mostly downhill stint through pine forest ends at interpretive sign no. 4 by the Kananaskis River, aka seepage from Can-

yon Dam. Here a bench overlooks a pool below some little falls. Cross a bridge and climb up the opposite bank. The trail then turns left and hugs the top of the canyon rim, which is fenced for your safety. At one time the river ran free through the canyon, gouging out potholes, splashing over rocks and against canyon walls. Now it is encased in that giant worm of a pipe on your right, sent silently on its dark way to the Pocaterra power plant. In winter the pipe is fringed with icicles.

Descend tiers of steps to the canyon bottom. After a quick look to the left to view a pool, follow the trail upstream, crossing the seepage another six times to the end of the canyon. En route look for dippers near a few tiny algae-ridden pools.

At a T-junction, turn left and cross the seepage for the last time. As you climb the bank ignore side trails heading right to B loop and arrive shortly at the T-junction. Go straight for the campground access road.

The pool below the steps.

54 LOWER LAKE — map 5

Half-day hike
Official trail
Distance 4 km one way to Elkwood
Height gain N-S 30 m (100 ft.)
Map 82 J/11 Kananaskis Lakes

Access Kananaskis Lakes Trail (road).
North Canyon day-use area.
The trail starts by the boat ramp.
South William Watson Lodge.
East Elkwood parking lot.

An easy stroll along the east shore of Lower Kananaskis Lake Reservoir between Canyon day use-area and William Watson Lodge and on to Elkwood parking lot. For views I prefer starting from Canyon and

Top: Lower Kananaskis Lake, looking south to mounts Fox, Foch and Sarrail.

Bottom: stumps at low water.

walking the trail north to south. Low water reveals unattractive mud flats dotted here and there with tree stumps.

HISTORY NOTE The lake's original name was Thorpe, after a director of Wisconsin's Eau Claire Logging Company who were sizing up the timber berths back in 1883.

NORTH TO SOUTH
To junction 2.7 km
The trail heads west, passing through a walk-in picnic area to the promontory marking the boundary of the sheltered

The trail to Elkwood parking lot.

backwater near Canyon Dam. Turn the corner and travel south along the lakeshore in the pines, making forays now and then to the waterline (however far that is) for rather stunning views of mounts Fox, Foch and Sarrail and the cliffs of Indefatigable Outlier rising in front of Indefatigable North.

In 2.7 km come to a T-junction with paved trails. Where you go next depends on your final destination. Regardless, all trails in the area are paved for easy access by wheelchairs users.

1. To William Watson Lodge 0.8 km
Keep right. In a minute or two come to another T-junction. Go straight on Bill Bensen trail that climbs the bank. (To right a trail heads out to a man-made promontory.) Bill Bensen trail climbs past memorial benches, then zigs left. Almost straightaway turn right. The next section of trail wanders behind chalets H-A, giving access to them and to four parking lots before ending up at William Watson Lodge.

2. To Elkwood parking lot 1.3 km
Turn left inland. The trail climbs up a cool valley of old spruce to a T-junction. Turn left. (Trail to right leads to the camping area.) Keep right at the next junction with Marsh Viewpoint trail. At the following T-junction turn left. (Trail to right leads to the chalets and William Watson Lodge.)

Cross a powerline right-of-way, which is Braille ski trail to the left. At the junction with Lodgepole ski trail keep right and come to Kananaskis Lakes Trail the road. Cross and in a few minutes arrive in Elkwood parking lot at the biffy.

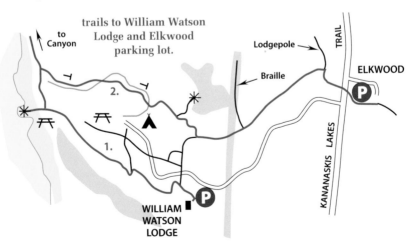

55 MARL LAKE interpretive trail — map 5

Half-day hike
Official trail
Distance 3.4 km return
Height gain 15 m (50 ft.)
High point 1716 m (5630 ft.)
Map 82 J/11 Kananaskis Lakes

Access Kananaskis Lakes Trail (road) at Elkwood parking lot.
Also accessible by trails from Elkwood campground: from D loop between sites 114 and 115; from C loop between sites 78 and 79; from A loop between sites 24 and 15. The interpretive trail crosses the loop B campground between sites 52 and 53, and 45 and 46.

Easy forest walking on a wheelchair-accessible paved trail leads to a lake with a spectacular backdrop. Morning light is best for photographs.

Through the campground 1.1 km
From the far right corner of the parking lot a wide trail curves past the amphitheatre. Keep straight (trail from loop A to right), then turn left (ahead is a trail leading to the main campground access road). At the next junction keep left (trail from B loop to right). The trail winds through a mossy forest of fir, spruce and pine, crossing loop B access road twice. Keep left (trail from loop C to right). Shortly stay left again (trail from loop D to right). Finally you arrive at a trail sign.

Marl Lake loop 1.2 km
Straightway pass a fen on the left where the chance of spotting a great blue heron is 100% if you're with the park interpreter. Come to a junction with the return loop.

Keep left. The trail passes more fens and interpretive signs. At a split in the trail definitely go left to the lakeshore viewing platform with its spate of interpretive signs. Across the lake is a stunning lineup of high mountains: Mt. Fox through Mt. Foch to Mt. Sarrail. Close at hand, inspect the water for leeches and scuds, and feel the marl on the lake bottom. It may feel like sand, but it's actually a by-product of algae, which find the calcium in the water indigestible.

Continue alongside the lake a way, then turn right and ease over a pine ridge back to the junction. Turn left and return the way you came.

Looking across Marl Lake to mounts Fox, Foch and Sarrail.

56 BOULTON CREEK interpretive trail—map 5

Half-day hike
Official trail
Distance 3 km loop
Height gain 24 m (80 ft.)
Map 82 J/11 Kananaskis Lakes

Access Kananaskis Lakes Trail (road) at Boulton Bridge parking lot.

A forest and river walk about Boulton's Creek, an old name pre-1914 that appeared on a Department of the Interior sectional map. Some easy hills.

HISTORY NOTE En route you visit the historic Fish & Wildlife cabin that was relocated from the valley bottom prior to tree clearing for Lower Kananaskis Lake reservoir in 1954/5. Lost were the original ranger cabin and several carvings on living trees made by Jack Fuller Sr., who in the 1920s worked as a summer guide taking parties on trips to Kananaskis Lakes. All that remains of his most popular carving—a nude woman with "wanton eyes, blue-stained lips and nipples of a soft red"—are photos in the Glenbow Archives taken by such notables as Lizzie Rummel and George Edworthy. Or are they lost?

By some fortuitous chance the nude resurfaced just a few years ago after residing for 50 years in a Calgary garden. Even more remarkably, it was a friend's husband's co-worker's father's garden, the co-worker's dad having rescued the carving while helping to clear the land back in 1955. Unfortunately, the list of names at the bottom of the carving is missing, namely of guides George Harrison and Guy Gano, of guests, and of 21 pack horses and 2 dogs.

From the near end of the parking lot cross the bridge over Boulton Creek. Immediately keep straight (left is the ski trail) and climb the bank to the Fish & Wildlife cabin.

At the T-junction turn right. Heading south through the lodgepoles, the trail undulates below what used to called Baseball Diamond Meadow, a once popular training ground for Jackrabbits that spawned not a few provincial and national X-C ski racers before there was the Canmore Nordic Centre.

Keep right (a side trail to left leads to A loop of Boulton Creek campground) then just beyond sign no. 2, skirt the edge of the bank with its view towards Mt. Indefatigable. Not long after joining Moraine ski trail (keep straight) you pass sign no. 3, where rock flakes have been found, pointing to the area's occupation some 8,000 years ago by Neolithic peoples of the Mummy Cave Complex.

The trail then moves away from the edge and zigs left, then right up a much longer uphill to a higher terrace. Descend slightly to a T-junction just past no. 7 sign. Turn right and zig down the bank to Boulton Creek. Cross the bridge to a T-junction at no. 8 sign and turn right.

Now on Boulton Creek ski trail, simply follow it back to the parking lot. It's a mainly flat walk alongside the creek with the chance of spotting dippers.

Boulton Creek from the return leg.

57 KANANASKIS LOOKOUT—map 5

Day hike, bike 'n' hike
Official trails with signposts
Distance 6.7 km from Boulton Bridge
parking lot, 4.7 km from Hwy. 40
Height gain 432 m (1417 ft.) from
Boulton Bridge,
274 m (900 ft.) from Hwy. 40
High point 2118 m (6950 ft.)
Map 82 J/11 Kananaskis Lakes

Looking south from the lookout to the
mountains of the Elk River.

There are two reasonable routes to Kananaskis Lookout. Both are wide forest trails, ski trails in winter, that join for the final steep pull to a fabulous viewpoint. If I'm on a bike I much prefer to zip along the fire road from Highway 40. But as this is a hiking guide I'd have to recommend starting from Kananaskis Lakes Trail at the Boulton area, which has campsites, an eating place and lots of people looking for a walk. Starting from Boulton Trading Post parking lot cuts out a little height gain.

Access

1. Kananaskis Lakes Trail (road)

1a. Boulton Bridge parking lot.

1b. Boulton Trading Post upper parking lot. From the southeast corner get onto a paved ski/bike trail and turn right. Follow it to a 4-way junction with biffies where the route from Boulton Bridge comes in from the right. Turn left.

1c. Boulton campground. The access road to A loop crosses the trail as does the access road between loops B and D.

2. Hwy. 40 (Kananaskis Trail). Park at the entrance to the fire road on the west side of the highway at 370118.

HISTORY NOTE The present, second, lookout was built in 1976, the first in 1952, five years after Joe Kovach blazed a trail along what is now the fire road. Interestingly, he followed in part a secret Indian trail that crossed East Elk Pass into the country of the Elk. For enthusiastic readers of *The Buffalo Head*, this was the route George Pocaterra, Adolf Baumgart and R.M. Patterson took in 1931 to escape the watchful eye of the ranger McGregor!

FROM ACCESS 1a
To the fire road via Whisky Jack ski trail 4.3 km

From the near end of the parking lot cross the bridge over Boulton Creek. Immediately keep straight (left is a ski trail) and climb the bank to the old Fish & Wildlife cabin. At the T-junction turn left past the garage. (To right is Boulton Creek interpretive trail.) At the following T-junction with Whiskey Jack ski trail, which is paved, turn right (the trading post can be seen to the left).

Climb a short hill to a 4-way junction with biffies where the trail from Access 1b joins in from the left. (To right is the amphitheatre.) Go straight on a wide, gravelled trail.

Climb a steep hill. At the top cross the campground access road to A loop (Access 1c). Climb alongside the campground road, then cross the road between B and D loops (Access 1c). All campground clutter left behind, continue on Whisky Jack ski trail, which is uphill though undulating because you keep crossing Spotted Wolf Creek and all its tributaries. The most interesting part of all this is the name of the creek, which honours George Pocaterra's blood brother Paul Amos.

At 4.3 km come to the T-junction with the fire road that has come in from Highway 40 and is signed "Pocaterra."

Kananaskis Lakes from the lookout, Mt. Indefatigable at right.

Lookout trail 2.4 km

Under its various guises you're going to be following the fire road all the way to the lookout. Turn right on Pocaterra ski trail. In half a kilometre turn right onto Lookout trail. (Ahead is Tyrwhitt trail, which follows the next section of the secret trail to the Elk. Nevertheless, I don't recommend it for summer hiking: boggy meadows and grizzlies just about sums it up.)

Coming up is the longest climb of the day, a steep grind up the north ridge of Lookout Hill, where total humiliation is to be passed by a mountain biker. The incline eases into a long straight, at the end of which you climb out of the trees to picnic tables. The hill top has been shaved, a green meadow allowing a 360-degree view if you stand by the lookout. Look south to the mountains about Elk Lakes (that's mounts Cadorna and Swiderski through the gap), west to mounts Fox, Foch and Sarrail and Kananaskis Lakes, and north down the Kananaskis Valley to Mt. Kidd.

FROM ACCESS 2

The fire road is followed in its entirety. In detail, cross Pocaterra Creek by bridge (Lionel ski trail) to a junction with Pocaterra ski trail. Keep left and make a gradual climb to Whisky Jack junction. Keep left and follow directions under "Lookout trail" two paragraphs back.

58 WEST ELK PASS – maps 5 & 7

Day hike, bike 'n' hike
Official & unofficial trails
Distance 5 km to pass
Height gain 213 m (700 ft.) to pass
High point 1905 m (6250 ft.) at pass
Map 82 J/11 Kananaskis Lakes

Access Kananaskis Lakes Trail (road) at Elk Pass parking lot.
Also accessible from #60 at Elk Lakes Provincial Park entrance, and from #61 Upper Elk Lake to West Elk Pass.

HISTORY NOTE I can't imagine why all those early explorers and travellers insisted on going over North Kananaskis Pass when Elk Pass was so glaringly obvious. Although the editor of *Survival on a Western Trek* surmised the John Jones Overlanders crossed North Kananaskis Pass en route to the gold fields of British Columbia in 1858, most people believe they went over the Elk. Myself, I'm convinced they crossed Highwood Pass. The mistake is understandable. In the days before photogrammetry and Google Earth, the fact that the Elk Valley and the Highwood Valley ran parallel but on either side of the Divide caused a lot of confusion, even to veteran mountain travellers like George Dawson and Walter Wilcox, and has resulted in

West Elk Pass below Mt. Fox.
Frozen Lake lies in the cirque at centre.
To its left is Taiga Viewpoint. Photo Vern Dewit

mountains being misplaced. For instance, is Mt. Fox really Mt. Tyrwhitt?

But back to Elk Pass, which surveyor Arthur O. Wheeler named in 1915 after being astonished to find it was nameless. Elk Pass is actually three: East Elk, Elk and West Elk. East Elk harbours the secret trail through to Tobermory Creek. Elk Pass (the highest) is now followed by the powerline right-of-way. West Elk Pass (the lowest) was the usual route and was crossed by an old Indian trail headed to hunting grounds in Nyahe-ya-Nibi. Deadfall was always a torment. In 1901 it took Walter Wilcox's party six hours to travel between the pass and Kananaskis Lakes. And this was in the downward direction! Even 20 years later, in the days of early tourism, forest rangers were always hacking out the trail.

TRAIL NOTE Today, travel is easy ever since Calgary Power put in the powerline access road and a road built for a tramline that never came about. So 95% of the route to West Elk follows the road (officially Elk Pass ski trail), and 5% the old trail, all of which is an easy plod through mainly spruce forest. NOTE Mountain biking is allowed on the road only.

To Blueberry Hill junction 4.4 km
Set off along the powerline access road, ignoring Boulton Creek ski trail on the left near the start. The road climbs over a ridge at the powerlines, which sing in the wind, then descends into Fox Creek. Keep straight (Fox Creek ski trail to left).

Follow a stretch of road built specifically for skiers. Cross the creek twice more, then settle into a long stretch tucked under the flowery east bank of Fox Creek that gets dug up regularly by grizzlies. Or by the sasquatch? Footprints 17 inches long were reportedly seen here in 1998.

It's interesting to note the main volume of water enters the valley at the halfway point. Thereafter you're actually following the southeast fork, a slow-moving stream overhung by willows.

Just after Patterson ski trail comes in from the left, the hiking trail shortcuts over a small ridge back to the creek and the ski trail. The forest is opening up, allowing views of Mt. Fox and The Turret, both climbed by the Boundary Survey in 1916. Level with a beaver house is the junction with Blueberry Hill ski trail marked by a signpost, picnic tables and resident whisky jacks.

To West Elk Pass 0.6 km
About 300 m after this junction, just before the road starts its final climb to Elk Pass, is a small sign on the right side reading "Lower Elk Lake." So you chain up your bikes here and on foot follow a trail up the open draw. Higher up, switch to the west side of the meadow and arrive shortly afterwards at West Elk Pass on the Great Divide. This important place is marked by a kiosk and a boundary cutline crossing the pass at right angles. On your left is the start of a very long, longitudinal meadow from where, with boots slowly sinking in the ooze, you get a tantalizing glimpse of the mountains of the Elk River rising up above the horizon.

For the Elk Lakes Provincial Park entrance go straight. For Upper Elk Lake via Fox Lake and Frozen Lake turn right.

One of the old monuments at West Elk Pass that defined the boundary between Alberta and British Columbia. If you head to Frozen Lake you'll pass a number of them.

*A wide-angle view of Frozen Lake below Mt. Fox.
The scrambler's ascent route follows the right arm.*
Photo Vern Dewit

OPTION

58A Frozen Lake

Unofficial trail
Distance 1.9 km from pass
Height gain 280 m (920 ft.)
High point 2185 m (7170 ft.)

If you're just hiking to West Elk Pass, why not visit Frozen Lake, a truly worthy objective after the ice melts. True to its name, this gorgeous lake remains frozen for about nine months of the year, so plan on visiting from late July on. The trail is quite clear and unremittingly steep. It is also the scrambler's access route to Mt. Fox.

HISTORY NOTE On the way you will pass a few "monuments." Designed by A.O. Wheeler, monuments were constructed during the boundary survey to delineate the Alberta/British Columbia boundary at important passes. Elk Pass was assigned the letter M, so with the pass being so wide there's a whole slate of monuments and cairns extending from Mt. Fox to Mt. Tyrwhitt, all with different numbers up to 23. The monument

at the lowest point of a pass was always numbered 1. The Elk Pass bunch were constructed on the spot in 1916 using cement and gravel gouged from a nearby creekbed to make concrete. Unless a flat rock was handy, the concrete base generally extended a metre underground. The heavy zinc cover was painted bright red and filled with concrete, the whole weighing an incredible 2700 lbs!

From the kiosk head right (west) up the boundary cutline. Where #61 to Fox Lake turns off to the left just after '1M' monument, stay on the cutline. Cross a wet meadow (flagging both ends) and continue up the cutline that climbs very steeply to 2M monument. (Just before 2M a trail starting between two blazed trees on the left side descends to Fox Lake. Use it as a shortcut to trail #61, should you be headed that way on returning from Frozen Lake.)

Another, longer climb brings you to the end of the cutline in the vicinity of 4M.

171

Here the trail turns right, then left into another steep climb. The gradient eases at a newfangled metal boundary post, that also marks the start of meadow and larch country. Traverse a grassy shelf between outcrops (view of Elk Pass and Fox Lake), then climb one final hill into the cirque.

Cradled in the precipitous arms of Mt. Fox, the deep blue water of Frozen Lake is an awesome sight, extremely difficult to photograph unless you have a lens with a wider angle than 28 mm. The right (north) arm is a difficult scrambler's route up Mt. Fox.

When we were there last, a good hour's entertainment was provided by another party having an epic circumnavigation of the lake, which involved climbing up the little glacier below Mt. Fox (not marked on any map). Instead try Taiga Viewpoint.

GOING FARTHER

58B "Taiga Viewpoint"

Unofficial trail, route
Distance from lake 0.7 km
Height gain from lake 215 m (705 ft.)
High point 2360 m (7743 ft.)

This one's for scrabblers. Rough trails lead to the col on the south arm of Mt. Fox at 348034 and up the outlier at 349035.

To the col 0.5 km
Starting from the lakeshore head left on a trail that heads diagonally uphill, traversing two shale gullies into some trees. Climb the tree ribbon to below a rock band, then make an ascending traverse twixt rock and scree to the col.

To Taiga Viewpoint 0.2 km
From the col or before transfer to other game trails that ascend Taiga Viewpoint, that heap of rubble on your left. The summit ridge is beautiful, though, being narrow, long and grassy, and capped by a cairn built by the Boundary Survey, who used the outlier as a camera station in 1916.

You'll be thrilled by Frozen Lake, which from this vantage point looks more like a caldera lake than a lake in a cirque. Peeking over the top of the north arm are the Kananaskis Lakes. Less exciting is the forested expanse of all three Elk passes, their complexities made clear. To the south lies Lower Elk Lake backdropped by Mt. Aosta, and the sweep of the Elk Valley enclosed by the wall of the Elk Range.

Return the same way, or if headed for Upper Elk Lake via #61 try the following shortcut descent.

Shortcut descent to route #61, 1 km
A prolonged steep drop of about 457 m (1500 ft.) to trail #61. Before you start, know the route is a grizzly hot spot.

Return to the col and turn left (southeast). Descend the grassy, flowery avalanche gully, which is not as easy as it looks, because lurking under the vegetation are ankle-breaking rocks that roll. At a steepening a trail appears and takes you into the stony creekbed. Lower down where the incline eases, use the meadow on the left side. Intersect #61 about 1.2 km from Upper Elk Lake.

Looking up the gully from trail #61.
Photo Brenda Everitt

Frozen Lake from Taiga Viewpoint. Upper Kananaskis Lake and Mt. Indefatigable (right) can be seen above the north arm of Mt. Fox.

The summit of Blueberry Hill, looking through trees to Upper Kananaskis Lake. Mt. Putnik at left.

173

59 BLUEBERRY HILL — maps 5 & 7

Day hike
Official trail
Distance 3.5 km one way from Elk Pass trail, 7.9 km from trailhead
Height gain 162 m (530 ft.)
375 m (1230 ft.) from trailhead
High point 2051 m (6730 ft.)
Map 82 J/11 Kananaskis Lakes

Access Via #58 West Elk Pass at Blueberry Hill junction.

I cannot figure out why, in 2001, Blueberry Hill was on nearly every club's list of hikes. It may be a great ski trail, but in summer it's an uninteresting forest plod to an imperfect viewpoint of Kananaskis Lakes. But here it is anyway...

HISTORY NOTE Way back, there was a lot of talk of making a ski trail down the north slope back to Elk Pass parking lot. Everyone loves loops don't they? That never happened, and in its stead I offer bushwhack #59A.

To Blueberry Hill 7.9 km
Follow West Elk Pass trail for 4.4 km to Blueberry Hill junction.

Turn right and cross the tiny southeast fork of Fox Creek on a bridge. The trail, 4 m-wide and dark under spruce, climbs gradually uphill and rightward. On bridges cross two forks of Fox Creek that rush headlong from the cirque between Mt. Fox and The Turret. After a prolonged ever-steepening uphill the trail flattens. Pass a ski sign "easy" on the left.

At the next sign, "more difficult," the trail makes its final approach to Blueberry Hill summit up a slabby ridge. After hours of plodding you are almost back to where you started from, only 300 m higher!

The summit is equipped with a picnic table and a memorial plaque on a tree. Kananaskis Lakes are largely obscured by trees—you really do need that couple of metres of snow to stand on.

OPTIONAL DESCENT

59A to Upper Kananaskis Lake & trailhead

Distance 2.2 to Elk Pass parking
Height loss 344 m (1130 ft.)

For those who find the long plod back unbearable, an option exists. And despite the horror stories, it can be done fairly easily, but you must be able to navigate without trails in steep bush. Rather than head blindly for the parking lot (seen between trees from the summit), I prefer the short descent to Upper Kananaskis Lake, because you KNOW that somewhere you're going to hit Upper Lake trail.

To Upper Kananaskis Lake trail 1.1 km
Return down the ridge to the trail sign "more difficult." Turn right onto a game trail heading through an open draw—a good beginning. As the slope gradually bows over, stay on the same line, keeping a steep upslope to your right. The trail peters out just before a dark area of spruce with no underbrush. Just below this a mossy water course starts up and is the key to the steepest part of the descent. Descend the right side of it; the footing is good. On the flat below, follow bits of trail on the right bank of the tiny stream and dodge around deadfall. Emerge on Upper Lake trail just west of the gravel pit. Turn right and walk a half kilometre to Upper Lake parking lot.

To Elk Pass parking lot 1.1 km
Make for the other side of the parking lot where a gated 4-m-wide ski trail starts to the right of the biffy. In 200 m the much narrower Lakeside ski trail comes in from the left. Thereafter, the trail undulates a little and crosses two tiny creeks en route to a gate signalling the south end of Elk Pass parking lot.

60 WEST ELK PASS TO ELK LAKES PROVINCIAL PARK ENTRANCE — map 7

Day hike, backpack
Official trail
Distance 4.1 km from pass
Height loss 177 m (580 ft.)
High point 1905 m (6250 ft.)
Map 82 J/11 Kananaskis Lakes

Trail access Via #58 West Elk Pass.
Road access Elk Lakes Provincial Park entrance is accessible by road if you have a few days to spare. Start from Highway 3 on the BC side of Crowsnest Pass. At Sparwood turn north on Hwy. 43 and drive 35 km to Elkford. Continue on the unpaved Elk River Road, another 67 km of very rough driving. At the end, keep left into the parking lot.

The usual way for backpackers to Elk Lakes Provincial Park is from Peter Lougheed Provincial Park via #58 West Elk Pass. This is the southern continuation of that route, an upgraded old Indian trail with one steep section. Bikes are not allowed on this trail, so bikers wanting to access Elk Lakes Provincial Park will have to take the powerline access road over Elk Pass, which very conveniently ends up at the park entrance.

ACCESS NOTE If the Highway 43 Association had their way, the pass would be crossed by a paved highway, thus doing away with routes #58 and 60, not to mention a half dozen ski trails. One can imagine the park filled to bursting by tourists catered to by one of those fast turnover eateries with attached gift shop selling scenic placemats. Luckily this has not yet happened and Elk Lakes remains a quiet place to visit.

From the kiosk, the trail keeps to the west edge of the longitudinal meadow. You cross the infant Elkan Creek trickling out of Fox Lake and about a kilometre farther on draw close to the bank of that creek,

which by now has plunged into a deep valley labelled "Canon" on the boundary survey map of 1917. Wind steeply down a hill and at the bottom recross Elkan Creek on a log. In case you haven't twigged, the word "Elkan" is an acronym of Elk and Kananaskis.

Come to the big meadow (swamp) where I remember lurching from one tussock to another. Now there's this tremendously long boardwalk, so rather than have your eyes glued to the ground, you're free to admire many-buttressed Mt. Aosta, seen in all its Gothic splendour across the Elk Valley — the best view of the day. The final stretch of trail heads down a ribbon of firm ground to join the main park trail at a signpost. Turn right for Lower Elk Lake. Turn left for the park entrance and Elk Lakes cabin, located half a kilometre away at the end of Elk River Road.

The kiosk at West Elk Pass. Photo Brenda Everitt

61 WEST ELK PASS TO UPPER ELK LAKE — map 7

Long day hike, backpack
Official trail
Distance 4.3 km
Height gain 55 m (180 ft.)
Height loss 152 m (500 ft.)
High point 1980 m (6496 ft.)
Map 82 J/11 Kananaskis Lakes

North Access Via #58 at West Elk Pass.
South Access Via #62 at the northeast end
of Upper Elk Lake.

This pleasant forest trail is the quick way
in and out of Upper Elk Lake and the
Pétain Creek area.

NORTH TO SOUTH

From West Elk Pass head west up the
boundary cutline towards Mt. Fox. A
few metres beyond 1M monument, turn
left at a signpost. The trail crosses bog on
boardwalk and makes a gradual climb to
the east shore of Fox Lake. While chiefly
of interest as a watering hole for sasquatch
(footprints 17.5 inches long recorded here
in the summer of 1961), it does have a
rather fine backdrop in Mt. Fox. You can

distinguish the cirque holding Frozen
Lake and to its left the large, grassy outlier
known as Taiga Viewpoint.

Continue up the trail to its high point at
the 1.5 km mark, then start the descent to
Upper Elk Lake. Glades allow fine views
looking down the Elk Valley. Cross a creek
with deliciously icy water, and lower
down is a wide, grassy avalanche track
where the trail has been rebuilt following a thorough mashing by trees toppled
in a 1991 avalanche. Grizzlies have been
spotted here, so it's not a good place for a
picnic. (It is, though, the optional descent
route from Taiga Viewpoint.)

Nearing trail's end, you cross a talus
slope and are treated to a view of Upper
Elk Lake backdropped by Mt. Elkan and
the Castelnau Glacier to the right of Mt.
McCuaig. Cross the bridge over the Elk
River at the outlet and join route #62 at
a T-junction.

Turn left for Lower Elk Lake and the
park entrance, right for Pétain backcountry
campground and Pétain Falls.

First view of Upper Elk Lake.
Mt. Elkan at right. Photo Brenda Everitt

62 ELK LAKES TO PÉTAIN FALLS—map 7

Day hike from park entrance, backpack
Official trails
Distance 1.2 km to Lower Lake
backcountry campground, 5.5 km
to Pétain Creek backcountry camp-
ground, 7.6 km to Pétain Falls
Height gain to falls 244 m (800 ft.)
High point at falls 1981 m (6500 ft.)
Map 82 J/11 Kananaskis Lakes

Trail access Via #58 West Elk Pass and #60 West Elk Pass to Elk Lakes Provincial Park.
Road access Start from Hwy. 3 on the BC side of Crowsnest Pass. At Sparwood turn north on Hwy. 43 and drive 35 km to Elkford. Continue up the unpaved Elk River Road, another 72 km of very rough driving. At the end, keep left into the parking lot.
Also accessible from #61 West Elk Pass to Upper Elk Lake.

This is the main valley trail, and it is easy. Make of it what you will: a stroll to Lower Elk Lake with a side trip to the viewpoint, a full day hike to Pétain Falls, or as access

Lower Elk Lake. The triangular hill with cliff is The Viewpoint (#62A). Photo Evelyn Ko

to tougher trails climbing into the cirques. NOTE No horses or bikes are allowed on this trail.

HISTORY NOTE See the log cabin at the trailhead? There used to be two such cabins, built sometime before the Second World War by coal prospectors working for the CPR. In the 1930s they were used by hunting guide "Old Man" Frank Phillips and became known as the Phillips cabins. He in turn passed them on to guide Mike Baher, who had built a string of cabins up and down the Elk River and into Cadorna Creek. Later, the more habitable cabin, sleeping six, became the winter headquarters of the Elkford Snowmobile Club, according to their sign above the door, and while they may have looked after it, the cabin was generally "used and abused" by an ignorant public and was ultimately razed to the ground by three drunken snowmobilers who had sneaked in over Elk Pass.

Lower Elk Lake to The Viewpoint trail junction 1.8 km
The trail leaves the parking lot opposite the park entrance camping area. Walk past the kiosk, turn right—Elk Lakes Cabin ahead—and descend to meadows. Cross a small creek to the junction with route #60 to West Elk Pass. Keep straight.

The main trail crosses Elkan Creek and its meadows, then runs alongside the Elk River, a rushing, glacier-fed stream emanating updrafts of icy cold air, to Lower Elk Lake (1 km from the parking lot). This tranquil body of water is sheltered from westerly blasts by a high wall of forest, the highest bump with cliff being "The Viewpoint." Rising up above the forest wall are the peaks of the French Military Group. Across the lake to the south is fabulous Mt. Aosta.

A boardwalk takes you along the north shore past Lower Elk Lake backcountry campground to the inlet, crossed on bridges with handrails. On the west bank of the river is a junction. Turn right for Upper Elk Lake, go straight for The Viewpoint.

To Upper Elk Lake and junction with Fox Lake trail 0.8 km
The main trail more or less follows the left bank of the Elk River to the junction with route #61 near the outlet. Keep left and arrive at Upper Elk Lake. Your attention is riveted on Mt. Fox across the water, from this direction an awesome precipice cleft by gullies and knife-edge ridges.

To Pétain Creek backcountry campground 2.9 km
The Upper Elk is 2 km long and fjord-like, squeezed between the forest wall on the left and precipitous, slabby slopes on the right, which rise over 1000 m to the ridge between Mt. Elkan and Mt. Foch. It's one of those places improved by a rain. Layers of clouds trailing across the flanks hide starting points of dozens of rills that burst into life and pour in parallel lines down the sodden slabs. At such times the trail tends to be inundated by rising water.

Boardwalk on the soggy trail alongside Upper Elk Lake. Photo Brenda Everitt

Upper Elk Lake and Mt. Fox. Photo Alf Skrastins

Pétain Falls from below.

At 0.8 km watch for the side trail to Upper Aosta Lake, a fishing tarn located 200 m away over a ridge on a bench. The dark waters are pretty well enclosed by forest, with just the odd view here and there of Mt. Aosta.

Leaving Upper Elk Lake behind, you crunch along a gravel outwash plain to Pétain Creek backcountry campground on the left, the starting place for Coral Pass (#64).

To Pétain Falls 2.1 km
Cross the bridge over what is now Pétain Creek and continue in much the same way as before along the west bank. Round the bend in a belt of spruce. You break out of the trees into a meadow and stand spellbound by the scene of not one but many falls plummeting down the cliffs from Pétain Basin.

Pétain Falls from afar. Since this photo was taken, the meadow has been largely torn up by grizzlies after the bulbs of the Glacier lilies.

At a junction with signpost go straight. (To right is the fainter Pétain Basin trail.) Head towards Pétain Creek, but don't cross it, because poised above your head like the sword of Damocles is the snout of Castelnau Glacier. Pieces break off regularly with loud bangs that scare the hell out of you and can be heard from as far away as the park entrance. Stay on the trail marked by cairns, and at the end rock hop to the base of magnificent Pétain Falls, which, at a collective 375 m, is one of the highest falls in Canada.

You've noticed how almost everything else around here is called Pétain: the creek, the basin, the glacier and the mountain next to Mt. Joffre. Five too many Pétains, according to historian Donald Smith, who wants a name change. He is not the first to wonder why Philippe Pétain, the "Hero of Verdun" in the First World War turned Nazi collaborator and traitor in the Second, should be so honoured. There's actually a precedent for replacing the name. In 1940 the station of Pétain on BC's Kettle Valley line was changed at the CPR's urging to Odlum.

SIDE TRIP

62A The Viewpoint

Distance 3 km return to junction
Height gain 130 m (426 ft.)
High point 1865 m (6120 ft.)

The hilltop at 348012 is a worthwhile add-on to Lower Elk Lake for anyone wanting a short day.

From the junction on the west bank of the Elk River, the trail follows the west shore of Lower Elk Lake. At a bay the official trail turns right and, climbing steadily, approaches the summit of the knoll from the back side. On your right is a drop-off and another at the summit facing east, so keep an eye on the kids and the dog. The best view is of Lower Elk Lake and the Elk Valley stretching away to the south.

63 PÉTAIN BASIN—map 7

Waterfall below the Pétain Glacier.

Day scramble from Pétain Creek campground
Unofficial trail & route, creek crossing
Distance 2+ km from Pétain Falls
Height gain 503+ m (1650+ ft)
High point 2286+ m (7500+ ft.)
Map 82 J/11 Kananaskis Lakes

Access Via #62 at Pétain Falls viewpoint.

This is one tough climb, a relentlessly steep climber's access trail to the basin below Mt. Joffre. Expect some easy scrambling with no exposure and snow in the basin. Start early if you want to explore. Alternatively, bivy at the campground on the edge.

At the signpost, fork right on the fainter trail that enters some trees. Cross a gully and start up the headwall, a tortuous crawl up vertical bush on the left edge of the gully. In your desperation you'll be glad to haul yourself up with anything at hand: branches, roots, even gooseberry bushes. The terrain eases fractionally at some fallen trees, then continues in much the same sort of way as before.

Three quarters of the height gain behind you, scramble up a grassy rib

that leads into a narrow, stony channel between bushes. Ascend the channel for only a few metres before branching left towards a small cairn marking the beginning of the traverse.

Traverse left on grass below talus slopes, then rock bands. The trail descends slightly to the base of a two-tiered buttress that you climb to a cairn. Possibly easier routes can be found to the right; certainly harder variations exist to the left. Topping out into the basin, head left to where Pétain Creek shoots out into space. Pétain Basin backcountry campground is located across the creek and is more safely reached by a lengthy upstream detour below another waterfall.

To reach the basin proper requires a scree scrabble between cliff bands around to the right. What unexpected pleasures it holds: a heady mix of flowery meadows and bedrock scored by *rillenkarren*, a dozen tarns in the bedrock and an artesian spring dubbed "The Fountain of Youth" bubbling out of a hump of gravel. You can wander quite high to within 380 vertical m of the summit of Mt. Foch. From here, the view of the Pétain Glacier with Mt. Joffre at its head is spectacular.

181

64 CORAL PASS — map 7

**Day hike or scramble from Pétain
Creek campground
Unofficial trail, route, creek crossings
Distance 6 km to pass
Height gain 780 m (2560 ft.)
High point 2515 m (8250 ft.)
Maps 82 J/11 Kananaskis Lakes,
82 J/6 Mt. Abruzzi**

Access Via #62 at Pétain Creek backcountry
campground.

The scramble crux of the headwall route.

Coral Pass is located between Pétain Creek
and Cadorna Creek on the Great Divide at
318956. Of all the hikes I've had to do for
this book, this was one of the most horrible
because we didn't start from the campground at Pétain Creek and it was pelting
with rain both going up and going down
the headwall. The headwall is the steepest part of the route, which is otherwise
fairly easy-angled. There's an alternative
to the headwall, which is the avalanche
slope of BC bush. But whichever route
you take, getting to Coral Pass is for the
experienced off-trail hiker who can hack
BC bush, steep slopes, tricky routefinding,
the odd creek crossing, snow, scree and a
little easy scrambling. A GPS unit is useful
for following the track log on the return.

The reward for all this trauma is wild,
untrammeled uplands with glaciers, the
most spectacular fossil beds you have ever
seen (hence the name Coral), and a fantastic view of the Italian Group of mountains.

To Nivelle Cirque 3 km via 1.
From the campground, a little upstream of
the bridge, a trail heads south into the forest
and is good to where it crosses a small side
creek. Not far after this crossing the two
routes up the initial steep diverge:

1. Via the headwall The direct route with
one pitch of easy scrambling.

Cross the alluvial flat on a faint trail
that follows an old river channel leading
straight to Nivelle Creek. Pick your way
along the left bank (bushes, rotting logs)
to the bend of the creek at 329982. Blocking the way ahead is the headwall. Don't
even think of following the lower canyon
choked by snow, tempting though it may
be. This route tackles the forested slope
just left of the canyon, which appears
quite innocuous with its staggered rock
bands. The route may still be flagged, but
don't depend on it. Rather, look for signs
of struggle with the vegetation. Possibly a
trail exists all the way!

Start from a small meadow to the left
of the lower cliff. Wend left initially, then
crawl straight up under menziesia bushes,
gradient and bushes easing as you approach the middle cliff band. Here, turn
right, following the rising base of the rock.
It gets quite steep and when the cliff ends
it's a straight-up thrutch to a terrace for a
brief respite.

Resume climbing, wending left below
a small crag and up to a strip of meadow
running below the top cliff band. At a

T-junction, traverse right on a trail midway between the trees and the bottom of the cliff. This trail leads to the one place where you can break through the cliff at its lowest point, right at the angle of the north- and west-facing slopes. Climb a 5-m-high grungy groove, a bit difficult to start but handholds are good. Next up is the crux traverse high above the canyon. Just as the situation becomes airy, the trail turns uphill and dissipates on easy ground. I need hardly tell you it's essential you hit this traverse line on the descent. The alternatives are to search for the avalanche slope or return via Cadorna Creek and the Elk River.

The final slope is easy going through forest, flats alternating with steps. The trail reappears at the top of the slope and heads slightly right and downhill through forest and meadow to Nivelle Creek, which is reached about 300 m back from the lip of the lower canyon. Continue up the left bank of the creek.

The final approach to the pass up the scree basin. In the background is the Elk Glacier below Mt. Nivelle.

2. Via the avalanche slope I'm told it's the easiest route, "which does not mean this is an easy route," says BC ranger Jack Paterson, who has struggled up it.

Not too far along after the first side creek crossing, climb the avalanche slope to the left of the headwall for 300 vertical m. Then traverse right between rockbands, following a game trail through the upper band onto treed benches. Continue to head southwest until you reach Nivelle Creek between canyons.

To the pass 3 km
Just below the right-angle bend at 327968, cross Nivelle Creek to the west bank and follow a trail alongside the river into larch and meadow country. Emanating from the upper canyon ahead is the thunder of waterfalls. The trail climbs above the first fall, then heads off up the hillside. Level with a crag on the left, keep left. Above the crag, turn left onto a good traversing trail that peters out in meadow not far above the confluence at 323967. This is a heavenly spot, bright-green grass and flowers in startling contrast to the glitter of glacier, névé and rushing stream.

Wade Nivelle Creek. As you climb out of meadows onto rock the lie of the land becomes clear. You're in a huge basin rimmed by a semicircle of ridges draped with permanent snow. To your right the Elk Glacier sticks out a white tongue between mounts "Gamelin," Nivelle and "De Gaulle." Farthest away, the low point in the ridge is Coral Pass.

Ribbons of bedrock streaming towards you offer obvious ascent routes. However, crags immediately below the pass make a direct approach impossible. We gained the pass from the right.

At the pass you're looking into what George Pocaterra always referred to by its Stoney name, Nyahe-ya-Nibi, meaning "Go-up-into-the-mountains country": Cadorna Creek (the lake is out of sight) and the "three giants of Nyahe-ya-Nibi"—mounts Cadorna, Swiderski and Battisti. Walter Wilcox called them Goldwin Smith, Duchesnay and Steele.

Directly across the valley the mountain with horizontal cliffs is called Misty Mountain by old-timers. After crossing

Pass in the Clouds in 1901, Walter Wilcox and Henry Bryant climbed Misty and looked across to Coral Pass. "Aha, a shortcut to Kananaskis Lakes," they thought. They returned to camp and the whole pack train moved down Abruzzi Creek and up Cadorna Creek. Wilcox carried on alone above Cadorna Lake and with field glasses pressed to his eyes, noted "no trail led up to the pass." So his party retreated down to the Elk River. There is a way, actually.

Descent

Going down you can vary the route a bit by exiting the pass to skier's right via a scree ramp. Lower down you're sure to run into a huge fossil bed several kilometres square where horn coral is scattered all over the rock like grass seed. Just as exciting for me was the karst we encountered, which extends across to the meadows and down into the trees. Dropping into one sinkhole and popping out another can give you hours of childish fun.

The three giants of Nyahe-ya-Nibi (mounts Cadorna, Swiderski and Battisti) from the pass.

65 INTERLAKES interpretive trail — map 5

Half-day hike
Official trail
Distance 2.2 km loop
Height gain 104 m (340 ft.)
High point 1813 m (5950 ft.)
Map 82 J/11 Kananaskis Lakes

Access Kananaskis Lakes Trail (road) at White Spruce parking lot below Upper Lake Dam. In detail: drive past Upper Lake day-use area access road: then, at the 4-way with Mt. Sarrail campground access road, turn left.

A scenic trail that loops over a hilltop between Upper and Lower Kananaskis Lakes. Though easy, this trail has hills and lots of benches. Among them you'll find the Wendy Elekes memorial bench (same plaque, different bench), moved from its rightful place on Indefatigable trail.

Also plentiful are interpretive signs that cover geology, First Peoples, first climbers and even first Canadian Everesters. That's because in 1984 the trail was renamed the "Mount Everest Expedition trail" to honour the 11 men of the expedition that made the first Canadian ascent of Mt. Everest in 1982. Understandably, most people, including the Everesters, prefer the original name of "Interlakes," which is descriptive and dates back to 1916 when the Boundary Survey used a twin hilltop to the north as a camera station.

Descending the south ridge. Looking towards Upper Kananaskis Lake, Mt. Foch (left) and Mt. Sarrail.

On leaving the parking lot keep right. (Track to left leads to Upper Lake Dam and Upper Kananaskis Lake trail.) In spruce forest the trail undulates past interpretive signs to a T-junction with the return leg. Keep straight.

The trail wanders along the damp east side of the hill (mosses, lichens, wintergreens and Labrador tea), then climbs a steeper slope via zigs and steps onto the north ridge. Here it turns south and continues in much the same sort of way to a rocky summit.

A little beyond is a viewing platform with a slew of interpretive signs. While one can look down over Lower Kananaskis Lake to the Opals, the best view is to the west across Upper Kananaskis Lake to a line-up of mountains between Mt. Fox and Indefatigable.

Continue down the more open, dryer south ridge of juniper and kinnikinnick. Enjoy a last view of the lake from a bench, then head back into spruce forest. The trail levels off just before the T-junction. Turn right and return the way you came up.

185

66 UPPER KANANASKIS LAKE CIRCUIT—map 5

Day hike
Official trail with signposts
Distance 16.2 km loop
Height gain ~61 m (200 ft.)
High point 1768 m (5800 ft.)
Map 82 J/11 Kananaskis Lakes

Northeast outlier of Mt. Lyautey from the east shore.

Access Kananaskis Lakes Trail (road).
1. North Interlakes parking lot. Walk down to the trailhead at the kiosk.
2. Upper Lake day-use area, a complicated collection of parking lots. Keep left (boat launch to right), keep right, turn next right into parking lots nearest the lake. For south shore trail, turn left and drive to the far end. For east shore trail turn right.
3. White Spruce parking lot. From the start of Interlakes interpretive trail, a wide track climbs to the dam.
Also accessible from #67, 69 and 71.

Who can resist circumventing a lake, even if it is a reservoir? This easy trail also serves as access to Rawson Lake, Aster Lake and Mt. Lyautey, and as alternate access to Three Isle Lake trail. Bikers can use a short section of the north shore to Point backcountry campground.

HISTORY NOTE In 1883, the fledgling Eau Claire & Bow River Lumber Company hungered after the mature trees that grow around the lake, but stayed only long enough to name the lake "Ingram" after C.H. Ingram of C.H. Ingram Associates, who'd advanced capital for the trip from Wisconsin.

Then Walter Wilcox in 1901: "A revelation of beauty hardly equalled anywhere... has four large islands and several small islets, all densely wooded, which give an endless variety of views from various points." A.O. Wheeler in 1916: "One of the most beautiful, of a glorious blue, studded with little timbered islands. Nestling below the towering rock precipices of Mt. Sarrail, 10,400 feet in altitude, on a bright summer day it is a thing of beauty and of joy." The Canadian National Parks Association in 1931 after the lakes were removed from the national park to become storage reservoirs: "People of future generations will curse us—or, we hope, bless us for what we are doing for them." R.M. Patterson post-reservoir: "A scene of wreckage to be shunned or hurriedly passed by en route to the Palliser... Nobody in their right mind would willingly visit the place now as an object of a trip."

Okay, so he was wrong, but knowing nothing better we continue to come to the heart of Kananaskis Country.

ANTI-CLOCKWISE
North shore to Point backcountry campground access trail 3.6 km

Follow Three Isle Lake trail along the isthmus. You may have seen the cabin that was built here in 2007 for the German TV series set in 19th century Canada *Im Tal der wilden Rosen (In the Valley of the Wild Roses)*.

Cross the intake pipe by bridge, noting North Interlakes Power Plant below at Lower Kananaskis Lake, then swing left onto the fire road. Almost straightaway the unsigned Indefatigable trail turns off to the right.

A little farther on veer right, then in 900 m from the trailhead turn left off the fire road onto a soft forest trail that descends to the shoreline within sound of the slap of waves. Offshore is Hawke Island, its few scraggy larch trees a mere remnant of those "small islets, all densely wooded."

After 1.5 km of enjoyable shoreline walking, a trail comes in from the fire road above, bringing in bikers bound for Point backcountry campground. After this junction the trail climbs into the blinding glare of a large boulder field—the Palliser Slide—where craftily constructed steps facilitate passage across its humps and hollows. While still in the boulder field, now disguised by a sparse covering of vegetation and trees, a spur trail to Point backcountry campground turns off to the left and services 20 sites scattered up and down the peninsula. Keep straight.

To the old Lyautey junction 0.9 km
The main trail continues past a viridian-green pool, so still and clear it looks like glass. A few minutes later, you contour around the head of a deep inlet and head up the east bank of the Kananaskis River, at this point a boisterous stream culminating in Lower Kananaskis Falls. Stop awhile at a bench in memory of Bernie Kathol, who was a district supervisor for Alberta Transportation.

The trail crosses the river above the falls and in a couple of minutes reaches the junction with the decommissioned Lyautey trail (no signpost). Keep straight.

The trail crossing the Palliser Slide.

West shore to Aster Lake trail 1.7 km
The word "shore" is a misnomer here. The trail lies so deep in forest you're without views unless you count cliffs glimpsed from time to time above the treetops. Begin with an uphill and 2 km later, at 285086, hit the Hidden Lake T-junction, fortuitously marked with a sign saying "keep ahead."

South shore to Access 2, 5.6 km
The trail rises, then descends to the lakeshore. Just before the shore access, a secondary trail to Hidden Lake takes off to the right at 289084.

Take a break here and scramble down a few rocks to the lake. Across the water is the easily recognizable Mt. Indefatigable. To either side are tree stumps by the hundreds. Walk left a short way and come to the many resurgences of Foch Creek, which are identified by lush vegetation and flowers. The strangest resurgence sits atop a high mound—an island at high water. Springs bubble up into the pool at such a rate that the water cascades down two opposite sides of the mound and into the lake. Pre-reservoir, the resurgences emptied into the Kananaskis River.

Lower Kananaskis Falls.

Return to the trail, which stays fairly close to the lake for the rest of the way to Upper Lake parking lots. It's quite a boring plod below the steep, mossy slope of spruce forest. Watch for bald eagles holding station on the tallest trees overlooking the lake and a rowan tree at the bottom of an avalanche gully. You may see a few loons, but they won't nest here because of the fluctuating water levels.

Cross Rawson Creek. A little farther on, the Rawson Lake trail takes off up the slope to the right. Keep straight.

In another 100 m cross the Sarrail Creek bridge below a small waterfall. The final kilometre undulates in and out of every indent, then straightens out for the final stretch to the southernmost Upper Lake parking lot.

East shore 4.4 km
Walk through to the northernmost parking lot where the trail continues. Cross a bridge at interpretive signs, then cross the boat launch road onto Upper Lake Dam.

I loathe walking along the dam, because it reminds me of all the beautiful features I won't see, like Twin Falls instead of a pathetic little canal carrying seepage.

At dam's end, the track from Access 3 joins in from the right and you wend left across a grassy "bay". In the trees, a side trail to the left leads to a rock chimney out on the point, all that's left of Geoff Gaherty's honeymoon cabin. (Gaherty was president of Calgary Power at the time of the dams.)

Finally you gain the east shore, which is characterized by rocky headlands and the half-moon curve of bays. When strong west winds send waves racing across the lake to break with a thump on the shore, it's easy to imagine yourself by some inlet of the ocean. Heightening that impression are terraces of shingle shaped by someone hitting a computer key. Across the water Mt. Sarrail and the Mt. Lyautey massif rise in great precipices, while farther away the distinctive shape of Mt. Putnik is revealed through the gap of the Kananaskis River.

Near the Foch Creek resurgences.

For all the fine scenery the east leg is a depressing section to walk. When the plug's out, the bones of the drowned forest are exposed and offshore islets are seen once again as headlands of the former shoreline. The deeply indented bay next to the treed "island" joined to the mainland by a causeway of stumps was once a lake. Near here archaeologists have recovered a few prehistoric flakes.

At the halfway point the trail comes close to the highway (old road connection), then continues around what's left of a promontory, a splendid viewpoint 80 years ago for a half dozen islands that crowded this half of the lake. Schooner lay about half a kilometre out, a boat-shaped island whose few trees were so arranged to resemble the masts of a sailing ship. On windy days, the dash of spray against the rocks gave the illusion it was the island itself that was moving.

Turn the corner into the large artificial bay, thus completing the loop when you reach the kiosk at Three Isle Lake trailhead. Turn right for North Interlakes parking lot.

Sarrail Creek bridge below the falls.

67 LYAUTEY—map 8

Day hike, backpack
Unofficial trail, creek crossings
Distance 2.2 km
Height gain/loss 30 m (100 ft.)
High point 1750 m (5740 ft.)
Map 82 J/11 Kananaskis Lakes

East Access Via #66 Upper Kananaskis Lake Circuit just south of the bridge above Lower Kananaskis Falls.
West Access Via #71 Three Isle Lake & South Kananaskis Pass.

Lyautey connects Upper Lake trail (north and south sections) to Three Isle Lake trail and is used mainly by backpackers camped at Points backcountry campground and by paddlers looking for a shortcut to Three Isle Lake trail.

It was decommissioned some years ago, all boardwalk and bridges removed, which means you're in for a bit of a paddle. However, the north end is still in excellent shape. Expect the odd fallen tree to step over or go around.

FROM EAST ACCESS

As soon as you've crossed the bridge above Lower Kananaskis Falls, leave the trail around the lake and turn right onto Lyautey. There's no signpost and branches are lying across the trail.

The trail ambles through forest to three creek crossings. Cross no. 1 on a tree, no. 2 on logs. Wade the third. The creeks all emanate from boggy ground and small tarns in the forest.

Shortly emerge into a meadow alongside a much quieter Kananaskis River with sandbars. The trail then moves away from the river and crosses the base of a large alluvial fan below the great northern wall of the Lyautey massif.

After passing through a few bands of trees you climb across an avalanche slope into old forest where the trail undulates all the way to the junction with Three Isle Lake trail. Again, there's no signpost and branches are lying across the trail. Turn left for The Forks.

Wading creek no. 3.

68 RAWSON LAKE—map 7

Short day hike
Official trail
Distance 3.9 km to lake from trailhead
Height gain 305 m (1000 ft.)
High point 2027 m (6650 ft.)
Map 82 J/11 Kananaskis Lakes

Access Kananaskis Lakes Trail (road) at Upper Lake parking lots. Via #66 Upper Kananaskis Lake circuit south shore section.

The trail, steep enough to make you sweat, leads to a beautiful jade lake under Mt. Sarrail. Know that grizzlies frequent the trail and lake area—one good reason why camping is not allowed on the lakeshore (though there is a biffy) and why you should not walk this trail alone.

Follow Upper Kananaskis Lake trail clockwise along the south shore. You undulate in and out of every indentation and in 1.2 km, just beyond the Sarrail Creek bridge and waterfall, come to a junction. Turn left onto the Rawson Lake trail.

A wide-angle view of Rawson Lake and Mt. Sarrail from the outlet. Photo Bernie Nemeth

Almost straightaway you're into zigzags, climbing through musty old spruce forest. The gradient eases half a kilometre before the lake and it's here you encounter boardwalk. Near the outlet hop down a paved side trail for the classic viewpoint of the lake backdropped by the vertical east face of Mt. Sarrail.

The main trail continues along the southeast shore below a line of cliffs, en route passing a biffy. Officially it ends half-way along the lake in a strip of meadow with interpretive sign. Some of you may recognize the sign as coming from the decommissioned King Creek interpretive trail.

All clear? Follow the ongoing trail on scree to the far end of the lake, from where you get a new perspective of this gorgeous piece of water. En route, flower aficionados should look for the elusive mist maiden growing on rocks near a small tarn.

GOING FARTHER

68A "Rawson Ridge"

Unofficial trail, route
Distance 1.4 km
Height gain 366 m (1200 ft.) from lake
High point 2392 m (7850 ft.)

The ridge at 301064 bounding the cirque to the northwest may not look up to much, and getting there is a steep, strenuous flog, but it is one fantastic viewpoint for Upper Kananaskis Lake. But first, with binoculars carefully scan the grassy slopes below the ridge for griz.

The trail continues, making for the right side rib of the prominent gully immediately left of the forest edge. Not far up, break away right into a shallow draw that offers a more reasonable way upward. Just below the gully split, the trail heads back left onto the rib and after the split climbs the right-hand gully.

At the top, head up right through lush flower meadows to a spectacular piece of ridge sandwiched between rock towers, so you can't walk too far in either direction. What you've come for is the bird's-eye view of Upper Kananaskis Lake and surrounding mountains. The colour of the water will have you drooling.

Top: Upper and Lower Kananaskis Lakes from the ridge. At centre left is Mt. Indefatigable.

Bottom: Looking down on Rawson Lake from the flower meadows.

69 ASTER LAKE—maps 5 & 8

Long day scramble, backpack
Unofficial trail
Distance 11 km from trailhead
Height gain 570 m (1870 ft.) from trailhead
High point 2292 m (7520 ft.)
Map 82 J/11 Kananaskis Lakes

Access Kananaskis Lakes Trail (road) at Upper Lake parking lots. Via #66 Upper Kananaskis Lake circuit. Follow the south shore section for 5.6 km.

Aster Lake and the high glacial valleys under Mt. Joffre aren't easy to get to. If you're hoping for an easy park trail with lots of zigs up the woody slopes of Foch Creek's west bank, you're out of luck, though I've known people who've given the slope a go, usually on the descent, like Henry Bryant did in 1901.

Unaccountably, the trail takes a thrilling line up the east bank, crossing scree slopes poised above cliffs that aren't for anyone whose legs turn to jelly in such places. Unless you're happy crossing steep snow,

Aster Lake and the Lyautey massif from the south shore. Photo Alf Skrastins

wait until August. To steep slopes and narrow trails add navigational problems. Obviously this trail is not for novices.

The trail is mostly used by experienced backpackers doing a three-day trip incorporating Northover Ridge and Three Isle Lake. Scramblers/climbers use it as access to Mt. Joffre, Mt. Sarrail, Mt. Northover, Warrior Mountain and Mt. Cordonnier. Waterfall lovers can visit Fossil Falls without climbing the second headwall. Campers can explore a stack of places from the campground. See Options.

NOTE New since the third edition: a small backcountry campground located alongside Aster Creek just below Aster Lake. (The oft seen grizzly doesn't seem to bother anyone.) Also new is a secondary trail to Hidden Lake from the trail around Upper Kananaskis Lake.

HELP NOTE Should you require help, there likely won't be anyone manning the patrol cabin. Be self-sufficient.

To Hidden Lake 0.5 km via 1.
There are two ways in to Hidden Lake:

1. By far the easiest way in, being flat with minimal deadfall.

The trail leaves Upper Kananaskis Lake Circuit at the hiking sign intended to keep you on the official trail. The words "Aster Lake" and "Hidden Lake" with arrows have been scratched on. So you turn left here on a much narrower trail. Cross a meadow (go either way at the split—right has no deadfall) and follow the stoney overflow channel, keeping right, to the northern tip of Hidden Lake. In a mess of driftwood go either way at another split.

Before Joe Kovach cut the trail on October 12, 1945, access from the shoreline to Hidden Lake was described by Walter Wilcox as "an hour of the most difficult bush work I have ever seen." Of course, he started from the shore of the original lake, which was a lot lower down in 1901. He and Henry Bryant were on their way to discovering Aster Lake by way of Fossil Falls.

2. Overall, the newer way in to Hidden Lake is a little shorter. While it is flagged and obvious, know that it climbs up and over a ridge and is peppered with deadfall for all of its 900 m-length. So until someone goes over it with a chainsaw, it offers no advantage.

It leaves Upper Kananaskis Lake Circuit at 289084 near the resurgences of Foch Creek and arrives on the east shore of Hidden Lake at 285079. Just before it reaches the lake, a side trail goes off to the left. I have never followed this, but obviously it's meant as a bypass trail for when the lake overflows into the forest.

Hidden Lake, first headwall 2 km
Hike clockwise around the grey-coloured lake to the southern tip. But how's the water level? Hidden belongs to the bathtub class of lakes, so you never know what to expect. At high water you're in for a dif-

ficult bushwack through the trees. When the water's gone down the drain, you can slop across mud flats blotchy with scarlet copepods. In between the extremes, there's a trail through a fringe of grass, ragworts and cow parsnips interspersed with a few stoney sections.

Starting from the south end of the lake at a large boulder, a dirt trail twists relentlessly up the first forested headwall. Out in the open the gradient eases and you reach a sort of col at 282064 (cairn and rock seat). Look back to Hidden and Upper Kananaskis lakes, and forward to your first view of Fossil Falls. This is where Wilcox and Bryant took off to take a closer look.

Second headwall 1.3 km
From the col, the "goat trail," as Wilcox called it, climbs diagonally across low-angle scree to a gully with water. Tighten boot laces, adjust packs and stagger up the right bank of the gully below thin waterfalls coursing down the slabs and cliffs of Mt. Sarrail. Cut right to below a rock island. Endure a few metres of powder scree, then head diagonally left up a ramp to reach the top of the island. A right turn up a corner gets you onto the proper traverse line. (If you want, continue flailing up scree and join the traverse to the right of the island.) Traverse steeper scree and one slab, then climb onto the first of those hanging scree slopes. Another climb leads to hanging scree slope no. 2 with cliff bands peeling off immediately below the trail. It's here, going down, where the exposure grabs you by the throat.

The trail continues its amazing line, descending to much less vertiginous ground at a boulder field. Cross a side creek, climb up the right bank, then traverse below a waterfall. (Snow lingers on the traverse until August usually.) A short scramble gains you a grassy terrace. Climb the cliff above via the dirty black gully, which some consider the crux of the route. From the top is a remarkable last view of Fossil Falls and a first view of Warrior Mountain.

Going around Hidden Lake.

The second headwall from above.

Descending the second headwall. Since this photo was taken, the trail has become more distinct.

To Aster Lake and backcountry campground 1.6 km

The trail dips into the trees. The contrast is astonishing, the savagery of the headwall replaced by the beauty of alpine meadows with flowers, larch and spruce; a hugely complicated terrain of miniature ribs and valleys all sloping in a northwesterly direction. People getting lost here have made a surfeit of trails.

The first feature you come to is seasonal Foch Pond, with its dazzling glacial backdrop of Mt. Marlborough. Follow a trail along the right bank. Then cross a meadow down the centre of which dribbles a fork of Foch Creek, a tiddly little thing you can step over. In 1916 the Boundary Survey made a blunder compounded ever since by every edition of the topo map. They named what is really boisterous Aster Creek after a trifling tributary. Left of the meadow and hidden in trees is the patrol cabin with no obvious trail leading to it.

Warrior Mountain reflected in Aster Lake.
Photo Sonny Bou

Climb over a rib. Cairns on the left side precede a T-junction. Turn right (trail to left blocked by branches). Almost immediately turn off left down a miniature rock band—two trails to choose from—and cross a miniature creek running through one of the miniature valleys. Wend slightly left into a parallel valley, which is dry at this point and marked by two cairns. Turn right. (Left heads towards Marlborough Tarn. See option.)

Descend the dry valley towards Aster Creek. At three cairns turn left uphill.

But first, anyone interested in hydrology, should visit the "confluence" at a pool and stand on the shingle. Far beneath your feet is the rumble of a waterfall, the subterranean waters from the tarn passing *beneath* those of Aster Creek.

This final climb up the left bank of Aster Creek is alternately flat and scrambly. If you're a sucker for pools and waterfalls like me, you'll be continually rushing over to the creek to see what it's doing. A biffy is the first sighting of Aster Lake backcountry campground (five sites with bearproof locker, no picnic tables), located on a flat below Aster Lake and sheltered somewhat from katabatic winds that blow nightly off the Mangin Glacier.

Climb a little higher to Aster Lake with its surround of meadows. Disappointingly, the water is grey from glacial silt deposited by the braided streams of the gravel flat upstream. But the mountain scenery is superb: Sarrail, Foch, Lyautey and Warrior were first climbed in July 1930 by Katie Gardiner with guide Walter Feuz.

But back to Walter Wilcox. While Wilcox was getting off a few photos of Fossil Falls, Bryant wandered off and climbed a gully to join today's access trail. Wilcox followed later and independently of each other they wandered all over the meadows, although only Wilcox ventured up to the lake "half a mile long at the base of a long glacier." So Wilcox was the first discoverer.

Fossil Falls in mid summer.

69A Fossil Falls

Route
Distance 2 km return to col,
18.2 km return from trailhead
Height gain ~76 m (250 ft.) return to col
High point ~2012 m (6600 ft.)

Although K Country's premier waterfall lies close to the beaten track, few people have time to make it a side trip. Why not consider it a day trip from the trailhead? A paddle 'n' hike works even better.

Leave Aster Lake trail at the cairn above the first forested headwall.

Walk straight through a gap between the scree and a treed knoll on the right. Descend a little, then traverse a wide scree slope, keeping just above a patch of tall trees, to a perpendicular band of thick vegetation on either side of a side creek. Push through to a small meadow below a crag. Cross diagonally upwards to some flagging which signals the crux—a

much longer, harder push through head-high bushes on a slant. Emerge on easy ground below "Alberta Falls" as Wilcox called them.

Return the same way. Don't emulate Wilcox and Henry Bryant by trying to rejoin the "goat trail" from the falls. The gully, sadly, was the scene of a recent fatality.

69B Marlborough Tarn

Unofficial trail, route
Distance 2.1 km via 1.
Height gain 168 m (550 ft.) via 1.
High point 2393 m (7850 ft.)

There are two routes in that can be combined to make a loop.

1. Descend the Aster Lake trail to three cairns and turn right up the dry valley. At two cairns leave the main trail and continue up-valley into meadows. Water is now running lively in the creek bed with lots of small waterfalls to delight in

Marlborough Tarn below Mt. Marlborough. Photo Alf Skrastins

before you reach the spring at the foot of the moraine. Climb the terminal moraine and continue on to an overlook for the bright-blue lake tucked under the glaciers of Mt. Marlborough.

2. Alternatively, from the campsite climb the hill to the south and contour in to the valley above treeline.

69C Hanging Valley & Waka Nambé Viewpoint

Unofficial trail, routes
Distance 3.2 km to tarns, 2.9 km to viewpoint, 7.6 km round trip
Height gain 317 m (1040 ft.) to tarns, 460 m (1510 ft.) to viewpoint
Height loss 91 m (300 ft.) to tarns
High point for tarns 2588 m (8490 ft.) at pass, high point for viewpoint 2731 m (8960 ft.)

The lower tarn in the hanging valley. In the background is Mt. Onslow.

This trip has two parts to it that can be done as an "either or."

Follow the Northover Ridge trail (see #70) to the high pass at 252041 between Warrior Mountain and Mt. Northover. Leave the trail here and stroll down scree and grass into the hanging valley on the BC side of the Divide, which harbours two tarns first visited by George Pocaterra and his dog MacDuff in 1911. A few metres from the lower tarn the ground drops away in a repulsive downfall of screes and crags streaked yellow and black. Giorgio did some gold panning in the valley below, but he got there via Joffre Creek.

Return to the col, then head southwest up scree, grass and likely snow for 152 m (500 ft.) to the flat-topped hill at 247037. There is the option of going farther up the north ridge of Warrior for a closer-in view of the astonishing Waka Nambé, which overhangs Joffre Creek 1200 m below. The "Great Spirit Thumb" or "Hand of God" was named by Pocaterra, who photographed it from the lower south ridge of Northover.

Waka Nambé. Photo Alf Skrastins

Climbing the scree scoop to Northover Col. Below is the pass at 252041 (centre left edge), and the twin tarns in the hanging valley. Above the tarns is the hill at 247037, the Waka Nambé viewpoint. The white fang of Mt. Joffre (3450 m) rises to the left of shadowy Warrior Mountain. Photo Alf Skrastins

70 NORTHOVER RIDGE—map 8

Scramble, backpack
Unofficial trails & route, creek crossings
Distance 10.8 km
Height gain 619 m (2030 ft.)
Height loss 731 m (2400 ft.)
High point 2850 m (9350 ft.)
Map 82 J/11 Kananaskis Lakes

Access from the south via #69 Aster Lake at Aster Lake.
Access from the north via #71 Three Isle Lake & South Kananaskis Pass at Three Isle Lake.

Northover Ridge is to Jasper's celebrated Skyline trail what Smirnoff is to any other vodka, or so the ad goes. It's a sublime ridgewalk! Don't thank me for telling you about it; thank Alf Skrastins, who first traversed the ridge in 1979 and brought it to everyone's attention in the *Foothills Wilderness Journal*. (As far as I can ascertain, the Boundary Survey in 1916 just visited the northwest tip to set up a camera station.) Combine it with routes #69 and 71 (and even routes #72 and 73) to experience the best backpacking trip, not just in K Country, but in the whole of the Canadian Rockies.

View from the southernmost high point of Mt. Joffre, Warrior Mtn. and Waka Nambé. Photo Sonny Bou

Amazing to me, the ridge plus trails #69 and 71 has recently been promoted as a one-day class 5 run by mountain runner Bob W, who gives tips on how to make an even longer day of it! While it is true that between editions of this book a trail has developed that sometimes travels below the crest, does it make it THAT easy? Only in some places. The thing is, there's no actual scrambling where you can cling to comforting rocks. In places the ridge is as narrow and airy as it ever was. Don't go if you're a klutz with two left feet or are bothered by heights. Know how to read grid references—your life depends on it. Wait for good conditions and pick a relatively calm day.

FROM THE SOUTH
To Northover Col 4 km

Wade Aster Creek at the outlet and follow the north shore trail onto a grassy bench offering a first view of Mt. Joffre. At talus return to the flat and cross the creek issuing from the glaciated pass to the east of Mt. Northover, which according to Alf offers good skiing. The mountain itself looks terrifyingly sharp from this direction, and it's hard to believe it's rated a difficult scramble.

Ahead is a knoll with trees, stepping-off point for the grassy slope above. Climb the slope from right to left, aiming for a scree gully at 256037, where cairns mark the start of a good trail up the right bank. A short way up the gully, the trail turns right up a more confined draw towards the pass at 252041 between Warrior and Northover. High up, the trail traverses some cement shale, which can be avoided by a simple walk up the draw bottom on scree, then snow to the pass. A sign reads "Height of the Rockies." Down left is a hanging valley with two tarns which make a pleasant side trip from the campground. Of course, a pass implies you can travel through to Joffre Creek, and while I know someone who's done it, I can guarantee you'll be petrified.

Continue along the trail (easily regained from the true pass) that traverses the west face of Mt. Northover on scree. Enter a scree scoop with permanent snow patches and plod up to the col immediately west of Mt. Northover at 242054.

What a fantastic viewpoint for Mt. Joffre, which sticks up like a white tooth with a distinct lean to the right. In 1901 Wilcox suggested it be named Mt. Walcott after the director of the US Geological Survey, but it got shot down and is named instead after a French general. To its left a glacier can be seen snaking through a gap from the Pétain Glacier.

Northover Ridge 2.6 km
Follow the ridge to the left (west). At the high point a narrow 10 m stretch is a taste of the ridge to come: almost a three-km-long tightrope of scree poised between the névé of Northover Glacier, and scree slopes plunging over 1200 m, or nearly 5,000 ft. into Joffre Creek (Fury Stream to Wilcox). At first, though, the rolling, rounded ridge and the thickness of the ice buffer the drops on both sides.

The easy stretch ends at 232062. WARNING! Don't think for one minute you can exit the ridge before the col at 221065. Enticed by a first view of Three Isle Lake or perhaps intimidated by the ridge ahead, some people have rushed off down the alluring side ridge at 232062, which traps you in its fatal embrace. Slips on ice lower down have resulted in injuries and one fatality. I don't want this to happen to you. So ignoring the false trail, *keep left at 232062, following a line of cairns* built in 1994. As you pass, add a rock.

The ridge narrows, rising elegantly to the northernmost high point. Where névé is replaced by cliffs above the névé you run into vertigo-inducing places where careful footing is required, and at the crux a bum shuffle if the pack is heavy and the wind is howling cross wise. This is the place where you might encounter a traffic jam.

On the far side either take the trail down left or continue the excitement by walking along the crest to the northernmost tip. Look out if you dare across the gulf of the Palliser River Valley to the Royal Group framed between mounts Onslow and Defender (Battle of Jutland destroyers nicknamed "the Cripple and the Paralytic" by Rudyard Kipling). To the north, Sir Douglas rises above Three Isle Lake. To the south, the spectacular wall of the Great Divide is seen continuing past Mt. Joffre to the White River.

All too soon the glorious ridge comes to an end and you drop about 183 vertical m (600 ft.) to the col at 221065.

To Three Isle Lake 4.2 km
Turn right (north) and on glissadable scree, descend to meadows and finally to the flat valley floor of an unnamed stream arising from the glaciers of Northover Ridge. A trail takes you out to Three Isle Lake (where you might just discover that third isle) and along the south shore past the patrol cabin to the campground.

Looking back from near the crux to Mt. Northover (above the hikers) and Mt. Joffre at right. Photo Alf Skrastins

The final stretch of ridge. At lower right you can see the escape col at 221065. In the background the Royal Group is framed between Onslow Mtn. (left) and Defender Mtn. Photo Clive Cordery

203

71 THREE ISLE LAKE & SOUTH KANANASKIS PASS — maps 5 & 8

Long day hike, backpack, bike 'n' hike
Official trail
Distance 7.8 km to forks, 11.6 km to lake
Height gain to lake 487 m (1600 ft.)
High point before lake 2200 m (7215 ft.)
Map 82 J/11 Kananaskis Lakes

Access Kananaskis Lakes Trail (road) at North Interlakes parking lot. Walk down to the trailhead at the kiosk.
Also accessible from trails #66, 67, 70, 72 and 73.

Three Isle Lake is the most popular overnight destination of all the trails radiating out from Upper Kananaskis Lake. Although you can hike there and back in one very long day, it is far better to backpack in to the campground for a long weekend and spend time looking around some fantastic high country. Alternatively, camp at The Forks below the headwall.

Consider biking the fire road section to Invincible Creek. The trail remains easy to the forks, then climbs steeply over a ridge to the lake. Despite improvements, and

Three Isle lake and the unnamed peak at 229086. Photo Leon Kubbernus

realignments (the latest after a washout in 1993), the headwall still exacts its pound of sweat.

TRAIL NOTE Bikes can be ridden to Invincible Creek.

HISTORY NOTE Unlike North Kananaskis Pass, South Kananaskis Pass is thought to be a pass of no historical significance. Precipitous slopes on both sides would seem to preclude it as a logical route to Oregon, or even as a good trading route to the west. Nevertheless, a legend persists that 50 years ago hunting guide Jim Tegart found Sinclair's abandoned wagon wheels in the bush on the east side of the pass. And R.M. Patterson DID get a pack train up the headwall to Three Isle Lake in 1938. And they were carrying not only camping gear but also a Faltboat.

To Invincible Creek 4 km
Head north across the isthmus, stopping en route to read three bronze plaques on a boulder paying tribute to Lt. Col. Donald

G. Worthington and Lt. Col. William Hart-McHarg, both commanders in the British Columbia Regiment, Duke of Connaught's Own, though both died in different world wars. The dedication ceremony was held on August 13, 2006, by members of their regiment "The Dukes." You'll be seeing mounts Worthington and McHarg later.

Moving on, cross the intake pipe by bridge (bikers use the trail to right) and swing left onto the fire road, which is a boring, undulating track that gives you sore feet. If someone were to start a ferry service across Upper Kananaskis Lake, I'd be the first to get in line.

Just after the bend, marked by a rock in the middle of the track, keep straight at Indefatigable trail junction (no signpost). Shortly veer right and in 900 m km from the trailhead keep right again on the road. (The descending trail to left is Upper Kananaskis Lake trail.)

At the next junction, at km 2.3, keep right on the fire road. (To left a trail descends to meet Upper Kananaskis Lake trail in the boulderfield.)

This junction occurs at the celebrated Palliser Slide where two big chunks of Mt. Indefatigable collapsed at different time periods and flowed to the north shore as catastrophic sturzstroms. What's left is a big slab with a couple of routes on it. Geologists tell us we're in for more bedding plane failures someday, so best pass the danger area quickly.

Plod stonily on back into the bush, ultimately descending to Invincible Creek at bike locks, which is where you leave the fire road.

To Lyautey trail 1.8 km
Cross Invincible Creek on a footbridge. After what's gone before, walking a soft forest trail under the cool canopy of climax forest is heaven. Somewhere among the spruce is a stand of Alberta's oldest lodgepole pines, which sprang from seed after a fire in 1586. To put it into perspective, this occurred during the reign of England's Elizabeth I.

Cross the Kananaskis River by a fine log bridge just upstream of Upper Kananaskis Falls. A few minutes later the T-junction with Lyautey (no signpost) is reached at the 5.8 km mark. Keep straight.

To Forks backcountry campground 2 km
Shortly cross a side creek. After this the trail stays within earshot of the noisy Kananaskis River, at one point rounding the bottom of a talus slope offering a view of Mt. Putnik and a more distant one of the headwall below Three Isle Lake with Mt. Worthington peeping over the top. Pass a bewildering array of cliffs and towering peaks on your left that are all part and parcel of Mt. Lyautey. A wonderfully clear spring bridged by the trail is the best place to fill up the water bottles, because the next side creek you cross—Three Isle—is milky from glaciers and so is the Kananaskis River.

The true Three Isle Creek just below the springs.

Steps up the headwall.

In the shadow of Mt. Putnik the trail splits, with Forks backcountry campground located in the angle. Just past the junction, on the right-hand trail, is a table chained to trees and food lockers—the logical place for refuelling and attending to feet, knees etc.

Headwall to Three Isle Lake 3.8 km
Turn left at the trail junction. After a flat stretch the trail climbs through an area of monster Engelmann spruce, then drops down to the inaptly named Three Isle Creek. Shortly the main valley turns a right-angle to the SSE, aiming for the glacial pass east of Mt. Northover. The trail, however, continues due west, climbing towards the headwall. The gradient eases momentarily and the resurgences of Three Isle Lake come bursting out of hillside to your left.

Climbing again, the trail twists up a bushy avalanche slope turning to scree. Keep right where the old trail went left and arrive at the lowest rockband, which is equipped with wooden steps and chain handrails—the whole assembled in a factory by people seven feet tall with correspondingly long legs.

At the top, walk a narrow ledge between rockbands, at the end of it scrabbling up and up until you meet the old route on the traverse below the long rockband. Turn right. At the end of the traverse climb a set of small zigs, traverse up left, then traverse up right to the summit of the ridge. Through all of this, you wonder what Lawrence Grassi would have done here — rock steps? more zigs? And, more puzzling, what route did Patterson's horses take?

Drop 30 vertical metres down a draw to the east tip of Three Isle Lake. I have a confession to make: I don't find the lake particularly beautiful. The shoreline reminds me too much of a reservoir. And where is the third isle? The setting is undeniably grand, though, with Mt. Worthington presiding at the head.

The trail to left leads along the south shore past the patrol cabin (built in 2000 "to improve security of staff and visitors"), and on into the valley below Northover Ridge. Trails to right lead to backcountry campgrounds. The first is "Three Isle Lake" and the second is "Three Isle Creek," which lies beyond a small creek on a promontory and has lakeview lots available. The same trail continues on to South Kananaskis Pass.

GOING FARTHER
You're settled in at the campsite and looking for places to go. Apart from the following two suggestions, other possibilities described in this book are the north end of Northover Ridge (#70), Beatty Lake for a swim and Beatty Col for the view (see # 72), which are reached by continuing on from South Kananaskis Pass.

71A South Kananaskis Pass

Half-day walk
Distance 2 km
Height gain 122 m (400 ft.)
High point 2301 m (7550 ft.)

Top: Looking south from South Kananaskis Pass to Three Isle Lake and Northover Ridge at centre. To left is peak 229086. Photo Wendy Devent

Bottom: The meadows of South Kananaskis Pass. Photo Wendy Devent

An easy walk through meadow and forest to a pass on the Great Divide—the jumping-off point for peak 193107, Beatty Lake and the backpacker's traverse to North Kananaskis Pass.

From the far campground the official trail continues along the north side of Three Isle Lake, at times following the shoreline of bays. Looking across the lake, ridge walkers will be motivated by an end-to-end view of Northover Ridge showing its glaciated aspect.

Ahead rises the bulwark of Mt. Worthington and to its right the little scree summit 193107. From this viewpoint Mt. McHarg is hidden behind Worthington. Both are rubble plods from the col at 204081. So it is baffling that a team of nine soldiers from the Duke of Connaught's Own Regiment failed to get up the peaks on the 10th of August, 2006, three days before the big ceremony down at the trailhead. Or maybe not, because in the September 2006 issue of *The Duke* it shows a photo of the unnamed peak at 229086 as being Mt. Worthington! So until some scrambler finds their high point cairns containing summit registers, which peak the soldiers had a go at is likely to remain one of K Country's enduring mysteries.

But back to the trail. From the west end of the lake it turns right, the lake quickly lost to view as you climb steadily through trees to South Kananaskis Pass at the demarcation of meadow. A signpost marks the Great Divide.

A trail through meadows lures you on. Anyone with a whole day to spare should seriously consider going on to Beatty Lake or Beatty Col. See #72.

OPTION

71B Peak 193107

Day scramble
Distance 3.8 km to summit, 6.4 km loop
Height gain ~558 m (1830 ft.)
High point 2798 m (9180 ft.)

Although the peak at 193107 is a modest summit compared to everything else around it, you'll be ecstatic at the views it reveals of the Royal Group. While the recommended loop can be done in a half day by starting before dawn, why return to the parking lot at North Interlakes looking like a dropout from the Iron Man triathlon? Reserve a whole day.

Expect oceans of scree, some snow, some easy scrambling and mild exposure. Missing out the first part of the ridge does away with the exposure. Regardless, you've got to be familiar with loose rock and adept at routefinding.

HISTORY NOTE It was from this very peak that George Pocaterra discovered the Royal Group in 1911. I have never understood why, when Walter Wilcox's party went down the Palliser River from Palliser Pass in 1901, he made no mention of this fabulous group of mountains. I can only assume they were so intent on finding the trail up to North Kananaskis Pass, they never looked to see what was to the right.

Anyway, Pocaterra was so impressed with this "country of burnt timber and hanging glaciers" that he immediately contacted the Geographer General about his discovery and sent photos. In 1913 the Boundary Survey were sent into the area (Wheeler, of course, claiming first discovery) and on their return, the Geographer General wrote Pocaterra asking him to give the group an Indian name. Because he knew an "Indian name would be cruelly mutilated," GP wrote back suggesting they choose an English name.

As luck would have it the number of peaks coincided with the members of Britain's Royal Family. Though if I'd been Prince George I'd have complained at being given a sub standard peak you can walk up. To sort out the various summits you need to carry the Gem Trek map of Kananaskis Lakes.

To the second draw 1.2 km
Start from South Kananaskis Pass.

Head up steepening meadows on the west side of the pass. The aim is to gain the cirque north of Mt. Worthington, which means that at some point high up on the grass you're going to have to traverse left. When you hit a draw follow it up to the lip. The feeling is one of total astonishment at the scene in front of you. Once again the topo map is wildly wrong and any idea you may have of a simple scramble to the top of Worthington from this direction is shattered by glaciers plastering the entire north face. Due west beyond a bewildering mess of moraines, your summit rises in an ungainly heap of scree and bedrock.

When the draw you're in starts to go downhill, haul yourself out of it onto the moraine to its left (hoof prints) and head off in the direction of the col at 196095, keeping the draw to your right. When this particular moraine ends, tackle the low rock step above. Sidestep a second step by a weakness farther to the right. Enter a second draw, likely covered by névé.

This second draw is where the descent route comes in.

View from Beatty Col of peak 193107 at right. The option descent follows the right-hand skyline ridge. To left are mounts Worthington and McHarg. Photo Eric Coulthard

The ridge between the col, seen at upper left, and peak 193107.

Peak 193107 taken from the same place as the photo above.

To Col 196095, 1.3 km

If game for the ridge walk, straightaway climb onto the sharp-edged moraine to the left of the draw. Follow it to its end below a higher, steeper step. Luckily, a diagonal R–L scree ramp offers a way into the basin above. Watch out for some nasty, tottery boulders en route. On gaining the basin, walk up left on low-angle névé to the col between McHarg and peak 193107.

Perhaps you'll be thinking tuna salad sandwiches and a sit down and be totally unprepared for the stunning view. Unlike other Royal Group viewpoints, this lofty col is perfectly located for looking straight down the Palliser River Valley. Bounded on the left by the great wall of the Divide and on the right by the superb Royal Group, it is a scene as sacred to view specialists as Mt. Assiniboine.

Traverse to Peak 193107, 1.3 km

From the col the entire ridge to 193107 is revealed. Névé reaches almost to the ridgeline of the first section, which is occasionally scrambly and narrow. If necessary, it can be omitted by crossing the basin lower down and rejoining the ridge at 195099.

After this the going is easy, though the final approach to the summit requires some desperate grovelling up fine scree. Top out at two cairns.

Some of the new things you can see are the Royal Valley, Tipperary Lake, Mt. Assiniboine, Palliser Pass slung between Mt. King Albert and Mt. Sir Douglas, and farther to the right the pocket handkerchief of the Haig Icefield. Some might say the best view is of Three Isle Lake.

Descent to second draw 1.4 km

From the summit head down the rubble of the broad east ridge. At ~198107 descend off the right side, heading diagonally right on whatever line appeals between slabs. Arrive in the second draw. Turn left and follow it out to your ascent route.

OPTIONAL DESCENT

71C to Beatty Lake

Distance 2.6 km, 8.4 km loop
Height loss 619 m (2030 ft.)

A tricky descent of the north ridge from the route-finding point of view.

Head down the east ridge initially to avoid some steep névé, then cut back left onto the broad north ridge. Lower down, curve right with the strata into the bottom of a basin. At this point you're 300 vertical m above Beatty Lake and stymied by cliffs.

Traverse right until stopped by a line of perpendicular cliffs. It's a little worrying, but all is well. From here a ridge drops towards the lake, unravelling beautifully in little rock steps and grassy platforms.

Low down, drop off into the small valley on the right and head north on game trail into spruce forest to—another dropoff. Far below is a glimpse of blue water. By walking right you'll find obstacle-free grassy slopes descending to the east shore of Beatty Lake. Now for that swim!

Cooling off in Beatty Lake.

72 SOUTH KANANASKIS PASS to NORTH KANANASKIS PASS VIA LEROY CREEK—map 8

Backpack
Unofficial trails, creek crossings
Distance 10.4 km
Height gain S-N 738 m (2420 ft.) via route 1. Add 213 m (700 ft.) for route 2.
Height loss S-N 655 m (2150 ft.)
High point 2362 m (7750 ft.) via route 1.
Map 82 J/11 Kananaskis Lakes

South Access Via #71 Three Isle Lake & South Kananaskis Pass at the pass.
North Via #73 Turbine Canyon & North Kananaskis Pass trail at the pass.

On the BC side it's possible to traverse from one Kananaskis pass to the other without dropping all the way down to the Palliser River. Except for one missing section, the old trail is in fairly good shape, much better than when A.O. Wheeler did the trip in 1916 during the Boundary Survey. Nevertheless, this is still a strenuous trip, in parts rocky, bushy and very steep,

The meadow between South Kananaskis Pass and Beatty Lake. In the background is Beatty Col.
Photo Eric Coulthard

with a humongous height gain coming at the end of the day. Most people hike the route south to north.

This is the key section of a popular four-day backpack starting from Upper Kananaskis Lake that takes in Aster Lake, Northover Ridge, Three Isle Lake, South Kananaskis Pass, Leroy Creek, North Kananaskis Pass and Turbine Canyon.

To Beatty Lake 2 km
From South Kananaskis Pass the ongoing trail through meadows makes you yearn to carry on, the walking easy and slightly downhill to a gem of a lake rimmed by spruce and larch and enclosed on the south side by a high, craggy wall.

To LeRoy Creek 5 km via 1.
There are two ways downward into the valley of LeRoy Creek:

1. Via the shoulder The easier route attempts to follow the old trail.

Cross the lake's outlet and turn right with the creek, shortly entering a dry canyon bed, Beatty Creek having sunk underground in the meantime. The nice, safe canyon ends cold turkey above a steep rockslide down which the trail picks a tenuous line into the wild middle reaches of Beatty Creek. Here, rockfall has created a miniature "valley of rocks", a cataclysmic mix of trees, boulders, sinks and tiny blue tarns. Amongst the chaos Beatty Creek resurges into the light of day.

Drop-off number two is supposedly unassailable, although I did hear of a mad mountain biker downclimbing the route with the bike wrapped around his neck. The trail gets around this impasse by *ascending* the hillside to your right onto the flat shoulder at 177133 of the mountain above Beatty Lake. The terrain funnels you to the escarpment edge for useful views of Palliser Pass and your objective.

The final zigzag descent to LeRoy Creek has been lost in some horrible over-the-head willow bush and deadfall. Meanwhile, another trail has developed over the years, one that traverses right (northeast) to an avalanche slope that offers a more reasonable descent to the creek. Cross LeRoy Creek and on the far (northwest) bank pick up an excellent trail come up from the Palliser River. Turn right.

2. Via Beatty Col The crossing of the col requires skill with scree on the other side, so is reserved for scramblers. It may cut the corner off, but it's no shortcut.

But like R.M. and Marigold Patterson in 1938, you too will be lured by the grassy slope rising to the col on the southwest ridge of Mt. Beatty at 201137. At 2484 m (8150 ft.) it is amazingly easy to get to. From low down you get classic views of Beatty Lake backdropped by the Royal Group. Nearly 300 m higher up, the col gives birds-eye views of the trail seen snaking up both passes. Mt. Joffre has

Beatty Lake back dropped by Mt. Prince Edward and Mt. Queen Mary. Photo Alf Skrastins

View from the shoulder of Palliser Pass below Mt. Queen Elizabeth.

The north side of Beatty Col. The route descends the obvious chute. Photo Eric Coulthard

come into view as well as the Haig Icefield, out of which flows LeRoy Creek.

The north slope is very steep initially, the obvious scree chute a mix of atrociously loose rock and cement shale where it's easy to go for a bit of a skid. Early and late in the season this stuff is covered by snow, which is a whole new ball game.

After the gradient eases there's miles of scree to pick your way over before you reach the vegetation. The best thing here is to just head on down the forest to LeRoy Creek. Most likely you'll pick up the trail from the Palliser River on the near east bank.

To North Kananaskis Pass 3.4 km
The trail on the left bank of LeRoy Creek crosses to the right (east) bank at 188148. (Disregard a fainter trail carrying on along the left bank. Possibly it continues up the main valley between mounts Maude, LeRoy and Monro to the moraines of the Haig Icefield.)

The main trail begins a gradual climb away from the river. As soon as you've crossed the tributary arising from the pass, the trail steepens dramatically and climbs straight up the tributary's left bank on a mix of grass and scree. Behind you the scenery is growing in magnificence and no excuse is needed for frequent stops to admire the Royal Group framed between the canyon-like walls of the valley.

Near the top the trail crosses to the right bank. Nowadays the creekbed carries hardly more than a trickle, but before landslides blocked Maude Lake's exit to the west, the white rushing water must have been a fine sight.

Unlike the south pass, North Kananaskis Pass is a bleak ridge of tundra slung between mounts Beatty and Maude. Where once there was nothing, it now sports an array of signs and cairns marking the various boundaries.

For Turbine Canyon backcountry campground keep right of Maude Lake.

73 TURBINE CANYON & NORTH KANANASKIS PASS—map 8

North Kananaskis Pass with its various cairns and signs. Looking west to Mt. LeRoy at right.

Backpack
Official trail
Distance 8 km to Turbine Canyon
backcountry campground from the
forks, 15.8 km from trailhead
Height gain 427 m (1400 ft.) to
campground from the forks, 518 m
(1700 ft.) from trailhead
High point 2240 m (7350 ft.) on bench
Map 82 J/11 Kananaskis Lakes

Access Kananaskis Lakes Trail (road) at North Interlakes parking lot. Via #71 Three Isle Lake & South Kananaskis Pass at the forks. **Also accessible** from #72.

A moderately strenuous trail with one long climb to a popular backcountry campground and a pass with a history.

LONG HISTORY NOTE It all started in October, 1854, when some 100 men, women and children struggled over Mackipictoon's secret pass, walking their horses and stumbling over boulders made treacherous by a heavy fall of snow. This new route for Red River immigrants under the Oregon Emigrating Scheme elicited such comments as "our rascally guide took us by a pass over the mountains (known only by himself), which he represented as the best and the shortest (10 days instead of the usual 30)," and "altogether it is the worst road I ever travelled."

Mackipictoon (or Mas-ke-pe-toon), known as Broken Arm because of a conspicuous infirmity, was a very great Cree warrior of ungovernable temper. Miffed because Hudson's Bay boss Sir George Simpson had not engaged him to lead his party over Simpson Pass, he inveigled chief trader James Sinclair into trying a new route over the Rockies, faster even than the White Man Pass he had shown him a few years earlier. Unfortunately, when they got to Kananaskis Lakes the Cree admitted he was lost and Sinclair was forced to take over the role of guide as well as leader, so who knows where they really went?

Incidentally, if any filmmaker is reading this, Sinclair (Brad Pitt) was "brave, restless, ambitious," and constantly at odds with the rather pompous Simpson (Anthony Hopkins). Only two years later, in the Columbia River Valley, he was killed while trying to save a party of American settlers besieged by Snake Indians. The survivors were about to take a boat into the rapids and perish together rather than under the cruel hand of the Indians when, like in all good westerns, help arrived in the nick of time. Too late for Sinclair, though, who was finally thinking of settling down with his family to farm.

If it hadn't been for this trip it's unlikely the Palliser Expedition would ever have travelled up the Kananaskis Valley and the place would be called something completely different.

Anyway, in 1858 Capt. John Palliser and party crossed what they thought was the same pass in search of a southern trade route across the Rockies. I say "apparently" because there's a move afoot,

spearheaded by Longview's Larry Boyd, to show that Palliser took another route entirely. Some description fits North Kananaskis Pass, but there are glaring discrepancies. Other parts of the description fit South Kananaskis Pass and Highwood Pass. Interestingly, the altimeter reading of 5,985 feet at the pass correlates to none of the above. This was borne out by George Dawson, who in his *Preliminary Report of the Physical and Geological Features of that portion of the Rocky Mountains between latitudes 49° and 51° 30'* corrected Palliser's reading to 6,200 feet, the almost exact height of—Elk Pass. A year later the John Jones Overlanders intended going over North Kananaskis Pass using the sketch map given them by James Hector, but most historians are agreed they went over Elk Pass (although I'm convinced it was neighbouring Highwood Pass, an understandable error).

If only all these people had taken an artist along!

Approaching Lawson Lake on the bench. In the distance are the two summits of Mt. Maude, the Haig Glacier and mounts French and Jellico.

In 1901 Walter Wilcox couldn't even find North Kananaskis Pass from the Palliser River end and finally arrived at Kananaskis Lakes via Pass in the Clouds and Elk Pass. He decided to pay the missed pass a one-day flying visit and fell prey to one of Palliser's discrepancies, as you'll read. In July 1916 the Boundary Commission's Richard Cautley, alone and on snowshoes, reached the pass after many attempts and determined once and for all that it was absolutely useless as a route through the mountains. Since then the old trail has seen sporadic use, a faint revival occurring in the 1960s and '70s with the growth of a new breed called backpackers.

When K Country took over, the trail was upgraded and realigned at the avalanche slope, destined to be trodden by a torrent of grateful hikers and skiers clad in Gore-Tex and Spandex. You are guaranteed to make the pass every time. Don't emulate Wilcox, though. A long weekend camped at Turbine campground is recommended for seeing the sights.

To Turbine Canyon 8 km
Follow #71 to the forks.

Here, head up the right-hand trail for a stretch of riverside walking alongside the Kananaskis. Level with a pretty waterfall, start a tedious climb up and across wide, steep avalanche slopes covered in head-high willows and alders that have a permanent downhill lean from the weight of the winter snowpack. Reenter forest and climb some more to the stream exiting the cirque between Mt. Putnik and "Razor Flakes". Cross and drag yourself up a final set of switchbacks to treeline.

The payoff for all the hard work is kilometres of joyous wandering along an almost level bench through meadows and larches. The Haig Glacier comes into view ahead, enclosed by mountains shaped like battleships. A tarn is where Walter Wilcox and packer Jim Wood lunched in 1901 and where Wilcox went on alone and on foot, telling Wood he'd be back in an hour. Wood probably said, "Oh sure." A little farther on, the trail undulates across a boulder field, then descends through

North Kananaskis Pass from the lower slopes of Mt. Maude. To left is Maude Lake below glaciated Mt. Beatty. To right, LeRoy Creek and the Royal Group rising above the Palliser River Valley.

larches to Lawson Lake, named by Wilcox, who thought at first it was the lake at the pass.

Follow the west shore, the trail then descending farther past the patrol cabin access trail to Maude Brook. Cross on a bridge. On the north bank is an important T-junction. Go right for 100 m to Turbine Canyon backcountry campground. (Left leads to North Kananaskis Pass.)

Back at Lawson Lake in 1901, a perplexed Wilcox, though realizing his hour was up, was determined to find the wretched pass, and after divesting himself of his field glasses and later his jacket, then his camera on various "scrubby spruces," broke into a run down the hill "splashing through an icy stream" with no time to see what lay downstream.

The campground trail leads through the camping area to the dizzying brink of Turbine Canyon. Supposedly it can be jumped across in one or two places as it twists its way down 330 m of hillside to the Upper Kananaskis River. But don't try it, okay?

Turbine Canyon.

217

GOING FARTHER

73A North Kananaskis Pass

Official trail
Distance 2.2 km from campground
Height gain 152 m (500 ft.) from campground
High point 2362 m (7750 ft.)

A fairly easy walk into alpine meadows about the pass. This is also the backpacker's route to South Kananaskis Pass (see #72).

Return to the T-junction on the north bank of Maude Brook and go straight.

The trail gains height slowly through alternating meadow and forest, passing to the right of huge morainal mounds hiding South Maude Lake. What's left of Beatty Glacier is still a thrilling sight below the shapely peak of Mt. Beatty. A steeper pull onto a forested knoll reveals the classic view of Maude Lake and North Kananaskis Pass backdropped by mounts LeRoy and Monro, "a desolate lake surrounded by bare cliffs and the awful solitude of that halfway belt, which has neither the beauty of the green valleys nor the grandeur of the great snowfields," said Wilcox. Palliser called it "our little teakettle lake," though nobody knows which lake he was referring to. The Stoneys know it as Îyârhe Apadahâ Îyabize, or "lake by the pass." It's a popular playground for grizzlies, which have been seen rolling down the steep east shore to go splash in the water.

The trail follows the west shore past a spate of prohibitory notices to the northwest corner, where a line of cairns leads you into the windswept passage between mounts Beatty and Maude. Here are more notices held up by cairns.

Back in 1901 Wilcox was still running, along the muddy shore and over snowbanks, finally gaining the pass at the mindboggling hour of 4 in the afternoon! I bet he rued not bringing his camera.

OPTIONS

73B Haig Glacier

Day hike
Unofficial trail with cairns
Distance ~3.2 km from campground
Height gain ~533 m (1750 ft.)
Height loss 30 m (100 ft.)
High point ~2713 m (8900 ft.)

The skier's trail to the Haig Glacier via the Beckie Scott High Performance Training Centre is a fairly strenuous slog on moraines with the odd patch of bedrock where the trail is less obvious. Luckily the way is well-cairned and there's a bridge over Haig Creek.

To Beckie Scott High Performance Centre 1.4 km
From the campground follow the trail to Turbine Canyon that starts at the junction of Maude Brook and a small creek issuing from moraines.

The trail crosses the small creek and turns left up a forested rib right (east)

The Haig Glacier trail below the gully.

of the creek. There's a steep bit in the middle of this section, then the trail eases off to treeline. Climb left of a big heap of moraine and enjoy your first view of the glacier and three shiny white Quonset-style huts perched on the ridge below Mt. Jellicoe. Not far now.

Descend right to Haig Creek, which is crossed by a metal bridge. The glacier snout has retreated and is now locked behind high rock walls penetrated by a gorge cut by the glacial stream. Below the gorge the waters slow down and make plaited patterns across a flat, then below the bridge gather together and picking up speed, pass under a rock arch and shoot out into space over a 300-m-high cliff. Half way down, the water passes through a second arch. Unfortunately, none of this exciting stuff can be seen from the bridge. See option C.

Pick your way up a ridge of bedrock to the helipad and the huts (at 218176), a CODA training facility for Canada's national and provincial X-C ski racers. To right is the same drop-off, to left the swim hole down on the flat.

To the Haig Glacier ~1.8 km

Continue up the bedrock ridge above the huts, then turn left and traverse scree slopes sandwiched between the southeast ridge of Mt. Jellicoe and cliffs falling to the glacier. (I have never climbed Jellicoe but I'm told it's an easy scree scramble from the trail.) At one point there's a steep climb up a bit of a gully, and later on a steep descent on the final approach to the ice.

While the Haig appears safe compared to such crevassed horrors as the Athabasca, casual wandering can be dangerous. I know of someone who almost disappeared down a moulin near this spot. And on no account follow ski tracks, as you're liable to be set upon by irate skiers. So unless you're properly equipped for crossing the glacier to either the French or the Robertson glaciers, end the walk on the moraines. From the high point of the trail there are astonishing views back to Lawson Lake on the bench and ahead to mounts Sir Douglas, Robertson and French towering over the icefield.

The Beckie Scott High Performance Centre from the approach. In the background are the Haig Glacier and Mt. Jellicoe.

73C Kananaskis Glacier

The view from near Jellicoe Shoulder of the Kananaskis River Valley, the Lyautey massif, Mt. Joffre and Mt. Putnik above Lawson Lake.

Day scramble
Unofficial trail, route
Distance ~4.3 km from campground
Height gain ~366 m (1200 ft.)
Height loss 213 m (700 ft.)
High point 2454 m (8050 ft.)

Getting to the glacial birthplace of the Kananaskis River requires easy scrambling and finicky route-finding. But what a valley! Hidden away and not easy to get into, it possesses an aura of wildness quite unlike that of other valleys in the area. Mid summer is best for waterfall viewing.

To Jellicoe shoulder 1.1 km
Follow #73B to the training centre.

First off, you're going to hop over the cliff below the huts! It's easy if you know where to go; it takes humans about 20 minutes, grizzlies about three. First thing is to reach the broad ledge below the initial drop-off. This is most easily gained by walking along the top of the drop-off in a southeasterly direction to where a stony draw heads down left. Below it, some easy

slabs deposit you on the ledge. Turn left. There's a narrow bit, then the ledge broadens out and slants downwards, eventually merging with easy-angled slabs. Walk down the slabs to the scree.

Follow the grizzly trail that climbs diagonally across the scree slope onto the verdant shoulder of Mt. Jellicoe. Take time to detour onto the rib to the right and walk south a bit for a spectacular view of the Kananaskis River Valley. It has to be one of my favourite viewpoints: on the left the great west wall of the Spray Mountains; on the right Mt. Beatty and its glacier, Lawson Lake on the bench and nearer at hand the cliff down which tumbles the waterfall. And blocking the end of the valley is the massif of Mt. Lyautey, behind which rises the white tooth of Joffre.

To head of the valley 1.8 km
But back to the grizzly trail that heads north below the unsuspected eastern cliffs of Mt. Jellicoe. From the route's high point is a first view into the upper valley: a mix

of meadow and scree with a winding stream. Presiding over the scene is Mt. Smith-Dorrien at the valley head.

From the shoulder a grassy rib leads almost but not quite into the valley bottom. Low down, the rib ends at a small step. Continue down scree or use an easy gully in the rock to the left. Hereabouts is a sizeable marmot colony.

There is much to explore. Ahead and left you discover a green tarn fed by twin waterfalls pouring off the glacier between mounts Jellicoe, Smith-Dorrien and French. Farther along and on the opposite side of the valley are little morainal hills covered in dryas—exceptional viewpoints for looking back down the valley to Mt. Joffre. Above them rears the west wall of Leaning Mountain and its hugely impressive rock tower. Yet another option is to flog up scree to the col between Smith-Dorrien and Leaning Mountain to take a peek at Hero Knob a thousand feet below.

Top: View from near Jellicoe Shoulder showing the descent route from the training centre. The route traverses the top ledge from left to right then descends the area of lighter coloured slabs below the shadow.

Bottom: Kananaskis Glacier below Mt. French.

74 UPPER KANANASKIS RIVER VIEWPOINT—maps 5 & 8

View of the Mt. Lyautey massif. Photo Gillian Ford

Day hike
Unofficial trail & route
Distance 7.4 km from trailhead
Height gain 500 m (1640 ft.) from trailhead
High point 2225 m (7300 ft.)
Map 82 J/11 Kananaskis Lakes

Access Kananaskis Lakes Trail (road) at North Interlakes parking lot. Via #71 Three Isle Lake & South Kananaskis Pass at Invincible Creek at 4 km.

The promontory overlooking the forks of Upper Kananaskis River at 256114 is one of the very best vantage points in the park, discovered back in 1916 by the Boundary Survey, who set up a camera station called "Lyautey N" on the point. Getting there requires careful routefinding in rough and complicated terrain, a challenge to anyone who's just completed Map Reading Level 1.

TRAIL NOTE Since the last edition, windfall on the fire road and tree growth has made route-finding even more difficult! But as my friend says, the view is well worth getting scratched up for. Wear long pants and take binoculars.

BREAKING NEWS Thanks to the Calgary Seniors Outdoor Club., the deadfall on the fire road may be cleared within the next few years. Watch the blog Kananaskistrails.com for updates.

At Invincible Creek cross the bridge on Three Isle Lake trail. Turn immediately right and follow a narrow trail alongside the creek back to the continuation of the fire road on the west bank. It takes just a few minutes. Turn left and follow the main fire road through old forest to its end at the bottom of a firebreak zooming up the hillside. En route ignore a side trail to right at 279117 (see Invincible Lake) and another at a cairn at 271119 (also see Invincible Lake). What you can't ignore is some particularly dreadful windfall between the two side trails that requires a chain saw and an army of volunteers. It's here where Tony declares it a shitty trail. "You're not putting this in the book again are you?"

So only the determined will arrive at the bottom of the fire break built to contain the Invincible Creek fire. Climb the break on single-track trail to what was once a small meadow, now ingrown with small spruce. Search for a cairn amid the greenery at the top left-hand corner.

From the cairn a trail heads left to the edge of a steep bank—cairn and blazes—then turns uphill and ends near treeline on an avalanche slope. Note this spot for the return journey.

Using fragmented game trails, traverse left across a rough mix of talus, grass and shrub until you are able to drop a little into the head of a tiny creek. Ahead rises the promontory, a complexity of knolls and sinks best handled by heading west up the draw of the creek, aiming for the low point between the promontory and the slope of the mountain to the right. Only then head south along a ridge to the camera station cairn at 256114 out on the point.

To anyone plodding along Three Isle Lake trail, Mt. Lyautey appears a hugely complicated massif, but from this viewpoint you're finally able to sort out which top is the true summit. The creek draining the glaciers is the base of a syncline with intense folding at its core where waterfalls plummet over the cliffs. As my geologist neighbour pointed out, it's worth a side trip from #71.

Another highlight is a rare view of Upper Kananaskis Lake backdropped by Elk Pass and the Elk Range. Best of all, you can follow route #73 from start to finish as it climbs onto the bench to Lawson Lake, then slips through the gap between mounts Beatty and Maude to North Kananaskis Pass. With binoculars you can even follow the route onto the Haig Glacier and over Jellicoe shoulder to the glacier at the head of the Upper Kananaskis River.

All this and larches, too.

Top: Unearthing the small cairn at the top left-hand corner of the "cutblock." Photo Gillian Ford

Bottom: Historic cairn on the point was built by the Boundary Survey in 1916.

75 INVINCIBLE LAKE—maps 5 & 8

Long day hike
Unofficial trails & route
Distance 7.7 km from trailhead
Height gain 707 m (2320 ft.) from trailhead
Height loss 107 m (350 ft.)
High point 2370 m (7775 ft.) at ridge
Map 82 J/11 Kananaskis Lakes

Invincible Lake. Photo Alf Skrastins

Access Kananaskis Lakes Trail (road) at North Interlakes parking lot. Via #71 Three Isle Lake & South Kananaskis Pass at Invincible Creek at 4 km.

This is a strenuous haul up over a ridge into the secluded valley west of Mt. Invincible, which has no easy way in. The main objective is a gorgeous blue lake, but just as exciting are the alpine meadows under Mt. Warspite and a traverse of little Mt. Nomad. To give yourself time to look around, start early. The old days are gone and you can no longer camp there.

TRAIL NOTE Since the last edition another route has developed up the west face to the ridge crest, but is little better than the old route. Has no-one ever heard of zigzags? Nevertheless, the ridge routes are less exhausting than a thrash through Invincible Canyon, believe me! Just know it takes as long to return as it does to get there and plan accordingly.

To the ridge

You must first gain the notch in the nameless ridge at 268129, because this is where the trail descends to Invincible Lake. There are two ways of doing this:

1. Up the ridge 2.6 km Overall, slightly shorter and less steep than route no. 2, but with more deadfall to contend with. NOTE Since the last edition the secondary fire roads starting you off up the ridge have filled in and become single-track trails.

At Invincible Creek cross the bridge on Three Isle Lake trail. Turn immediately right and follow a narrow trail alongside the creek back to the continuation of the fire road on the west bank. It takes just a few minutes. Turn left and follow the fire road as it winds through old forest with occasional deadfall.

In 400 m, at 279117, turn right onto a series of secondary "roads" that head up the ridge. A narrow trail marked by a rock starts you off. At a T-junction (road to left) continue ahead on a more obvious road up a steep hill. The gradient eases and you come to a similar junction. Continue ahead on a steeper trail marked with a cairn. Halfway up the rise, a tangle of deadfall is best tackled on the left. At the top, the road, now recognizable as such, turns up left. Follow it to its end, then turn uphill into the forest. Mark this spot as a waypoint on your GPS!

Shortly enter the open ridge, steepish but easy if it weren't for all the deadfall you have to weave between or clamber over. The ruins of a forest extend all across the hillside to the left and even up the west slopes of Mt. Indefatigable across the canyon to the right.

Pass to the right of the big solitary crag. After it's below you, the gradient starts to ease, the ridge tapers and curves around to the left (west). Still there is deadfall to contend with, the wind blowing out of the west making eerie flute music among the dead branches.

But despite its drawbacks, the ridge is one of the finest vantage point for Upper Kananaskis Lake and its mountains. Best of all, you can look into Invincible Valley above fronds of larches. Unfortunately, the lake remains hidden by Mt. Nomad—the mountain that stands alone in the angle of the two forks.

As you gain height a trail appears. At a second notch marked by a cairn at 268129 the trail descends the north flank.

2. Up the west face 2.8 km The steep direct line climbs about 457 m (1500 feet) in just over a kilometre and for the main part is on trail mercifully free of deadfall. If you hit the trail at the right time, the fireweed is spectacular.

At Invincible Creek cross the bridge on Three Isle Lake trail. Turn immediately right and follow a narrow trail alongside the creek back to the continuation of the fire road on the west bank. It takes just a few minutes. Turn left and follow the fire road as it winds through old forest with occasional deadfall. In 400 m ignore the side trail to right at 279117 and continue

Route 1 near the top of the ridge. Route 2 climbs the left-hand slope.

on the main fire road—which is also the route to Upper Kananaskis Viewpoint. The going becomes painfully slow, your progress held up by large fallen trees. In 1.3 km from Invincible Creek, you come to a large cairn at 271119. This is where you leave the road.

Climb the right bank to an adequate trail that wriggles up an open rib. Higher up, the gradient steepens and the trail gets scratchier. About two thirds up the slope the trail disappears in a willowy levelling with a few live trees and many recumbent ones, leaving you to pick your own route up a final grass slope cross-hatched with deadfall. We went straight up—though *en zigzag*—to the right of the crag and gained the ridge 400 m down-ridge of the notch.

Turn left and follow the trail over a couple of minor bumps to the notch.

To Invincible Lake 1.1 km

As long as you're going the same way as they are, animals generally pick the best line. This is what happens here. From the notch, elk have made a pretty good trail down the steep north slope of the ridge into the west fork. It takes a diagonal line from right to left, lower down crossing a shale slope, then a wider scree slope before fading out on grass near the valley bottom. Jump the creek and walk up easy-angled grass to the lake.

Long and blue, Invincible is bounded on the west by a line of sombre cliffs and on the east side by a grassy terrace under little Mt. Nomad. Crossing the low ridge beyond the lake gives access to the head of the main fork, where you can spend an hour of pleasurable wandering in the meadows below Mt. Warspite.

OPTION

75A Mt. Nomad

Half-day scramble
Distance 0.6 km from Invincible Lake
Height gain 229 m (750 ft.)
High point 2536 m (8320 ft.)

The little summit between the forks is an uncomplicated scree scramble via its south ridge.

It was named as recently as 1995 by "The Grand Fleet Expedition" (alias Calgary's 144th Lake Bonavista Sea Venturer Company), which in 1991 climbed a few of the ship mountains to commemorate the 75th anniversary of the Battle of Jutland. It is, of course, named after a destroyer sunk in the battle.

From the south end of Invincible Lake walk up the grassy south ridge, then up a steeper slope of scree to the summit ridge. Walk left to a cairn from where you look down on Invincible Lake and back to a snippet of Upper Kananaskis Lake seen through Invincible Creek canyon.

I'm told it's possible to descend the northwest ridge to the low ridge between the two forks of Invincible Creek, then work your way back along the terrace above the lake.

Summit of Mt. Nomad. Photo Sonny Bou

76 INDEFATIGABLE TRAIL—map 5

Half-day hike
Unofficial trail
Distance 2.7 km one way
Height gain 457 m (1500 ft.)
High point 2164 m (7100 ft.)
Map 82 J/11 Kananaskis Lakes

Access: Kananaskis Lakes Trail (road) at North Interlakes parking lot.

Indefatigable is a short trail that climbs onto the eastern escarpment of Mt. Indefatigable. If you had to choose only one trail in the Kananaskis Lakes area, this should be the one: the views of both lakes will have you reaching for your camera at every twist and turn. Many half-day trippers stop somewhere between Wendy Elekes Viewpoint and the high point.

It is disappointing, then, that in 2006 the "glorious" trail was without public consultation demoted to unofficial status and is no longer being promoted by park officials. Citing the trail could "no longer be maintained to safe standards," conservation officers promptly removed

Upper Kananaskis Lake from the Wendy Elekes Viewpoint.

all signage and memorial benches and put them into storage. Large white rocks were dumped across the entrance, thus ensuring that even without a signpost the trail is easily identifiable. So how bad is this "erosional nightmare?" Just wear hiking boots or approach shoes with good traction. As Dave Hanna puts it, "Don't be hiking it in your oxfords."

Indefatigable is the base trail for options A and B. Scramblers use it to access Mt. Indefatigable's north peak.

Head north across the isthmus on Three Isle Lake/Upper Kananaskis Lake trail (fire road) and cross the intake dam and spillway via the bridge Shortly after the fire road swings left, at precisely 320 m from the parking lot, turn right onto an unsigned trail strewn with white rocks at the entrance.

Initially, the trail winds gradually uphill through old forest. A rising traverse up left leads to the start of a moderately steep climb up the left side of a ridge and onto the top of the eastern escarpment. En route, the main trail is fairly obvious amid a wide range of variations—a hot, powdery tread-mill with occasional easy scramble steps. This section doesn't last long and soon the trail swings right onto a promontory. This is the superb Wendy Elekes Viewpoint with or without the memorial bench. Look across Upper Kananaskis Lake to the mountains of the Elk.

Descend a little, then continue climbing less steeply up the ridge between a gully on the left and the eastern escarpment on the right. As Upper Kananaskis Lake falls astern, so Lower Kananaskis Lake comes into prominence along with the whole of the Opal Range.

At 2.3 km the trail reaches its high point and levels off. The blue-flagged trail to Mt. Indefatigable South turns off to the left. Keep straight. In only 4 m a second trail turns off to the left. This is the trail to Indefatigable Outlier.

But why not bag another viewpoint? At the second junction, turn right downhill and continue another 400 m to the end of the trail. Here the view is of the outlier rising above cliffs.

GOING FARTHER

76A Indefatigable Outlier

Day hike
Unofficial trail
Distance 1.9 km from Indefatigable trail, 4.2 km from trailhead
Height gain 777 m (2550 ft.) from trailhead
High point 2484 m (8150 ft.)

Day hikers go farther: to the gorgeous flower meadows and larch forests of Indefatigable Outlier at 298132—the high point of the eastern escarpment. This is a very popular trail, probably because it is the scrambler's access to Mt. Indefatigable North. It is also the cross-country route to Gypsum Tarns.

With demotion, K Country is no longer issuing bear warnings and closures for the area. Instead turn to trailex.org. And yes, people hiking this trail and Option C do occasionally spot the male grizzly crossing back and forth from Gypsum Creek. Usually he is seen from afar minding his own business. There has never been an incident but just in case take the usual precautions and turn back if necessary. We want him to stay on his home ground.

Start from the high point of Indefatigable trail. Turn second left onto a narrower trail that climbs gradually up hillside into the larch and glacier lily belt. Keep straight at the next T-junction. (The trail to left joins with Mt. Indefatigable South trail.)

The trail then traverses steep hillside to a hanging valley crammed with Indian paintbrushes all the colours of nail varnish. En route a side trail to right heads down to a spring.

The trail continues along the right side of a seasonal pond and crosses the outlet. Climb through larch meadows to a junction. Keep straight. (To left is the trail to the col at 297329 between the outlier and Mt. Indefatigable—your descent route.)

The main trail makes for the south ridge of the outlier at last krumholtz. It's here you'll find long-stemmed fleabanes that blur to a purple haze on hillsides dropping away to the escarpment edge—an unforgettable sight for those lucky enough to be here at the right time.

The trail twists more steeply up the ridge, then, at the start of scree, traverses the left slope, finally climbing to the summit along the edge of cliffs. The cairn occupies an airy spot on the edge of the escarpment, which here attains its greatest height. A place to watch your step while taking photos.

Added to Kananaskis Lakes and the Opal Range is a new view up the Smith-Dorrien Valley, bounded by Kent Ridge on the right and mounts Warspite and Invincible to the left. Remarkably, the whole of the route from Gypsum Quarry

High up on Indefatigable trail, not far from the high point.

through to Gypsum Tarns and up to the col below you is visible. Straight west the view is blocked by the two Indefatigables and the connecting ridge. See option B.

Usual descent

Rather than return the same way, most people make a little loop, Heading southwest, walk down easy-angled scree and shale to the col at 297329 below North Indefatigable. Turn left and descend a shallow, shaley gully. A trail soon develops on the right side and takes you down a grassy slope to the junction with the ascent trail at the bottom.

Another variation occurs after the traverse below the tarn. At the first junction head right (blue flagging) and when you hit the trail to Mt. Indefatigable South turn left and follow it out to Indefatigable trail at the high point.

On the summit of the outlier.

Indian paintbrush and valerian in the meadow before the tarn.

A red box on the summit, looking extraordinarily out of place. Photo Dave MacDonald

OPTION

76B Mt. Indefatigable South

Day scramble
Unofficial trail & route
Distance 1.3 km one way, 3.6 km from trailhead
Height gain 938 m (3080 ft.) from trailhead
High point 2646 m (8680 ft.)

Did you know Walter Wilcox made the first ascent in 1901 after lunch? The fact is Indefatigable's south summit is little more than a strenuous walk up steep slopes. Nowadays a trail takes you almost to the south ridge. There's nothing to be scared of unless you count the final 200 metres, which are slightly exposed.

Wilcox suggested the mountain be named Mt. Merriam after Dr. C. Hart Merriam of the US Agriculture Bureau, but luckily the name was not approved.

Start from the high point of Indefatigable trail. Turn first left onto the narrower trail with blue flagging (as of 2007).

The trail trends uphill through open forest of spruce, larch and heather. At a junction in a levelling keep left. (Right leads to Indefatigable Outlier.)

Continue up through dwindling forest and onto a broad grassy ridge. Initially the trail veers right, but after the gully on the left peters out, it swings left onto another broad grassy ridge and follows it up to the rock below the south ridge of the mountain. Here the trail enters a shallow scoop on the left and climbs diagonally right to left up the scoop on good, firm rubble. Top out on the south ridge at a large cairn.

Ahead is a view to die for: Upper Kananaskis Lake with a backdrop of blue mountain shapes receding into the distance. When the sun is west of south it puts a glitter on the water and a shine on the icefields and névés about Mt. Joffre. Farther to the right you can pick out the routes to Aster Lake, Three Isle Lake and Invincible Lake, and identify such notable

Descending off the south ridge.

One of K Country's greatest views: Upper Kananaskis Lake from the summit. Prominent among the mountain shapes are Mt. Sarrail and Mt. Joffre (far right).

peaks as Sir Douglas and King George in the Royal Group.

Turn right and plod up a low-angle scree ridge to a summit with cairn. Into view comes the summit ridge and Firenet's VHF repeater station #103, consisting of solar panel, antennae, a large square green container and a large round red container the "size of a newborn calf shelter" according to Dave M. (And yes, people do use it as a shelter in bad weather.) The gaudy colour makes it a great attraction from the parking lot down below.

Either call it a day or carry on past the repeater station to the true summit, treading warily across Wilcox's "several hundred yards of knife edge." It gives you a taste of the moderately difficult scramble between the south summit and Mt. Indefatigable proper: a dramatic narrowing, a drop on the right, scree and slabs on the left, a sudden feeling of exposure. After setting up his tripod Wilcox found no room to stand behind his camera and "had to focus and expose plates by a method adapted to such emergencies."

77 BULLER PASS — maps 9 & 4

Buller Pass from the usually dry south fork.

Backpack, long day hikes
Official trail with signposts, bridges
7.4 km to pass, 10.1 km to Ribbon Lake
Height gain 670 m (2200 ft.)
High point 2484 m (8150 ft.)
Map 82 J/14 Spray Lakes Reservoir

Access Hwy. 742 (Smith-Dorrien/Spray Trail) at Buller Mountain day-use area. Use the first parking area on the right.
Also accessible from #25 Ribbon Falls and #31 Guinn's Pass.

The moderately strenuous Buller Pass trail was conceived as a backpacker's trail to the backcountry campground at Ribbon Lake. It's a varied trail taking in forest, flower meadows and a high rocky pass with a fabulous view.

Options! Options! People with two vehicles can make a one- or two-day trip to Hwy. 40, either via Ribbon Creek (21.4 km) or via Guinn's Pass and Galatea Creek trails (16.7 km).

Day hikers usually head to the pass and back. Others make a high-level loop around peak 213385 and return via North Buller Pass. This north pass route was the original route to the lake, but was superseded in 1981 when the official trail went in over the south pass. It's still available as a much rougher alternative.

The latest fad is to make a one-day (two-vehicle) trip over the north pass and through another pass to Sparrowhawk Tarns. En route, anyone with energy to spare can include peak 222406 into the mix.

There are a few other relatively easy mountains within reach of the passes such as Red Peak at 214404 and its neighbour 210395 (see #78) and the big grey peak at 217373. The other suggestion is to camp at Ribbon Lake and make more leisurely ascents to various peaks and passes.

The first part of the trail is the scrambler's access to Mt. Buller.

Waterfall and bowl in Buller Creek.

To the forks 4.5 km

Walk back down the access road to the highway. The trail starts from the far side and after crossing a bridge makes a bee-line for Buller Creek. Descend and cross on a bridge.

For the next few kilometres the trail climbs steadily along the north bank of Buller Creek Valley. Arrive at Engelmann Spruce Flat and a bridged crossing of the creek just upstream of the confluence with a "side creek." Here you discover most of the water comes from the side creek that has its source below Mt. Engadine. Just before the bridge a narrow trail heading left is the scrambler's access to Mt. Buller.

The trail then zigs up a step in the valley floor. At the top is a long traverse left back to Buller Creek at riverside meadows. Round a buttress below a scree slope and return to Buller Creek at the waterfall and bowl. It's a natural place to stop for a break. The creek above is where you should fill up the water bottles, cos the next guaranteed water is over the pass at Ribbon Creek springs.

Soon after, the trail crosses the usually dry south fork to a T-junction. Turn right. (To left is the north pass trail.)

Buller Pass 2.9 km

In an amazingly short time the landscape changes to a wide, flat valley floor hemmed in by arid ridges of grey scree. Underfoot are flower meadows with a sprinkling of larches. In no time at all, it seems, you reach the foot of the headwall, which is all scree.

The second big climb of the day is 168 vertical metres. The trail climbs up the left side, then make a long traverse right above a slabby area, finally turning left into the pass. Marking the high point is a large cairn. Ahead is the million dollar view of Ribbon Lake backdropped by the two summits of Mt. Kidd. To your right rises peak 217373.

To North Buller Pass cutoff 0.7 km

The east side of the pass is much steeper. Luckily a good trail weaves down the boulder slope, making a long traverse left to gain a grassy rib taking you all the way down to a draw. Just before the drop-off into the draw, cut left if heading for North Buller Pass.

To Guinn's Pass trail 0.7 km

The trail drops into the draw, crosses it and turns right and continues to the brink of another drop-off where you'll spot an unofficial trail shortcutting along a bench to Guinn's Pass trail. Part way down the slope, just after Ribbon Creek bursts out of the hillside in great spouts (Ribbon Springs), is a T-junction with sign. Turn left. (To right is Guinn's Pass trail to Galatea Creek.)

To Ribbon Lake 1.3 km

The trail descends all the way to the bottom of the hill into the green basin at the head of Ribbon Creek. Cross the creek on bridge and wander through alternating spruce forest and smelly flower meadows (it's the valerian) to the west shore of Ribbon Lake and its backcountry campground. En route, a side trail to left leads to the patrol cabin.

The first view of Ribbon Lake from Buller Pass. Rising above is Mt. Kidd to left and its south peak to right.

OPTION

77A North Buller Pass loop

Unofficial trail, route, creek crossing
Distance 5 km, 16.9 km return trip
Height gain 183+ m (600+ ft.), 853+ m
(2800+ ft.) return trip
High point 2484 m (8150 ft.)

This loop circles around the peak between the two passes, crosses North Buller Pass, which is the same height as the south pass, and descends the north fork to join Buller Pass trail at the forks.

It is a hugely popular option for a day trip which should always be taken in the anti-clockwise direction. Should you be seen toiling UP the north pass from the north fork, people will stop you and tell you you're crazy. Simply say you are heading left at the pass to Red Peak.

The trail is intermittent and the going enjoyable, mostly on grass, EXCEPT on the west side of the pass, which is steep and unpleasant. On the east side a cornice and snow persists into mid-July.

To North Buller Pass 1.5 km
Leave Buller Pass trail above the drop-off into the draw and head left across a few rocks to grass. Ascend the left side of the open draw to a gap at 217388 between peak 213385 and a grassy knoll to the right. If you can hack climbing another 100 vertical metres, I recommend taking in the knoll for a superb view of Ribbon Lake and the upper Ribbon Creek Valley, which features one sizeable tarn and lots of little ones. Descend slightly into the grassy basin below the north pass.

Next up is the climb to the pass, which is around the corner to the left. Many people just grit their teeth and make a rising traverse across scree and boulders, which is painful to watch when there is a much easier way: descend a little more into the bottom of the basin, and on grass walk to the base of the final steep rise. Climb a grass finger on the right side and pick up an obvious game trail that crosses the shale diagonally from right to left to the cairn on the pass. Easy!

Looking from the draw to the east side of Buller Pass below peak 217373. You can just make out the trail descending from left to right.

Looking up the north fork of Buller Creek from the waterfall. North Buller Pass at centre.

The view just misses seven-star status: the pointy peak far to the west being not Assiniboine (which is hidden behind Mt. Buller), but the infamous Mt. Eon. In the other direction the view is largely blocked by nearby ridges : it pays to wander a way up the ridge to the north, the south ridge of peak 210395, which is more easily climbed from the other side.

To Buller Pass trail 2.8 km
The west side of the pass is a steep, rubbly mess where scree has been shuffled about on hard underlying shale. (See the pic on page 238.) Slither down the first 30 m, then on reasonable trail traverse right to the top of a grassy strip. The trail corkscrews down the strip, the angle gradually easing as you near the flat valley floor.

The trail more or less continues to the right of the dry creek, then along the sandy creekbed. Just after passing the large patch of trees, use either the creekbed or bits of trail in the meadow to right. Look up right to what appear to be hoodoos or reefs.

Come to the waterfall at the head of a tiny box canyon. This signals the start of a good trail taking you all the way out to the forks. It follows the right banktop, then descends to the creekbed below the canyon. Don't cross yet! Continue alongside the creek through a meadow and into some trees where the trail crosses to the grassy left bank.

Shortly it climbs into open forest, then makes an ambling descent to the forks. A sharp left turn precedes the junction with Buller Pass trail at the bridge. Turn right and return the same way you came up.

78 the "RED PEAK"—map 4

Long day scramble
Unofficial trail, route
Distance 1.8 km from North Buller
Pass, 9.1 km from trailhead
Height gain 366 m (1200 ft.) from North
Buller Pass, 1036 m (3400 ft.) from
trailhead
High point 2758 m (9050 ft.)
Map 82 J/14 Spray Lakes Reservoir

Access Via #77 Buller Pass at the forks.
Also accessible from #78 Red Basin.

This is the brightly coloured peak at 214404 overlooking Sparrowhawk Creek Tarns and Red Ridge. In optimum conditions, meaning after August, it's a very easy climb from North Buller Pass, which is far harder than anything on the ascent route. Earlier in the season, getting through the cornice that fringes the summit ridge could be a problem. Regardless, it all makes for a very long day.

Returning the same way is easiest. For something more challenging try #79 Red Basin (15.6 km road to road), which requires two vehicles or bikes.

NOTE Grizzlies dig the grassy rib.

Climbing North Buller Pass.

North Fork to North Buller Pass 2.8 km
Rather than requiring you to read the last entry backwards, here is the description from the forks on the Buller Pass trail.

At the forks turn left and on trail begin an ambling ascent through open forest. Descend to the grassy right bank of the north fork and cross it into trees. The trail continues along the left bank into a meadow, then climbs above a tiny box canyon. Look down on a waterfall at the canyon's head.

The good trail ends here, Follow either the now dry creekbed or remnant trails in the meadow on the left side to the foot of the headwall—a wide band of orange scree and rubble.

On trail, corkscrew up a strip of grass just left of centre. From the top the trail traverses right, then disintegrates, leaving you to lurch another 30 vertical m to the top on scree and rubble shuffled about on a slippery layer of hard shale. Reach North Buller Pass at a cairn.

View from the grassy rib, looking down on the meadows and tarns of Ribbon Creek's north fork. To right the route from Buller Pass is shown crossing the grassy saddle to North Buller Pass (right). Mountains on the skyline: Mt. Kidd South, peak 237374, Guinn's Pass, peak 217373, Mt. Galatea.

Climbing the Red Peak 1.8 km

There is no need to descend the east side of the pass. From the cairn follow a game trail diagonally down left to a finger of grass. Then, descending slightly as you go, traverse the lower grass slopes of peak 210395 to a fork of Ribbon Creek—a wide, stony gully with water. Cross and climb onto the rib beyond.

Turn left (north) and walk up the broad, easy-angled grassy rib to the right of the gully. Make for the wide band of permanent snow you can see on the skyline. Where the gully turns left into a mess of pale-orange screes, continue ahead on the rib where grass is slowly being replaced by scree. High up, the rib steepens a little and narrows, delineating the right end of the snow bank. At the last, grovel up a few metres of steep scree (or snow) to gain the connecting ridge between peak 210395 and Red Peak.

Turn right and walk along the broad flattish ridge. At an unexpected burp, use a bypass trail on the right side. One last uphill burst on reddish-orange screes sees you at the summit. A small cairn with canister is perched on the edge of tottery red crags falling to the north and east. Even the soil nurturing tiny cushion plants is red.

The view to the west is panoramic: thunderstorms can be seen approach-

Red Peak from the summit ridge.

ing from 100 km away. Of course, Mt. Assiniboine is pre-eminent. The view east is blocked by lofty Mt. Bogart, which from the prairies is often mistaken for Assiniboine. To the south, The Tower, and mounts Galatea and Buller are standouts in a welter of lower peaks. To the north the main features are Spray Lakes Reservoir, the grey, sprawling mass of Mt. Sparrowhawk, the high point of Red Ridge and below you the Sparrowhawk Creek Tarns, the complexity of the cirque and its tarns made clear from this high vantage point.

79 "RED BASIN" — map 4

Day to long day
Unofficial trails, route
Distance 4.9 km one way to basin
Height gain 686 m (2250 ft.)
Height loss 107 m (350 ft.)
High point 2286 m (7500 ft.)
Map 82 J/14 Spray Lakes Reservoir

Access Hwy. 742 (Smith-Dorrien/Spray Trail) at Spray Lakes day-use area.
Also accessible from #78 Red Peak

Red Creek lies opposite Spray Lakes day-use area, and to the south of Red Ridge, the main fork of it curving into a basin between Red Peak and Mt. Buller.

Of all the valleys off Hwy. 742, this is the most geologically fascinating, its attractions including the two best examples of rock glaciers in K Country, possible

One of the boulders in the forest.

tension gashes (see explanation further on), and a boulder field to make boulderers drool. Pity it requires so much effort to get up there.

Access is not via the creek, but by way of an intermittent hunter's trail up the north ridge of Mt. Buller. In 2009, the lower section of trail was still flagged with pink and white tape decorated with mushrooms and pine beetles and bearing the words "pest mgmt. zone." After this you are on your own, so only experienced off-trail hikers should even consider this hike.

From the basin, hiker/scramblers who start early from the trailhead can climb onto the south ridge of Red Peak to join the normal route up the mountain. For more proficient rubble scramblers, peak 210395 is also accessible.

To Basin viewpoint 3.1 km
Most of the height gain occurs in the climb up Buller's forested north ridge to the viewpoint at 191407.

Start from the south side of Red Creek to the left of the survey marker. For the first half kilometre you angle across to the creek using bit trails through the forest. Alternatively, fight the willow bushes all the way along the creek until you come to the very obvious trail that climbs the bank to flagging. Beyond this point the bank rises steeply.

Shortly you climb another, steeper step onto the ridge proper, where the going improves considerably. Initially you follow the top of the bank some 30 vertical m up from the creek, then ease into a steady uphill plod, long stretches of good trail alternating with trail that is barely visible. Gradually, the ridge turns south and you meet your first larch. An oddity of the ridge crest high up is the series of massive gashes filled with spruce that are clearly seen on Google Earth. Gord, who has yet to check them out personally, thinks they might *possibly* be sigmoidal tension

gashes arranged *en échelon*, i.e., stress fractures caused by a large-scale change in orientation right around Mt. Buller. All except the last one can be avoided by staying right.

After one last uphill push you emerge on open ridge at 191407 and look down on Spray Lakes Reservoir. Ahead is Mt. Buller, its northern cirque blocked by boulders, some so huge they show up on the map as little circles of contour line. To the east rise Mt. Sparrowhawk, Red Ridge and Red Peak, the latter the source of two

Top: Red Basin from the Basin Viewpoint. Note two rock glaciers flowing down the west face of Red Peak at left and centre.

Bottom: From the same viewpoint, Spray Lakes Reservoir during the pine beetle burn of 2009.

tongue-like rock glaciers creeping down its west flank to the creek. Apparently, multiple lobes (seen beautifully on Google Earth) are what distinguish rock glaciers from regular rock slides and scree chutes.

If going no farther, it's worth either carrying on up the ridge of Buller a way, or exploring the boulder field for the boulder with the hole through the middle.

241

Into the basin 1.8 km

Descend to the col between your ridge and the north ridge of Buller proper, then head down left through trees at the edge of the boulder field. Rather than traverse into the basin, it's easier to descend the whole 100 m (300 ft.) to the flat above a small tributary of Red Creek (camping spot). Then follow one of the trails down the steep little bank into the tributary valley. There always seems to be water flowing just downstream of this point. (This tributary is shown on the topo map as a split in the main creek. Not so, as you'll find out.)

Turn right and walk up the valley to where it unfolds. Continue on and come to the main creekbed. Actually, you look *down* into it, an arid, stony swath below the steep end wall of the bigger rock glacier. Descend into the bed at a comfortable place, which may mean following the banktop to the right for a way, then simply walk up it into the basin. Below the headwall is an island of meadow and trees, which makes a logical turnaround point.

Photo showing route to Red Peak from the basin. Route climbs grass slope onto bench at far left, then heads diagonally right, finally climbing the rib to the left of the gully below the col. After this it's an easy walk along the ridge to the left.

GOING FARTHER

79A to Red Peak

Unofficial trail
Distance 1 km to col, 1.6 km to peak
Height gain 320 m (1050 ft.) to ridge, 503 m (1650 ft.) to peak, 1189 m (3900 ft.) from trailhead
High point at peak 2758 m (9050 ft.)

The following is based in part on Alf Skrastins's description.

From the end of the meadow, climb up the grass slope on the left to a bench, and from there follow a game trail all the way to the ridge between peak 210395 and the Red Peak. In detail: from the bench the trail climbs to the last patch of vegetation, then enters a gully (snow early and late in the season) leading through some small rockbands. It then heads right onto a scree rib and follows it straight up to the ridge. While the footing is firm on ascent, on descent the scree is a little too large to descend easily and you'll probably want to make a few zigs.

On gaining the ridge, turn left. In a short distance you meet up with the normal route up the mountain. Now read #78.

80 WATRIDGE LAKE—map 9

Watridge Lake and Cone Mountain.

Short day hike, bike 'n' hike
Official trails with signposts
Distance 3.7 km to lake
Height gain 60 m (200 ft.)
High point 1798 m (5900 ft.)
Map 82 J/14 Spray Lakes Reservoir

Access Hwy. 742 (Smith-Dorrien/Spray Trail). Turn west onto Mt. Shark Road, signed Mt. Engadine Lodge, Mt. Shark trailhead. Keep right at all intersections until you come to the end of the navigable road at Mt. Shark parking lot in 5.3 km. (The road ahead is gated and known as the Watridge logging road.)

An easy walk on ski trails and logging roads through the Mount Shark X-C ski area to Watridge Lake, one of "the finest Cutthroat lakes in Alberta." It is usually combined with a steeper trog to one of "the largest karst springs in North America."

NOTE This is the official access to Bryant Creek, the Spray River Valley and Mount Assiniboine Provincial Park. Also the scrambler's access to Mt. Shark.

To Watridge Lake turnoff 3.4 km
Straight off you can see the tip of Mt. Assiniboine from the parking lot, which bodes well. Start from the signboard and shortcut through to Watridge logging road beyond the gate. Turn left. The old road is obvious as it winds through the convolutions of the Mt. Shark X-C ski trails. In brief, keep straight at junctions 2 and 24. Cross Marushka Creek in a dip. Keep left at the top of the hill at 23. Intersect junctions 21 and 20 (fine views of Tent Ridge, Mt. Shark, Mt. Turner, Cone Mountain and Mt. Nestor from all along this stretch). Just past 14 keep right and descend past 13 to Watridge Creek bridge. Note that the creek is wide and rushing. Turn left at 12 up the hill.

Just before leaving the cutblocks, you are seamlessly transferred from logging road to a four person-wide ski trail built in 1988/89. Before then we followed the old trail to Watridge Lake and Bryant Creek, that ran below the bank to the left of the ski trail.

The trail rises gradually to an important T-junction with signpost. Turn left. (The trail ahead shortly enters Banff National Park and is the main access to the Spray River Valley, Bryant Creek and Mount Assiniboine Provincial Park.)

To Watridge Lake 0.3 km
The trail drops to the line of the old trail and turns right. At the T-junction with Karst Spring trail, keep straight and reach the pale green waters of Watridge Lake in a minute or two. You are looking northwest to Cone Mountain, a "sharp, symmetrical peak, with a conspicuous, oblique fissure on the south side" according to George Dawson in 1884. Around your feet the bog flowers are beautiful, particularly the white bog orchids.

If you have time walk along the north shore a way. Breaking the mountain silence is a continual roar emanating from somewhere in the forest to the south of the lake. You'd have to be a pretty dull person not to wonder what the hell is going on up there.

So on to Karst Spring!

GOING FARTHER

80A Karst Spring

Official trail with interpretive signs
Distance 0.8 km
Height gain ~122 m (400 ft.)
High point ~1905 m (6250 ft.)

A narrower steeper trail leads to one of the largest karst springs in North America.

Without experimenting with pyranine concentrate or rhodamine WT, one can only speculate on where the water comes from. From the valley between Mt. Shark and Tent Ridge? Unlikely. The snow-fed rivulets that vanish into the ground most likely reappear lower down as Marushka Creek. Or could it be the resurgence from Birdwood Lakes sited in the basin under Mt. Smuts and erroneously shown on maps as being inside Banff National Park?

A lake's water supply could well explain the spring's almost constant rate of flow throughout the year. Nevertheless, it boggles the mind to think of the subterranean stream coursing through stony labyrinths, maybe idling around in an underground reservoir for a while, changing valley and slope, and passing under Mt. Shark *for a distance of 6 km* before rising again at Karst Spring.

HISTORY NOTE Nowadays there's an official trail, but 40 years ago when Harry Connolly led us to Grotto Spring, as he called it, there was no trail and the thrill of discovery was still burning bright.

The first person to set eyes on the spring was Dean Marshall, then foreman of Spray Lakes Sawmills. While making a preliminary study west of Marushka Lake prior to logging in 1967, he stumbled across a creek "so unique" he returned the following day, approaching on a higher line to find the source of the noise.

Return to the last junction, turn right and cross the outlet to Watridge Lake on boardwalk. The trickle gives you a clue that this Watridge Creek as marked on the topo map (Gem Trek has it right) cannot possibly be the same as the one you crossed earlier. *Ergo* Watridge Lake is not the source of Watridge Creek.

The trail enters the humidity of old-growth spruce forest and heads across to Watridge Creek, which is racing pell-mell down the hillside. As you climb along the right bank the trail steepens and zigs to trail's end at a bench, viewing platform and interpretive sign. The mystery is solved! The REAL Watridge Creek glides out of a gloomy grotto on Mt. Shark and thunders down the mountainside in great waves as Elizabeth Falls. It's at its most spectacular during early summer; in fall and winter the rate of flow slackens somewhat and reveals boulders carpeted in bright green moss.

Scramblers bound for Mt. Shark continue uphill sans trail.

#80A. Watridge Creek below Karst Spring.

#81A. Lower Kirsten Tarn and Mt. Smuts.

81 MARUSHKA (SHARK) LAKE—map 9

Marushka Lake, looking towards Mt. Smuts at left and Mt. Shark at right.

Short day hike
Unofficial trail
Distance 3.7 km to lake
Height gain 36 m (120 ft.)
Height loss 68 m (225 ft.)
High point 1920 m (6300 ft.)
Map 82 J/14 Spray Lakes Reservoir

Access Hwy. 742 (Smith-Dorrien/Spray Trail). Turn west onto Mt. Shark Road. In 1.8 km park in a small parking area on the right side of the road.

This silky sheet of green water, which I persist in calling Marushka, lies in that strange valley between Tent Ridge and Mt. Shark. A revegetating logging road, then trail provides easy access.

HISTORY NOTE The name Marushka (NOT named after the vodka) came about donkeys years ago when the guru of the Spray, Harry Connolly, took Terry Beck, his cousin Myra Willey from England, and Jozef Turcan (a doctor of engineering and hydraulics at the Czech Academy of Science) to view the then unnamed lake.

"Is Myra the same as Mary?" Jozef asked, then suggested they use the lovely Czech name Marushka.

To Tent Ridge junction 0.7 km
About 100 m farther along the road beyond Monica Brook, turn first left onto the grassy Marushka Lake logging road that we used to drive by car. It starts off with an uphill, then flattens off to the junction with secondary logging road to the left. This is route #82 to Tent Ridge. Continue straight on the better road.

To Marushka Lake 3 km
In only 100 m a cairn on the right side indicates the trail to Mt. Shark parking lot and the helipad, which is okay in winter, but is of little use in summer. I mean, who wants to do all that extra climbing without the fun of a downhill run at the end of the day?

The road then climbs to its high point at a junction 1.4 km in. Keep right (cairns) and make a long gradual descent. En route, encroaching trees narrow the road to single track at several points. But overall this is a very pleasant section to walk, with views out over Spray Lakes Reservoir and ahead to Mt. Shark.

At the end cutblock, continue ahead on a narrower road to the edge of mature forest. A forest trail with step-over deadfall carries on, arriving at the lake's east shore not far from the outlet.

The colours of this lake will have you drooling: emerald green shot with azure, and delicate shades of orange and cream in the shallows.

Anyone headed across the outlet to Johnny Musco's historic cabin, Tony's Place, will be in for a disappointment. It's been burned down between editions.

GOING FARTHER

81A Kirsten Tarns

Distance ~2 km
Height gain 100+ m (330+ ft.)

HISTORY NOTE Back to Harry Connolly. Anticipating widespread logging in the area, Harry, starting in 1967, spent over 20 years of his life looking into and promoting Tent Ridge as a ski area. His company's proposal for "Assiniboine" was used in Calgary's successful bid for the 1988 Winter Olympics but was then unceremoniously dropped. I won't go into that here. But during the early days when Bob Niven was president of CODA and Frank King was chairman, Niven's daughter sadly succumbed to a rare heart condition at age 12. Harry suggested to Bob that, "it would be nice to name a little lake after your daughter."

He did. Walking farther into the upper valley is a fascinating, frustrating business: no creek, no trail and heaps of recessional moraines. But in two places the water surfaces in two lovely azure pools at the bottom of sinks called collectively Kirsten Tarns.

A trail more or less follows the shoreline around to the south shore. Jump the short-lived inlet and turn left. Climb the hill strewn with boulders via its right side. At the top descend off left into a sunken valley, one of a good many. Open and sprinkled with boulders, these intermittent valleys tend to follow the line of the underground stream, but not always. They also occur at right-angles to it. In addition there are hundreds of sinks in the forest separated one from another by ridges and small hills.

Luckily the route to the tarns is straightforward. Just continue up the valley ahead, slip through a gap to the left of another hill and descend to the sink containing the largest Kirsten tarn. The scene is fairy-tale, the clear, blue-green water of the tarn backdropped by Mt. Smuts and the long ridge from Mt. Shark.

Continue up the main valley, here and there listening to the stream gurgling under your feet. A short piece of creek emerging from rocks and disappearing into rocks precedes Upper Kirsten Tarn, which is much smaller and shallower and completely enclosed by boulders.

It's a good place to stop. Going farther to the valley head entails complex navigating around steep morainal walls of forest and all you see for your trouble is more moraines and more sunken valleys minus trees, grass and tarns. You've seen the best the valley has to offer.

Upper Kirsten Tarn.

82 TENT RIDGE—map 9

Day hike
Unofficial trails & route
Distance 3.6 km
Height gain 625 m (2050 ft.)
High point 2515 m (8250 ft.)
Map 82 J/14 Spray Lakes Reservoir

Access Hwy. 742 (Smith-Dorrien/Spray Trail). Turn west onto Mt. Shark Road. In 1.8 km park in a small parking area on the right side of the road.
Also accessible from #83.

If yearning for a great view that includes Mt. Assiniboine, take the normal route up Tent Ridge. It's a relentless uphill trudge using logging roads and a trail that climbs out of the trees onto an open ridge.

Tent Ridge was named, very aptly I think, by Harry Connolly and for a while was destined to be plastered with ski lifts, a gondola and the Fir Tree Day Lodge with restaurant. Snow depth indicator stations were scattered all around the ridge, including one at the head of Gawby Gulch, and recordings taken for over 20 years.

Summit view looking south towards the summits of the Tent Ridge Horseshoe (at left and centre right). In the background from left to right: mounts French, Commonwealth, Robertson, The Fist, Sir Douglas and Birdwood.

To Tent Ridge junction 0.7 km
About 100 m farther along the road just beyond "Monica Brook" (unofficially named after Monica Prociuk by Harry and Terry Beck), turn first left onto the grassy Marushka Lake logging road. It starts off with an uphill, then is almost flat to the junction with a secondary logging road to left (red flagging and stake in 2007). Turn left.

To Gawby Gulch 1.1 km
Your new logging road climbs and winds to the left, levelling out below what was cutblock no. 23 reaching far up the slope. It is now filled with small pines.

At a small clearing leave the logging road (which carries on less clearly into cutblock no. 26) and transfer to a trail running parallel to the road on the right side. Look for it on open ground between branches laid on either side. At the far side of the "cutblock", it turns right at a cairn and climbs up the left edge of the "cutblock" to the top left-hand corner. Here it turns left and enters old forest between two trees blazed with arrows.

In a few minutes reach Gawby Gulch. At the T-junction in the gulch turn right. (WARNING: on your return do not turn right at this T-junction. The alluring trail quickly degenerates en route to cutblock no. 26, leaving you to fight your way back to cutblock no. 23.)

To Tent Ridge 1.8 km
Walk up the easy-angled gulch to a flat meadow, site of a snow depth indicator station in the 1970s. Above rises the steep northeast face of Tent Ridge. Although you can't see it yet, ahead and in a direct line with Gawby Gulch is your ascent gully, one of several parallel gullies scoring the treed lower slope. (At this point, the very faint Tent Ridge connector heads left along the meadow. See #83 Getting Off.)

The main trail continues, veering left to get around a pile of deadfall, then heads right and climbs straight up the left side of the gully to a prominent white boulder

View of Spray Lakes Reservoir from the summit.

at the three-quarter mark, a useful marker during the descent when you want to be sure you're on the right route. Cross a game trail and continue uphill on dryas, crossing two more traversing game trails en route to a cairn below the steep open slopes of a bowl.

While you can stagger up the bowl almost anywhere to the summit, I advocate using the northeast ridge to your right, most easily gained by traversing right on the next available game trail above the cairn. Pass through a few larches.

The northeast ridge calls for nothing more than moderately strenuous effort up grass, then shale and stones with a zigzagging trail. On topping out at the tent apex you'll be thrilled by the magnificent view of Spray Lakes Reservoir. To its left you can trace the route from Mt. Shark trailhead up Bryant Creek to Assiniboine, the great peak itself peeping over the top of Mt. Turner. Glittering like jewels in the dark forest are the lakes of Marushka and Watridge.

Turn left and continue along the grassy ridgepole to the highest point, marked by a cairn, where you can have a fine time identifying the upwelling of shapely peaks suddenly disclosed to the south.

83 TENT RIDGE HORSESHOE—map 9

The north ridge of peak 154311.

Day scramble
Unofficial trails & route
Distance for circuit 10.1 km
Height gain 823 m (2700 ft.)
High point 2554 m (8380 ft.)
Map 82 J/14 Spray Lakes Reservoir

Access Hwy. 742 (Smith-Dorrien/Spray Trail). Turn west onto Mt. Shark Road. In 1.8 km park in a small parking area on the right side of the road.
Also accessible from #82 Tent Ridge and #84 Tryst Lake.

This is one of the most enjoyable ridge walks you'll ever do. It takes in three summits—Peak 154311, peak 146308 and Tent Ridge grouped around Monica Basin—and though occasionally narrowish and rocky, it is not exposed. Expect one short easy scramble step early on.

Getting to the ridge and back is easy on trails. However, knowing ahead of time the route to Tent Ridge will save time on the descent. Some hikers like to drop off the ridge into Tryst Lake cirque and return via #84 and Mt. Shark Road.

CLOCKWISE

To Monica Basin 2.8 km
From the parking area walk BACK along the road a short distance, then turn right (west) up a grassy logging road. Round a bend into what used to be cutblock no. 27. At a cairn and yellow flagging turn right onto a narrow trail that climbs through small pines towards old forest at the top of the "cutblock."

At the demarcation, cross an intersecting trail, then head up leftwards, stepping over much deadfall. Gradually the trail turns right and wanders through forest to a T-junction at km 1.6. Turn left. (The trail to right is the optional return route via the Tent Ridge connector. See Getting Off.)

Very shortly turn right at a 4-way junction with flagging. After a while the trail veers left and uphill to a T-junction. Keep straight and come to Monica Brook at the start of the meadows. The trail follows it up to a seasonal tarn in the basin below peak 146308. (Though the basin is lovely, I wouldn't say no to a GOOD trail up the ridge from the 4-way junction.)

To peak 154311 1.3 km

Gain the ridge to your left (east) at treeline. This is most easily achieved by a diagonal climb from right to left on grass then scree. Turn right (south) and start up the delectable north ridge of peak 154311.

Straight off climb a steep slope on trail. Then cross a narrow rocky section to the base of the scramble step. Tackle it direct: up a groove, left on ledges, then up right to the top.

After this the route unravels beautifully, long promontories alternating with scrambly rock steps. Rather disappointingly, this exciting form of progress stops short of the summit, which is the size of a tennis court with a Firenet repeater station (#108), dumped on top of it. But it would be hard to ruin such a fabulous viewpoint completely, even though the wires holding the tower in place have the annoying knack of appearing in every photo. The view south is particularly fabulous: Tryst Lake far below and all of K Country's shapeliest peaks grouped together in one frame: Robertson, French, Sir Douglas, Commonwealth, Birdwood, Smuts and The Fist.

Looking back to peak 154311 from the easy climb to The Hub. From the col you can escape right, into Tryst Lake cirque.

To The Hub at 146308 0.8 km

Stroll down the broad west ridge to a col touched by fingers of spruce thickets reaching up from the left side. This is where you can escape to Tryst Lake: a 244-vertical-m descent through larches that have a permanent lean from the weight of the winter snowpack.

the start and the Tent Ridge connector from Tent Ridge trail.

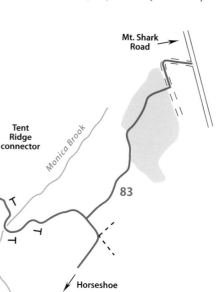

The upcoming climb to The Hub of the horseshoe is not as steep as it looks, the ascent helped in its upper stage by a winding trail in the scree.

At the summit a fresh view opens up of nearby connecting ridges to The Fist and Mt. Smuts. Down below you to the west are the sinks of upper Marushka Creek.

To Tent Ridge 1.6 km

Turn right (north). Not far along, vertigo sufferers may prefer to follow a trail below the ridgeline on the left (west) side. While this connecting ridge to Tent appears level, it's anything but. Unseen are two drops requiring well-scratched detours down the west flank on tippy rocks where it's easy to come a cropper.

The final pull up colourful Tent Ridge is easy, with several false tops to plod over before you reach the summit, a superlative viewpoint for Spray Lakes Reservoir. But far more satisfying is the view of the whole ridge walk you've just completed.

The ridge between The Hub and Tent Ridge (seen in the distance).

GETTING OFF

1. Via #82 Tent Ridge 3.6 km Fully 99% of people reverse the Tent Ridge ascent route down Gawby Gulch.

2. Via Tent Ridge connector 3.5 km While having the advantage of connecting to your ingoing trail, the 600-m-long Tent Ridge connector has a down side: some deadfall, a creek crossing and hills. Do you really want to climb uphill?

Initially, follow the standard route down the northeast ridge to the flat meadow. Here turn right and follow a faint trail through the meadow criss-crossed with step-over deadfall. Stay near the left edge. The meadow narrows to a draw (trail improves) and you reach the top of the high, forested bank above Monica Brook. Descend, traverse, then descend very steeply to the valley bottom. Cross Monica Brook and climb the far bank. After a relief section there's another steep uphill before the trail meanders along to the T-junction with flagging. Turn left and return the same way you came up.

84 TRYST LAKE—map 9

Short day hike, bike 'n' hike
Unofficial trail
Distance 3.3 km one way
Height gain 260 m (853 ft.)
High point 2149 m (7050 ft.)
Map 82 J/14 Spray Lakes Reservoir

*Tryst Lake backdropped by The Fist (L) and
The Hub of Tent Ridge Horseshoe (R).*

Access Hwy. 742 (Smith-Dorrien/Spray
Trail). Turn west onto Mt. Shark Road. In
1 km turn left onto a side road and park a
little way in.

A short climb on good trail to a cirque
lake. Being of the bathtub variety, it drains
underground and is disappointing in the
fall. Nonetheless, this is the time the trail
is at its busiest, with a procession of larch
lovers coming and going.

HISTORY NOTE Tryst is another of
those lakes formerly called "Lost" until
Harry Connolly arranged a lover's meeting
there some 50 years ago. Though June, the
lake was still frozen when Harry guided
Elizabeth Willey (Marushka Mary's sister)
and her fiancée, Jim Springer, to the lake.
Enamoured of the wonderful scene, Elizabeth and Jim embraced and Harry took a
photo for posterity.

Walk south along the flat grassy logging
road for 1.9 km. Exactly 170 m north of
Tryst Creek (marked incorrectly on maps),
a blaze and large cairn indicate the start of
the Tryst Lake trail.

Head off to the right through the trees
to the stream and follow it up the right
bank a short way. Cross to the left bank
(bridge) and for a while continue easily
up the valley. Higher up, the valley rises
in three distinct steps, the willow bushes
of the avalanche chute lower down giving
way to clumpy white heathers. The terrain
then levels, with larches signalling your
arrival at lakeshore meadows.

Tryst is wonderfully situated below a
peak shaped like a clenched fist, the whole
scene becoming magical in fall when the
larches turn colour. "The Chutes" to left
are a popular destination slope for skiers.
The larch slope to right is gaining popular-
ity as an escape route off the Tent Ridge
Horseshoe.

Return the same way. Now for afternoon tea at Mount Engadine Lodge!

85 "BIRDWOOD LAKES" — map 9

Lower Birdwood Lake and Smutwood Ridge from Smuts Pass. Photo Andrew Nugara

Long day hike, bike 'n' hike
Unofficial trail & route
Distance 7.3 km via 1
Height gain 497 m (1630 ft.) to lake,
549 m (1800 ft.) to High Col
High point at Smuts Pass 2340 m
(7680 ft.), at High Col 2393 m (7850 ft.)
Map 82 J/14 Spray Lakes Reservoir

Access Hwy. 742 (Smith-Dorrien/Spray Trail).
1. Usual Turn west onto Mt. Shark Road. In 1 km turn left onto a side road and park a little way in.
2. Shortcut Park at the side of the hwy. 2.2 m south of Mt. Shark Road opposite the mouth of Commonwealth Creek.
Also accessible from #88 Burstall Pass.

A Jekyll and Hyde route that starts with a fairly easy walk on trail up Commonwealth Creek Valley. The second half is a grunt up a headwall to Smuts Pass on the so-called Banff Park boundary. Most people don't end the trip here but continue on to High Col and up the lower slopes of

what Andrew calls Smutwood Ridge for the fantastic view of Mt. Birdwood.

On reaching the lakes, the superb alpine country will make you yearn to carry on. And with two vehicles you can do just that: continue over High Col to Birdwood Pass or on to Burstall Pass in one day. (See Options A and B.) Scramblers use the trail to access Mt. Smuts and The Fist. But whatever you do, start early.

There are two starts. The usual route is uncomplicated with no creek crossings. The shortcut, while reducing the one-way trip by at least 1.1 km, is soggy underfoot with two possible creek crossings.

1. Usual 2.4 km Walk or bike the grassy N–S logging road heading south. In 1.9 km Tryst Lake trail (cairn) takes off to the right.

Cross Tryst Creek and enter a large cutblock/plantation with a breathtaking view of Commonwealth Peak and Pig's Back up ahead. At a Y-junction keep right onto a secondary logging road.

2. The Shortcut 1.3 km Descend the bank and slosh across Engadine Flats and Smuts Creek, aiming for the obvious grassy avenue on the far side of the valley. At a sign (no camping, no fires, dogs on a leash) follow a trail (nee logging road) uphill and through a cutblock, wending left to the main N–S logging road at 171309.

Turn right and follow the logging road down to Commonwealth Creek (log crossing hopefully) and up to a Y-junction. Turn left. (The road ahead leads to Access 1.)

NOTE An even shorter shortcut exists that shaves off another 400 m. Starting from waypoint 171309, it crosses the road and follows a secondary logging road along the left (southeast) bank of Commonwealth Creek to the sawmill site at 168304. Head diagonally right into forest. A blazed trail runs above the creek past the waterfalls, to sort of join the main trail across the creek at the end of the narrows. Mostly used by skiers and snowshoers.

Up Commonwealth Creek 3.8 km
As you follow the new logging road into Commonwealth Creek Valley, keep left after a small side creek crossing and pass through a sawmill site to a cutblock. At the far forest edge, dump the bikes and transfer to a forest trail.

The trail descends to Commonwealth Creek at small waterfalls, then seesaws between boisterous creek and rocky outcrops through the narrows. This section ends in a bog. Continue at the demarcation of forest and flat wet meadows where the stream flows over gravel beds in great meanders. To your left is Pig's Back, while ahead rises Mt. Birdwood, revealing its diminutive north glacier.

Farther on you cross the runouts of horrendous avalanche slopes falling from The Fist and wade through fields of ragwort and cow parsley. Just ahead is another narrows, but you're not going through it. Instead, the trail climbs to a stony side creek with cairn at 150289.

Cross the side creek and on stones climb up the left bank to another cairn

Falls in Commonwealth Creek. Photo Roy Millar

where the trail resumes. Continue climbing fairly steeply up the left bank, then traverse left into the forest for a flat stretch where delicate foamflowers grow among showy rhododendrons. At a junction keep to the right. Two short rises bring you to treeline below the headwall.

Headwall to Smuts Pass 1.1 km
Coming up is the steep climb of the day. Make for the scree gully on the right side of the headwall and scrabble up a trail on its right side. Shortly the trail crosses the gully onto the wide, grassy slope and climbs the larch-scattered rib just left of the gully. Near the top where the headwall starts to rear up and become ugly, head off right across easier-angled ground to gain a large, flat terrace above the gully's left fork. High to the left, Mt. Birdwood rises like the thin blade of a knife. On the right the south ridge of Mt. Smuts looks equally terrifying and I can't believe it's a scrambling route, but this is where hardcore scramblers would set off up the first gully. For us walkers there's one last climb to Smuts Pass: a short step, which the trail traverses from right to left.

The grassy saddle between Birdwood and Smuts is not really a pass and certainly not the Banff Park boundary. The ground ahead slopes gently down to a sunken valley occupied by Lower Birdwood Lake. On the terrace above is another lake, frozen for a good part of the year. From it, a cord of white water pours into the lower lake, whose waters sink into the ground at the same phenomenal rate to join some vast underground drainage system. This giant sinkhole is bounded on the west by a high ridge that is the true boundary.

To High Col 0.7 km

The trail continues, climbing beside the stream to the upper lake, and from there to grassy High Col at 135279—the true pass—and a very fine vantage point for Snow Peak (looking its most spectacular) and the west face of Mt. Birdwood. For an even better view, wander up the lower slopes of Smutwood. My favourite viewpoint for Birdwood, though, has to be the terrace east of the upper Birdwood Lake, where an unsuspected tarn mirrors the mountain to perfection.

Birdwood Lakes from near High Col. Mt. Smuts in the background. Photo Andrew Nugara

GOING FARTHER

85A Birdwood Pass

Unofficial trails, route
Distance 1.9 km to pass, 17.3 km trailhead to trailhead
Height gain 167 m (550 ft.)
Height loss 107 m (350 ft.)
to High point at Birdwood Pass 2454 m (8050 ft.)

Making a point to point with Burstall Pass trailhead is a long day's hike. The trail is intermittent, the terrain steep in places, and in other places a wasteland of stones and snow patches that make navigation a nightmare in a whiteout. Throw in a bit of scrambling and bushwhacking at the end and you've got a route that only hard-core hikers will enjoy.

To Birdwood Pass 1.9 km

Start from High Col. Without losing height, head southeast across meadow to the trees on the skyline. Find the game trail that drops steeply through the trees for 10 vertical m, then cuts left through a diagonal rock band into a long, slightly

Upper Birdwood Lake (Ice Lake) and Mt. Birdwood. Photo Andrew Nugara

descending traverse. Between forested ribs you cross steep avalanche chutes crammed with flowers, the gorgeous scenes looking remarkably like a Neo-impressionist painting by Georges Seurat. At black shale the trail drops sharply to a flat meadow nowhere near Birdwood Creek (which is farther down the slope in a mini-canyon). This is the low point.

Restart the climb to Birdwood Pass between Mt. Birdwood and the precipitous northeast face of Snow Peak. Use the draw immediately under the west face of Birdwood, a simple walk up grass, scree and often snow leading directly to the pass at 146264.

This is a bleak spot, wide open to bad weather. Somehow I can't seem to get here without a thunderstorm gathering. Judging by his photographs, Alf Skrastins has the same problem. But the view is stupendous, not only of where you've come from but looking ahead to the fabulous karst country of Burstall Pass, the smooth slabs of Whistling Ridge leading the eye towards the great peak of Mt. Sir Douglas.

Birdwood Pass in good weather. Looking south to Whistling Ridge, Mt. Sir Douglas and South Burstall Pass. Photo Angélique Mandel

To Burstall Pass trail 1.5 km
The far side is a two-step scree, or scree 'n' snow slope dropping to a grassy bench. Gain a lower, narrower bench sited above the high cliff defending the pass from the Burstall Creek side. It was here, just as the storm was imminent, we came upon a couple of climbing acquaintances with a tent. Unfortunately, we couldn't cram another six people into a tent made for two and had to leave. This means walking to the far left end of the bench (as you look out), where a "trail" in scree leads down to a

Flowery avalanche chutes.

four-m-high rock step that can be managed holding an umbrella in one hand. After this you descend under the cliff, heading a long way right to grass where the trail, its duty done, vanishes. Descend where you fancy. The end result is always the same: some bushbashing to gain the Burstall Pass trail in the big meadow above the headwall. Turn left and follow it out to Burstall Pass parking lot.

GOING FARTHER STILL

85B to Burstall Pass

Route scramble
Distance 1.7 km, 19.3 km trailhead to trailhead
Height gain 91 m (300 ft.)
Height loss 91 m (300 ft.)
High point ~2423 m (7950 ft.) on south ridge of Snow Peak

At Birdwood Pass you make the decision whether or not to carry on to Burstall Pass and grab four passes in a day. The key section is a traverse of the east face of Snow

On the benches between Birdwood and Burstall passes, Mt. Birdwood behind.

Peak. You want as little snow as possible on this traverse. Check conditions by viewing Snow Peak from the east shore of Mud Lake near the Burstall Pass parking lot.

Start from the lower bench on the southeast side of the pass and head south, at the obvious place transferring to a higher bench, which is of varying width and slant. Halfway along is a small plot of Indian paintbrush featuring a showy bicoloured species.

Unfortunately, the bench peters out and you must climb steep broken ground to gain the broad south ridge of Snow Peak above. This entails climbing diagonally uphill, passing below, then up the left side of a permanent snow patch. The scrambling couldn't be easier. The danger comes early in the season when a more extensive snowfield forces you farther left onto ledges above a drop-off. (Even earlier you'd be plodding up a dangerous lee slope below a really huge cornice.)

Needless to say, finding the going down place from the other direction can be difficult.

On reaching the ridge, turn left and follow it up and down to Burstall Pass.

86 COMMONWEALTH LAKE—map 9

Day hike, bike 'n' hike via 1.
Unofficial trails, possible creek crossing
Distance 4.5 km via 1.
Height gain 198 m (650 ft.)
High point 2042 m (6700 ft.)
Map 82 J/14 Spray Lakes Reservoir

Access Hwy. 742 (Smith-Dorrien/Spray Trail).
1. Usual Turn west onto Mt. Shark Road. In 1 km turn left onto a side road and park a little way in.
2. Shortcut Park at the side of the hwy. 2.2 m south of Mt. Shark Road.

After an easy logging-road start, a moderately steep forest trail, cleared by Rudi Kranabitter, takes you to a body of water formerly called Jeanette, then Lost and now, officially, Commonwealth—a pretentious name for a small green gem.

There are two starts to this trail. No 2, though reducing the return distance by a whopping 4.4 km, is soggy underfoot. Take Tevas if your boots let in water.

1. Usual logging road 2.9 km Walk or bike the grassy N–S logging road heading south. In 1.9 km Tryst Lake trail (cairn) takes off to the right. Cross Tryst Creek and enter a large cutblock/plantation with a breathtaking view of Commonwealth Peak and Pig's Back up ahead. At a Y-junction keep left. (Logging road to right is the normal route up Commonwealth Creek.)

Descend and cross Commonwealth Creek, hopefully on logs. At the top of the hill at waypoint 171309 turn right onto a secondary logging road.

2. Shortcut 0.7 km Descend the bank and slosh across Engadine Flats and Smuts Creek, aiming for the obvious grassy avenue on the far side. At a sign (no camping, no fires, dogs on a leash) follow a trail (nee logging road) uphill and through a

Commonwealth Peak above Commonwealth Lake.

cutblock, wending left to the main N–S logging road at 171309. Cross.

To Commonwealth Lake 1.6 km
A secondary logging road heads along the left (southeast) bank of Commonwealth Creek to the flat sawmill site at 168304.

Start the uphill climb to the left of the forest edge in old cutblock. Amid a jumble of skid trails, your road is distinguished by tread. Remember this as it levels, bending right, then back left up a hill. Before it starts to curve even farther to the left around the top of a shallow gully, abandon it for a narrow trail that climbs into forest. Wind moderately steeply through fir and menziesia forest to a levelling where the trail makes a beeline for the lakeshore.

The lake is beautifully situated in the forest below Commonwealth Peak, and as I've mentioned, it's green, the colour of unripe Granny Smith apples.

OPTION

86A "Pig's Back"

Day scramble
Route, unofficial trails
Distance 2.5 km from lake
Height gain 427 m (1400 ft.) from lake
High point 2454 m (8050 ft.)

The fit hiker can extend the trip to the col between Commonwealth Peak and peak 163287, called Pig's Back, and from there climb Pig's Back for the view. Interestingly, the name was coined by K Country employees to be in keeping with Pig's Tail, which is the little peak between Commonwealth and Birdwood.

From the col there is the option of going farther and making a loop with Commonwealth Creek trail, which involves a paddle across Commonwealth Creek. Whatever you decide, all options travel through rough terrain with steep slopes, scree, bush and likely snow until mid-summer. After snowmelt the flower gardens below the pass are some of the best in the Rockies.

To the col 1.9 km
Walk up the valley beyond the lake through forest with flowery glades to the larch and boulder zone. At the obvious place depart the valley and take to the right-hand hillside. Climb steep grass, threading between slabs to gain easy-angled talus leading to the col at 163281.

When we arrived at the col the first time, a fierce rainstorm had just passed, the clouds parting theatrically to reveal the steaming rocks of Commonwealth Peak glittering in the sun like anthracite. Andrew Lloyd Webber couldn't have stage-managed it better.

Up Pig's Back 0.6 km
Anyone arriving at the col and not heeding the siren call of the little pointy summit to the north is missing out on a fabulous viewpoint. So, set out on grass, promis-

ing not to turn around until I say. After scree begins, the ridge steepens and narrows dramatically, with cliffs on the left side and on the right a convenient sheep trail running below the crest to the summit, which turns out to be false. Ahead stretches a wide, flat pig's back clothed in high altitude grass. Walk to its end and look back. What a place to view the north faces of Commonwealth Peak and Mt. Birdwood! In early July, winter's snow still lies heavy on the peaks, but here are green grass and flowers and picas running about between your feet. To the northwest is an equally impressive view across the valley of Commonwealth Creek towards Birdwood Lakes and Mt. Smuts.

Pig's Back.

GOING FARTHER
The loop (+peak) 13.6 km
From the col slither down scree into the barren valley on the west side. Follow this drainage down to the first drop-off via a game trail on the left side of the creek. Where a side creek comes in from the left, cross to the right bank. Above the second, steeper drop-off a trail traverses right across scree into forest, then plummets to valley bottom.

Wade Commonwealth Creek to the trail on the northwest bank. Turn right and follow trail #85 down Commonwealth Creek to the main logging road you started out on. Turn left and return to the trailhead.

#86A. The summit of Pig's Back. Looking back along the promontory to Commonwealth Peak.

#87A. First Hogarth Lake, looking towards the Kananaskis Range.

87 HOGARTH LAKES LOOPS — map 9

Half-day hikes
Map 82 J/14 Spray Lakes Reservoir

Access Hwy. 742 (Smith-Dorrien/Spray Trail) at Burstall Pass parking lot.
Also accessible from #88 Burstall Pass trail in two places.

87A Hogarth Lakes Loop

Distance 5 km
Official trails with red snowshoe markers, unofficial trails, creek crossings
Height gain 18 m (60 ft.)
High Point 1914 m (6280 ft.)

A flattish forest walk around a string of fishing lakes named after ranger Jock Hogarth. For the most part you follow the red markers of the snowshoe trail along logging roads. So while the walking is easy, you may be thwarted by Burstall Creek crossing if logs aren't in place. Just in case they're not, carry Tevas and hiking poles. Be alert for bears.

To First Burstall Lake turnoff 2 km
Forgoing the gated gravel access road, cross Mud Lake Dam on trail. Join the road briefly, then swing right at the hiking sign onto Burstall Creek logging road. Just after the logging road turns left and starts up a hill (hiking sign), turn right onto the Hogarth Lakes logging road (red snowshoe sign).

The road swings right into forest and after one flat kilometre arrives at Burstall Creek crossing. Early in the season this crossing may be impassable. Look for logs downstream. At the next four logging road junctions keep right, left (the good road to right is the return leg), right and down a slight hill with flagging, then left.

Disregard the post, which indicates the snowshoe trail turning off to the right into a bog. Stay on the major road that runs along the west shorelines of First and Second Hogarth lakes under the cliffs of a knoll.

Unlike muddy Mud Lake, the Hogarth Lakes are remarkable for their translucent green colour shading to cream in the shallows. Tom Thomson trees around the rims make wonderful foregrounds for the mountains of the Kananaskis Range.

Halfway along the second lake a side trail leads down to the water. Along the shoreline to the right a lone snowshoe hangs from a tree. Just after is a Y-junction. Stay right. (The uphill logging road to left is First Burstall Lake loop.)

the two loops

263

Return leg 3 km

Carry on past a smaller third lake. At its end keep right and round the end of it. After crossing its tiny outlet you are on the return leg, which is almost totally enclosed in old forest. The snowshoe trail comes in from the right off Third Hogarth Lake and is followed (red markers) to a T-junction near Burstall Creek. As you see by the map the slightly rolling logging road wends a fairly straight line amid a complexity of secondary roads infilling with small spruce.

At the T-junction near Burstall Creek turn right. (DO NOT follow the snowshoe trail to left unless you want to swim.) Keep left and arrive back on your outgoing trail. Turn left and retrace your steps back to the trailhead.

87B First Burstall Lake Loop

Distance 5.2 km
Official trails with red markers,
unofficial trails, creek crossings
Height gain 91 m (300 ft.)
High point 1975 m (6480 ft.)

A scenic loop with hills that takes in two Hogarth lakes, First Burstall Lake and the Burstall Pass trail. Two crossings of Burstall Creek can be problematical, so carry Tevas and poles. Be alert for bears.

First Burstall Lake from the east shore. Looking towards Whistling Ridge at left and Snow Peak at centre right.

To lake 3.5 km

Follow Hogarth Lakes loop to the Y-junction at Second Hogarth Lake.

Turn left up the hill and keeping left on a trail climb into a draw between the knoll and the east slope of Commonwealth Ridge, notable for its ice smears in winter.

The trail follows the grassy draw to a small meadow, then enters a spruce avenue. Ignoring a track to right, continue straight up a hill to an open area where the trail is vague. Go left a bit and pick up a grassy logging road that is followed down right, through what once was a huge cutblock covering the entire southwest slope of the knoll. Now it's infilled with young pines and offers no view.

Just before the road crosses Burstall Creek, push through a few trees to the east shore of First Burstall Lake. With luck you'll hit the meadow with a fallen tree to sit on. Unusual for the Rockies, the lake is almost colourless, flanked by Mt. Burstall on the left and Commonwealth Peak on the right. Straight ahead is Burstall Pass.

Return to the road and wade Burstall Creek. Climb a short hill to a T-junction with Burstall Pass trail logging road.

Return leg 1.7 km

Turn left and follow the Burstall Pass logging road down a long hill. At French Creek trail intersection the road curves left and down to the T-junction with the Hogarth Lakes logging road. Keep right and return the same way you came in from the parking lot.

88 BURSTALL PASS — map 9

Long day hike, bike 'n' hike
Official trail with signposts, creek
crossings likely
Distance 7.8 km
Height gain 472 m (1550 ft.)
High point 2362 m (7750 ft.)
Maps 82 J/14 Spray Lakes Reservoir,
82 J/11 Kananaskis Lakes

Access Hwy. 742 (Smith-Dorrien/Spray Trail) at Burstall Pass parking lot.
Also accessible from #86A and B, Birdwood Lakes.

The Burstall Pass trail takes you into that cheerful green and white karst country above treeline. Once you are up high, there are many enticing opportunities for off-trail exploration: see options and scramble #89.

Not all of this route is scenic trail. It kicks off with 3.3 km of tedious logging road that we used to drive pre K Country. Now you can bike it to a bike rack. This cuts down the hiking to 4.5 km one way.

Burstall Pass. In the background is Mt. Birdwood, Pig's Tail and Commonwealth Peak.

Okay, so you may be walking your bike up some hills, but coming down is a blast.

Creek crossings on the flats are unavoidable, but after September you can generally cross dryshod.

As Joe Kovach and Bill Balmer noted on October 6, 1948, the pass can easily be crossed to the Spray River. Nowadays there is the luxury of a trail, so anyone off to Leman Lake, Spray Pass or Palliser Pass can come this way in preference to slogging all the way up the Spray River trail from Bryant Creek. For details read *The Canadian Rockies Trail Guide,* by Brian Patton and Bart Robinson.

This is also the scrambler's access for Mt. Burstall, Piggy Plus and Snow Peak.

To bike rack 3.5 km
Forgoing the gated gravel access road, cross Mud Lake Dam on trail. Join the road briefly, then swing right at the hiking sign onto Burstall Creek logging road. To left is French Creek pouring out of two culverts

Burstall Pass (centre) from the lower south ridge of Snow Peak. To left is South Burstall Pass below Sir Douglas. At centre ridge 147230, showing both ascent and descent routes. To the right is Leman Lake between mounts Leman and Leval. The pointy peak is Talon Peak above Talus Lodge.

into a holding pond, diverted from its natural course into Smith-Dorrien Creek to Mud Lake, a receptacle for all the muck carried down from the Robertson and French glaciers. At another hiking sign curve left up a hill. (To right is the flat Hogarth Lakes logging road.) At the top is a four-way junction. Turn sharp right at the hiking sign. (Ahead is the French Creek logging road.)

Continue to follow the Burstall Creek logging road, which climbs past numerous re-vegetating logging roads and skid trails, the result of Balmer's visit to look over the timber. Down to your right, Burstall Creek is closeted in a canyon. A side trail just after an intersecting logging road leads to a vertiginous viewpoint. Don't sue if you fall over the edge. Okay?

After the road descends a little, keep straight at km 1.7. (A secondary road to right heads downhill and crosses Burstall Creek. See #87B.)

Below the avalanche slopes of Mt. Burstall, the going is mainly flat with a few small uphills. Pass a massive boulder, and down to the right the three relatively drab-coloured Burstall Lakes, which lie out of sight from the road. Though not out of earshot. On a left-hand bend the roar you hear comes from the cascade at the outlet of the middle lake. A short distance on, a side trail to right leads to waterlogged meadows surrounding the middle lake. (See side trip A, Avalanche Impact Pond.)

After another uphill, a cairn on the left side indicates the scrambler's route up Mt. Burstall. A few metres on, a short side trail to right leads to Third Burstall Lake, a detour worth taking for the view of Mt. Birdwood and Commonwealth Peak rising steeply above the water.

At about 3.4 km, a small meadow on the left-hand side—a former sawmill site—marks the end of the logging road. This is also where scramblers take off up a hidden valley to Piggy Plus. The road reverts to trail and dips sharply. Immediately after is the bike rack.

To the pass 4.3 km

From the rack, a rooty trail descends gradually to the valley bottom and runs alongside Robertson Creek to a bridge. Cross and navigate a large willowy alluvial flat extending from Robertson Glacier moraines to west Burstall Lake. This

*Mt. Robertson, Robertson Glacier
and Mt. Sir Douglas from the flats.*

entails following footprints in the gravel and signs on posts. During the summer glacier melt, paddling continually shifting braided streams is the norm.

Ahead is Snow Peak, the south ridge in profile. As you cross the mouth of Robertson Glacier Valley, look left for a view of the glacier slung between the vertical strata of Mt. Robertson and lordly Sir Douglas.

Enter forest again and climb the timbered headwall of Burstall Creek, which is a bit of a grunt with overnight gear and a six-pack. Some 120 vertical metres later you reach the long flat meadow below Birdwood Pass and Mt. Birdwood's Lizzie Ridge. This is where route 85A comes in.

Cross the meadow and climb steadily through open forest to a flattening where the trail turns right at a signpost. (The less worn trail ahead starts you off towards South Burstall Pass.)

The trail heads up right, zigs back below a rockband into meadows, then right again, ultimately approaching the pass from the south. A national parks signpost marks the spot.

When the cloud's down, Burstall Pass is a hugely complicated terrain of barren ridges, confounded by a deep sinkhole on the west side. In fine weather it's a marvellous place to be. Mountains encircle you, Mt. Birdwood to the northeast and The Fortress seen through the gap made by Burstall Creek. Sir Douglas is pre-eminent to the south, while to the west, Assiniboine lords it over a welter of lesser peaks. Bounding the pass to the south is the unnamed ridge 147230, and to the north the oddly named Snow Peak.

GOING FARTHER

88A Leman Lake Viewpoint

Official trail, route
Distance 0.7 km from pass

If not climbing Snow Peak or Ridge 147230, this is the next-best viewpoint and requires little extra effort.

Start at Burstall Pass. The same trail continues into Banff National Park, traversing the left side of the sink. Instead of turning right as for the Spray River Valley, continue ahead to a grassy shoulder. Keep walking until the peacock colours of historic Leman Lake come into view. In 1901 Walter Wilcox named it Lake Castelleia after the wild flower observed on its banks, i.e. the Indian paintbrush.

While Leman Lake can be reached from the Spray River Valley you can miss out the backpack by driving Hwy. 93 and the Kootenay-Albert forest road and walking for an hour over Spray Pass. For details read *Hikes around Invermere & the Columbia River Valley,* by Aaron Cameron and Matt Gunn.

*Right: The impact pond and mound above Third
Burstall Lake. Mt. Burstall in the background.*

OPTIONS

88B Avalanche Impact Pond

Half-day
Route, creek crossing
Distance 0.6 km from Burstall Pass trail, 3.2 km one way from trailhead

Close to the northeast end of Third Burstall Lake is a small pond marked on the topo map at 173272. As ponds go it's a bit of a rarity. It's full name is "snow-avalanche impact pool" because it's been excavated by climax avalanches shooting down the 580-m-high gully from the ridge above. The ejected material piled up in a mound on the downhill side and the hole filled up with water.

Landform enthusiasts should consider making the pond a half-day destination from the trailhead. Take Tevas and poles.

Start from Burstall Pass trail at 2.6 km from the trailhead. Head right on a narrow trail leading to a waterlogged meadow about Second Burstall Lake. Put on the Tevas and make your way around the left shore to Burstall Creek between lakes. Follow it

South Burstall Pass area below Whistling Ridge. Photo Alf Skrastins

up and wade the creek easily at the outlet to Third Burstall Lake.

Ahead is the grassy mound, and behind it a green pond about 9 m deep. The best viewpoint is from a little way up the gully (see photo.).

It's hard to think of a better lunch spot than the back side of the mound that slopes down to the lake at sun-bathing angle and gives fine views across the water to Mt. Burstall and Whistling Ridge. Alternatively, some cleverly constructed seats made out of large rocks and deadfall are available close to the shore.

88C South Burstall Pass

Long Day hike
Unofficial trail then route
Distance from main trail 1.7+ km
Height gain from main trail 168+ m
(550+ ft.)
High point 2454 m (8050 ft.)

The slightly higher pass at 155226 is really the culmination of the Burstall Creek Valley between Whistling Ridge to the east and ridge 147230 to the west. Much of it is a rough walk on rock, but an exciting one for karst lovers.

Leave Burstall Pass trail at the signpost at 150245 where a fainter trail heads south. After it peters out choose your own route, more or less following the draw to a wide flat area of fissured pavement which is the pass. At a cairn look back. The four dog-tooth mountains: Smuts, Birdwood, Pig's Tail, and Commonwealth Peak have lined up four abreast. What you've really come for, though, is the close-up of Mt. Sir Douglas, its north face mantled with glaciers.

If you have time continue southeast into a cirque "of shattered karst full of depressions and blocked shafts."

On the return explore farther towards Whistling Ridge and Burstall Slabs ("one of North America's finest friction climbing areas"),"where small streams plunge into beautifully sculptured elliptical shafts" writes caver Jon Rollins describing Burstall Pots. He surmises the water may rise again at Karst Spring, though no water tracing has ever been carried out. Also have a look for the wee tarn.

88D Ridge 147230

Day
Route, unofficial trail
Distance 2.3 km to South Burstall Pass
Height gain 244 m (800 ft.)
High point 2606 m (8550 ft.)

If motivated by fabulous views, traversing the ridge between the two passes is something you can't pass up. Most often it is combined with Option C.

Getting onto the ridge is not as straightforward as you might expect. From the signpost at Burstall Pass head southwest onto the big grassy rise 145239 through a break in the rock band. Steer south and gain a smaller rise by the left edge. Ahead rises the main body of the ridge. Sneak through the obvious draw on its left side, cut back right on steep grass, and finish with a simple scree plod on sheep trail.

Except for one short rise before the second cairn, the summit ridge is broad and flat, the right side falling away in cliffs to the Spray River Valley. You'll revel in the view that takes in the whole of the Spray Valley from Bryant Creek to Palliser Pass, plus Mt. Assiniboine and all the peaks you could see from Burstall Pass. Look *down* on blue-tinted Belgium Lake, and across the pass to Mt. King Albert, named after the King of the Belgians who died in a climbing accident and not, I hasten to add, a member of the Royal Group. Carry on to the very end, dropping slightly to a spectacular grassy promontory that gives you the best view of the day—the classic shot of Sir Douglas.

To regain the Burstall Pass trail
Most hikers drop off the left (east) side of the ridge onto South Burstall Pass. From the end point this is a fairly simple descent of alternating scree steps (the second is the steepest) and grassy terraces. Then turn left and wander back north through the valley karst.

Alternatively, head left along the lower terrace. Where the terrace slips a notch at mid point, descend to the flat meadow and pick up the Burstall Pass trail just below the pass.

View of Sir Douglas from the promontory.

89 SNOW PEAK—map 9

Long day scramble
Unofficial trails & route
Distance 19.8 km return from trailhead,
4.3 km return from Burstall Pass
Height gain 427 m, (1400 ft.) from pass
High point 2789 m (9150 ft.)
Map 82 J/14 Spray Lakes Reservoir

Access Via #88 Burstall Pass trail at the pass.

An easy scree scramble via the south ridge with variations lower down. Expect intermittent trails and a couple of hands-on steps near the top. While it can be climbed on a whim from Burstall Pass, most people should plan for this trip by starting early from the trailhead (it IS a nearly 20-km round trip!) and by waiting until the peak is snow free from mid-July on. And anyway, you're going to be spending a long time on the summit taking in the tremendous view.

Snow Peak from Ridge 147230. The route follows the right-hand ridge with the option of taking the grassy gully to the left of the big step.
Photo Alf Skrastins

NAMING NOTE Not exactly a glaciated peak, it was named after the extremely large cornice, which overhangs the east and northeast faces for half the year.

Start at the pass and head north along the very broad, undulating ridge of grass, slabs and last trees. On the left side are a series of depressions and holes. At the base of the mountain proper, below a small cliff and in line with the depressions, are the 3 D Caves, which are really two caves with three entrances. Don't even try venturing in. According to Jon, the bouldery passageways suddenly end in vertical ice. More obviously dangerous is the entrance to the elliptical pot.

Starting to the left of the elliptical pot, climb up alternating grass and scree to a wider, higher, sloping grassy bench.

Above is the big step leading to a shoulder. Some scramblers head right on scree towards the ridge line with the very much steeper east face, then make their way up rubble between small bands just to the left of the ridge and to the right of a crag. I like to traverse left, and when past the crag slog up the obvious swath of grass turning to scree at the top. (This is just left of the scree run descent.) Your choice.

Scramble up the second band.

Above the shoulder the ridge narrows and is banded. A twisty trail in scree avoids the first band by keeping to the left. The next band requires a scramble up its right edge above the northeast face. The third two-tier band is taken on the left side. All that remains now is a simple walk along the summit ridge above the cornice, perhaps, to the top (cairn, register). Some people carry on to a lower summit.

Of course you have been ogling the stupendous view all the way up. It's hard to imagine a more magnificent viewpoint for the Burstall/Palliser Pass area than this one. The standout peaks include Sir Douglas to the south, Talon Peak to the west and Assiniboine to the northwest. Down below you to the east you can trace the route from High Col to Birdwood Pass below the massive cliffs of Mt. Birdwood. By the time you tear yourself away from the summit, perhaps Leman Lake will be glittering in the late afternoon sunlight.

DESCENT TIP Return to the shoulder above the big step. From here a scree run is available at skier's right. Various trails lead into it.

The summit ridge. To right is the lower summit below Mt. Assiniboine.

90 FRENCH GLACIER—map 9

Long day hike
Unofficial trail, 1 creek crossing that is
avoidable via start 2.
Distance 7.7 km to high point
Height gain ~670 m (2200 ft.)
High point 2530 m (8300 ft.)
Maps 82 J/14 Spray Lakes Reservoir,
82 J/11 Kananaskis Lakes

Access Hwy. 742 (Smith-Dorrien/Spray
Trail) at Burstall Pass parking lot.

The trail up French Creek leads to larch
meadows and moraines at the foot of the
French Glacier. Getting there is not a
whole lot of fun, so you've got to be the
dedicated adventurous sort who enjoys a
long forest trudge. Skiing up this valley
is a lot simpler.

During its years of trampling by provincial and national team x-country skiers
en route to summer training camps on the
French Glacier, the old trail was improved
and in places carefully rerouted to miss
out the waterfalls. Now that skiers either
helicopter in or walk up North Kananaskis
Pass trail to a more permanent camp below
the Haig Glacier, the trail is again falling
into disuse. Nevertheless it is still follow-
able, but with more deadfall to step over
than one would wish for. There are also
variations here and there and I would be
surprised if your up route is exactly the
same as your down route.

French/Robertson Col from the high point.
The col is still 2 km distant.

Going farther from the end of the trail
through the French/Robertson Col to the
Haig Icefield and on down the Haig Glacier
to meet up with route #73B requires all the
paraphernalia of glacier travel. In summer,
those innocent looking snowfields have
snared quite a few people, including a
ranger fortuitously accompanied by two
search and rescue experts.

The alternative to the long trudge is a
visit to First Waterfall, or sorties to Second
and Third Waterfalls that often get missed
out in the rush to the glacier.

This trail is also used by scramblers
after Cegnfs and Mt. Murray. The latest
passion is to make a loop with Robertson
Glacier and the Burstall Pass trail via the
col between Piggy Plus and Mt. Robertson, which requires you be proficient on
steep snow.

TRAIL NOTE Nowadays there are two
starts. The regular start involves a crossing of French Creek, a calf-deep paddle
in summer. To avoid the paddle, use the
alternative start 2.

There are two starts to this trail:

1. Regular start 1.8 km The straightforward way on good logging roads entails an
extra hill climb and a crossing of French
Creek. Use if just going to First Waterfall.

The toe of the French Glacier and moss campion. Up right is Mt. Robertson.

Forgoing the gated gravel access road, cross Mud Lake Dam on trail. Join the road briefly, then swing right at the hiking sign onto Burstall Creek logging road. To left is French Creek pours out of two culverts into a muddy holding pond, diverted from its natural course into Mud Lake, a receptacle for all the muck carried down from the Robertson and French glaciers. Just after the logging road curves left, the very much fainter Hogarth Lakes logging road turns off to the right.

Keep straight and up the hill. At the top is a 4-way junction of logging roads with hiking sign. Go straight. (To right is the better Burstall Pass trail)

The unsigned French Creek logging road is more like a trail at this point as it climbs a hill, en route passing a side road to right. From the top it's a long, drawn-out descent into French Creek Valley. Amid vegetated side roads the main logging road is always obvious. Come to a T-junction on the bank of French Creek with cairn. Ahead rises the lower summit of Cegnfs. The name derives from the initials of the first ascent party: F, F, G, N, P and S (surnames), or C, P, M, J, P and B (first names.) Not only is the name unpronounceable, it is also unfathomable.

Go straight and wade French Creek. (The logging road to right leads to First Waterfall. See OPTION.) Since the last edition the remains of the bridge have departed downstream, replaced by a few logs that are inundated at high water.

Follow the logging road, which shortly intersects another logging road. The flagged road to left is the alternative start. (To right the less obvious "road" leads to an old camping spot with collapsible picnic table.) Continue ahead. Skip the next section of text and go to "To end of logging road."

2. Alternative start 2.1 km I like this route because there is no creek crossing, less climbing and you can easily bike the first 1.2 km, thereby reducing the return trip by 45 minutes or so.

Forgoing the gated gravel access road, cross Mud Lake Dam on trail. Join the gravel road and disregarding the hiking sign, simply follow the gravel road to its end. It takes 20 minutes on foot or five minutes by bike. Accompanying you on your right for most of the way is the French Creek diversion canal built in 1959. The road ends at the French Creek Dam that stops the water from following its natural course down Smith-Dorrien Creek Valley. Cross the overflow channel on a bridge.

Continue on the obvious logging road that wends rightish and becomes single track as it enters the forest of French Creek Valley. Near the creek, deadfall makes a diversion necessary. On the flagged trail climb up the bank to left, turn right at the top and descend back down to the logging road at flagging. Turn left. Shortly the logging road turns right and intersects the regular route (logging road) at flagging. Turn left.

To end of logging road 0.6 km
The logging road gains height up the left (east) bank of French Creek between Cegnfs and Mt. Burstall. Shortly beyond the road's high point at the narrows, you reach French Creek. The road crosses to the west bank above First Waterfall. Do NOT cross.

To Cegnfs/Mt. Murray turnoff 0.9 km
Transfer to a trail edging along the left (east) bank. Soon it climbs steeply up the bank into trees and then descends again to the willowy creekbed—a pattern to be repeated numerous times over the length of the valley. Make another uphill foray and descent towards the creekbed, only this time keep left everywhere on the forest bypass trail.

At a piece of red flagging the trail starts a longer, more gradual climb through dim, old-growth forest smelling like a newly opened bag of peat moss. En route cross two side creeks. Then listen for the roar of Second Waterfall below you. A little farther on descend and cross a side creek with grassy sides. To view Second

Waterfall, head down the side creek to its confluence with French Creek. If climbing Cegnfs and Mt. Murray, head up the creek. For French Glacier, continue along the trail.

To the headwall 1.4 km
The trail climbs the muddy far bank onto a flat with flowery glades, then makes a gradual return to the creek for a wet mossy stint. Again climb steeply up the bank for a longer stretch inland with much deadfall. Then round a right-hand bend of the river on steep hillside with one awkward step at high water.

For a while after, the trail is mostly creekside and is hard to spot on stoney ground. Then once again it climbs into the forest, soon arriving at a small meadow with a view ahead of a summit north of Mt. French that is nameless despite being prominent in all views. Soon after, the trail is blocked by deadfall and you must detour right (trail, flagging), then back left (no trail, no flagging). A flat leads to the foot of the forested headwall down which falls Third Waterfall in two steps.

To French Glacier 3 km
To get above the headwall, the old trail made a lengthy arc to the left. The newer version stamped out by athletes with superior VO_2 max, zigs straight up the steepest part of the headwall. Two-thirds up, go either straight or right at a split.

A relief section follows above a mini-canyon, ultimately returning you to creekside for an enjoyable stint alongside French Creek. Up ahead you can spot Sir Douglas poking up above the Robertson/Piggy Plus Col.

Opposite avalanche slopes falling from Piggy Plus the trail turns away from the river, cutting off the corner as it alternately climbs and traverses through meadows at treeline. A short descent leads into larch meadows below the hills and ridges of snow-streaked moraines. It's a gorgeous spot, but where is the French Glacier, you ask?

The trail carries on, turning left and leaving the meadows behind, follows a ridge of lateral moraine on the left side of the valley to its high point where it fades out. Still no view of the French Glacier.

Second Waterfall.

Third Waterfall, the upper step.

Descend a little, then climb the obvious snow-filled trough—longer and steeper than it appears—to last scree, the taking off point for the Robertson/French Col. (See the photo on page 273.) Finally a place to view the French Glacier, a little bit of the Haig Icefield spilling through the gap between mounts French and Robertson, which have to be two of the most spectacular mountains in K Country. Incredibly, the col is still 2 km away.

On the return, drop skier's left to the stoney flat at the toe of the glacier, where you will likely experience the glacier wind, a giant cooling fan on a stinking hot day. It's not as barren as you might suppose: dotting the flat are mounds of intensely coloured moss campions; springs bubbling up into small pools are fringed with grasses.

Unless you are crossing the ridge between Mt. Robertson and Piggy Plus to the Robertson Glacier, work your way back over the moraines to the trail, and return more or less the same way you came up.

The low ridge between Piggy Plus and Mt. Robertson is a scramblers route over to the Robertson Glacier which I have never done. Note the pools at the bottom of the photo.

OPTION

90A First Waterfall

Half day
Distance 1 km return, 4.3 km return to trailhead via route 1.

First Waterfall is usually missed in the haste to get to the glacier. Why not make it the destination of a leisurely half-day trip? Could also be combined with the alternative start to make a 4.6 km loop for those interested in river diversion techniques.

Hike the regular route, and at the T-junction on the bank of French Creek turn right, up another logging road that follows the right (west) bank of the creek. The road soon turns to single track. At a large fallen tree the trail climbs the bank to some flagging. Rather than carry on to another piece of flagging (beyond which all descents to the creek are STEEP), descend easily down left to the creek while the going is good. Turn right and edge your way along the bottom of the bank into a cliff-girt recess bisected by the two-tier waterfall.

First Waterfall.

91 RUMMEL LAKE — maps 9 & 4

Spray Lakes Reservoir from the upper cutblock.

Day hike
Unofficial/official trail, occasional sign-posts & markers
Distance 5 km to lake
Height gain 396 m (1300 ft.)
High point at lake 2210 m (7250 ft.)
Map 82 J/14 Spray Lakes Reservoir

Access Hwy. 742 (Smith-Dorrien/Spray Trail). Park beside of highway opposite the Mt. Shark Road.
Also accessible from #93 and 32.

To some people, this little lake, named after Baroness Elizabeth "Lizzie" Rummel, surpasses Chester Lake in both colour, setting and number of larches. It is one of the few trails with a biffy at its destination. Lest you get too excited, only winter camping is allowed.

TRAIL NOTE Since the last edition the trail has become semi-official. In 2007/8 the final section was rerouted for the benefit of snowshoers and skiers through avalanche-safe forest. For hikers this is not too exciting, and many still prefer to follow the old, unofficial trail along the south bank of Rummel Creek.

Lakes near timberline are often a stepping stone to the alpine above, in this case Rummel Pass and the opportunity to go right through to Hwy. 40.

To junction with trail #93, 3.5 km
The route starts from the east side of the highway at the winter camping sign.

Follow a logging road that heads southeast, paralleling the highway to a large plantation/née cutblock. At the Peter Lougheed Provincial Park boundary it turns left, and narrowing to trail width, climbs easily past the odd clump of white rhododendron and Labrador tea to the plantation's top left-hand corner. A gangway between mature forest leads into the upper cutblock, where the gradient steepens and you are treated to views of the mountains about Spray Lakes Reservoir through to Commonwealth Peak.

At the top of the cutblock you again turn southeast and slip into forest, following a broad, gently inclined ridge high above Rummel Creek. Here the forest is wonderfully open, with grouseberry and red heather underfoot. There are three major dips, then the trail turns sharp left at a T-junction marked with an arrow. (The trail ahead with a stump laid across it is the "wrong" route, but the "right route" if you're taking the grizzly trail to Chester Lake. See #93.)

To bridge junction 0.4 km
The trail, becoming rooty, descends to Rummel Creek and runs alongside it to a T-junction at a bridge. From here there are two routes to the lake that could be used to make a loop:

Rummel Lake via winter route 1.1 km
The official winter route is not scenic (except when the trees are plastered in snow), but it's completely free of avalanche danger should you be wandering up here near the end of the spring avalanche cycle. Look for yellow markers on trees.

Turn left and cross the bridge over Rummel Creek. A trail starts you off, then you navigate from marker to marker through forest with steeper sections. Near the end you again hit a trail that leads to the biffy from where trails lead down to the lake at the outlet.

Rummel Lake via summer route 1.1 km
Keep straight past an "avalanche area do not enter" sign. The trail climbs a bit, then runs alongside Rummel Creek. Just after a bit of meadow the trail turns sharp right and reaches the *mauvais pas*—the rocky bank above a cascade. The ledge traverse has got slicker with time, so much so that hikers have taken it into their own hands to develop a bypass trail. It starts back in the meadow at a small cairn, then heads right, cutting up and over a little ridge. Right now it's a little faint (look for branches laid on either side), but in time should get better IF EVERYONE GOES

Winter biffy!

THAT WAY. It rejoins the main trail just above the cascade.

Continue between a steep scree slope and shoreline willows to a tributary—often dry—issuing from the cirque to the right. After another stony stint you enter a small meadow distinguished by the "flag tree" that, sadly, keeled over in the winter of 1990. It must have been a quite magnificent tree in its time, but it's now a recumbent trunk of incredible girth, festooned with fluorescent wolf lichen and sheltering all kinds of creepy-crawlies within its rotting heartwood. The trail then climbs a short, steep hill into forest, shortly descending more gradually to Rummel Creek. Cross via logs. Now on the left bank, the trail climbs without pause to the lake.

Before you can say "Who's got the lunch?" it's mandatory to read the latest signs and check out the trail to the biffy. Then wander the grassy left shore of the lake, which is lovely, its translucent turquoise waters overlooked by Mt. Galatea and its southwest outlier which throws down cliffs and screes to the water's edge. And, as mentioned, there are larches.

Rummel Lake below the southwest outlier of Mt. Galatea.

GOING FARTHER

91A Rummel Pass

Unofficial trail, route with cairns
Distance 2.4 km from lake, 4.3 km to Lost Lake
Height gain 192 m (630 ft.) from lake
Height loss 375 m (1230 ft.) to Lost Lake
High point 2402 m (7880 ft.)

Getting to Rummel Pass, located between The Tower and Mt. Galatea, is fairly easy on grass and scree with no steep slopes to contend with. Most people return the same way or just go to the first tarn and back. To view the tarns before the water sinks underground, visit during the first half of July.

Going farther to Lost Lake in the southwest fork of Galatea Creek ups the difficulty a couple of notches and requires accurate routefinding. However, if you've got two vehicles and a willing party who can hack steep slopes and a little bush-whacking, why not continue on to Hwy. 40 via #32 and 30. Total kilometrage of the through route is 16.1.

To Rummel Pass 2.4 km

Follow the trail along the meadows of the northwest shore. Not too far along it turns left and climbs open forest to a bench. Turn right and continue through last trees into a big expanse of flat meadow. Make for the obvious gap between Mt. Galatea and The Tower, a name transposed from The Fortress. Around a big rock the trail peters out, and rather than tromp over scree, it's easier to cross the valley to the right side and pick up a cairned trail in grass that leads directly to the first tarn. From this direction The Tower is considered a walk-up, if 777 vertical metres of steep scree appeals. Personally, I would rather loll by the tarn and through binoculars watch someone else's struggle while slurping nectarines. Interestingly, in fall this tarn dries to a long swath of soft white sand that is a pleasure to walk on.

A second tarn lies beyond the upcoming scree field, one that in mid-summer is still rimmed by snowbanks and has mini-icebergs wafting about. A trail develops in the scree of the left shore

The first tarn in summer below The Tower. The route to the pass heads through the gap.

and continues beyond the tarn up a short scree rise to cairns. Walk through a stoney defile. At the far end the trail reappears in grass and winds around left onto the pass at the edge of a drop-off.

There is something in the configuration of the mountains at this spot that squeezes the air and sends it battering like a wild thing on the walls of The Tower. (Heaven knows what this place is like in a full-fledged gale.) So you hunker down behind a small crag and look ahead to a new dark landscape holding Alvin Guinn's lost lake.

To Lost Lake and beyond 1.9 km

The same trail continues down left over rubbly ledges and across a big scree slope. Before reaching a ridge, cut down a ribbon of grass into the bowl. Exit to the next level down via a sheep trail on the left side of a cement-hard slope littered with ball bearings. Boulders, dribbled down the slope, have fanned out across the flat at the bottom into the trees, which is a trifle disconcerting.

On the flat make for the grassy draw ahead. A trail develops on the right side of the fledgling stream that, without warning, plunges over a cliff. Now what? The trail crosses a side creek, descends to the lip of the drop-off, climbs to an overlook on the right, then drops over the edge. While there's no cliff at this point, it's a branch-clinging slither for about 35 vertical metres.

Arrive in forest just west of the lake. The question here is which way around the lake to go?

Right The right (southeast) shore lures until dense thickets and cliffs drive you up onto grassy bluffs. Follow a bit of a game trail along a bench and at lake's end drop down to the outlet. Pick up the valley trail at the forest edge.

Left My preference is to follow the game trail around the left (northwest) shore. Just beyond the lake proper, cross the creek on a beaver dam to the southeast bank and continue to a junction with the main trail. Turn left.

Now read #32 and 30 for the route out to Hwy. 40.

Rummel Pass, looking towards Mt. Galatea. At left you can spot The Fortress.

92 CHESTER LAKE—map 4

Day hike, bike 'n' hike
Official trail with signposts
Distance 4.3 km
Height gain 305 m (1000 ft.)
High point 2210 m (7250 ft.) at lake
Map 82 J/14 Spray Lakes Reservoir

Access Hwy. 742 (Smith-Dorrien/Spray Trail) at Chester Lake parking lot.
Also accessible from route #91 via #93.

This jade-coloured lake is a year-round popular destination and you are unlikely to be alone. In addition to the hiking crowd, scramblers use the trail to access mounts Chester and Galatea and Gusty Peak, and boulderers to access Elephant Rocks.

The start up steeply inclined logging roads is less than aesthetic, but after that it's a pleasant and mostly easy walk though alternating forest and flowery meadow. Biking to bike racks at the end of the logging roads reduces the hiking to 4.2 km total. However, if you're like me you'll be pushing a good part of the way

Chester Lake below the northeast ridge of Mt. Chester.

in, constantly reminding yourself that the return rush will be worth it.

NOTES 1. Since the last edition the route has reverted to the ski trail. 2. After decades of traditional camping by the lake, backcountry camping is no longer allowed anywhere.

To end of logging roads 2.2 km
The logging road leaves the top end of the parking lot near the biffy. After the gate keep straight, then veer left at the T-junction with Blue upper leg ski trail and cross Chester Creek.

Shortly after, the snowshoe trail turns off to the right. At the T-junction following, turn right. (The logging road to left is the skier's descent route, which is 20 m shorter!)

Between here and the next signpost at the "5-way" junction the winding route is obvious, taking every uphill option. You aren't likely to mistake overgrown skid trails for the road. At the "5-way" junction, stay on the ski trail, which is the middle fork in a prong of three. (The logging road to right is the old hiking route.)

At the end of the straight is a T-junction. Leave the bikes here and turn right onto a trail. (The logging road to left is the skier's descent route.)

To Chester Lake 2.1 km
A refurbished trail with rocks on either side to keep you from straying climbs through spruce and fir forest. After the terrain levels you alternate between forest and small hummocky meadows. A shorter climb brings you to a large meadow extending right across Chester Creek, now seen bubbling away to your right. Ahead is a clear view of mounts Chester and Galatea, Gusty Peak and The Fortress — all scrambles per Kane. This meadow is also the place of departure for route #93 to Rummel Lake trail.

A biffy on the left precedes your arrival at Chester Lake, where you'll no doubt be greeted by resident whiskey jacks after your lunch. At the outlet, the trail splits, with one trail bridging the creek into a larch clump and pica rockpile, the other following the west shoreline.

Lawns in Upper Chester Creek.
Photo Roy Millar

GOING FARTHER

92A Upper Chester Creek

Unofficial trail, route
Distance 2.3 km to tarn
Height gain 259 m (850 ft.) to tarn
High point 2454 m (8050 ft.) at tarn

The scrambler's access to Gusty Peak and the alternative descent route from The Fortress/Chester Col.

Follow the lakeshore trail past the turn-off to Three Lakes Valley. The trail climbs into a grassy draw below Gusty Peak, following the edge of the left-hand scree slope to the lip of a hanging valley.

The upper Chester Creek valley between Gusty Peak and The Fortress is filled with rocks of all sizes and shapes, piled up in great heaps like unwashed dishes. Going farther is unpleasant if you're aiming for the blue tarn at the valley head. Just before the tarn, the shale slope to right leads to Chester/Fortress Col. Nearer at hand, meadows as immaculate as city lawns border the infant creek, which sees daylight for perhaps 50 metres before sinking into the ground below a permanent snowbank and resurging at a waterfall lower down.

The second tarn in Three Lakes Valley. Looking out to mounts French, Robertson and Sir Douglas. Photo Annette Le Faive

92B Three Lakes Valley

Unofficial trail, route
Distance 2.2 km to third tarn
Height gain 244 m (800 ft.)
High point 2454 m (8050 ft.)

The picturesque valley to the north of Chester Creek holds three small tarns. It's the scrambler's route to Mt. Galatea.

From the lakeshore trail, turn left onto a well-used trail that climbs over the intervening ridge of larches and jumbo-sized boulders (Elephant Rocks) to the valley north of Chester Creek.

The trail continues upstream to the first tarn, whose damp shores are beautified by clouds of silky white cotton grass. Climb the grassy headwall above, noting tufts of goat hair snagged on knobbly boulders. The finger valley between Mt. Galatea and Gusty Peak is a goat hot spot and if you're lucky you can spot them feeding on delicacies in damp, slanting gullies high up to the right. Tarn no. 3 is a sink lake, often disappointing. Tarn no. 2, sited picturesquely on the headwall's brink, is a place to linger by.

Elephant Rocks. Photo Rachel Oggy

93 CHESTER LAKE TO RUMMEL LAKE—map 4

Day hike
Unofficial trail & route, creek crossing
Distance 3.6 km
Height gain and loss south to north
61 m (200 ft.)
High point 2277 m (7470 ft.)
Map 82 J/14 Spray Lakes Reservoir

Access Hwy. 742 (Smith-Dorrien/Spray Trail).
1. Via #92 Chester Lake.
2. Via #91 Rummel Lake.

Every time I've been to Rummel Lake I've always met a hiker who's come in from the Chester Lake trail. They are usually found recuperating at the junction and talking in a quivering voice about 'the grizzlies.' Don't let this deter you from following this route; there's never been a close encounter and the route between the two lakes, or to be scrupulously correct, between the two access trails, is surprisingly scenic. But with all those grizzlies around, it's best to be a group.

Leave Chester Lake trail at the third (last) meadow before the lake. Strike up-meadow to the left and through a few token trees on the watershed to a brown-coloured pond marking the southeast edge of a large, flat meadow, which is the middle portion of Three Lakes Valley. The whole hillside between this meadow and

Easy meadow-walking in the draw.
Looking northwest to mountains
beyond Spray Lakes Reservoir.

Elephant Rocks has been torn apart by grizzlies digging up yummy hedysarum roots. Yet, for decades happy campers at Chester Lake seemed blissfully unaware of what was going on less than half a kilometre away in Three Lakes Valley.

Pass left of the pond, following the left (south) edge of the meadow to Three Lakes Valley Creek. Cross the creek.

Indistinct at first, a good trail materializes in the grass of the far bank and climbs diagonally from right to left across steep, flowery slopes. As it turns northwest into the trees the gradient eases and red flagging appears, indicating keep right at questionable junctions. Cross over the watershed and emerge (red flagging marking the spot) in a draw filled by an extremely long longitudinal meadow between larches. Through the V are blue mountain shapes. To your right rise steep, grassy slopes that I like to check for big brown shapes.

The trail continues down the centre of the draw, which seems endless. But there comes a point when the meadow fills up with bushes and it's here (flagging) where the trail climbs the bank on the right past a large dead tree into spruce forest. The final stretch is slightly downhill and straightforward to the junction with Rummel Lake trail.

94 HEADWALL LAKES — map 4

Day hike, bike 'n' hike
Official & unofficial trails, route
Distance 7 km from usual access
Height gain 457 m (1500 ft.) to upper
lake from usual access
High point 2341 m (7680 ft.)
Map 82 J/14 Spray Lakes Reservoir

Usual Access Hwy. 742 (Smith-Dorrien/Spray Trail) at Chester Lake parking lot.
Shortcut Access Park 1 km south of Chester Lake parking lot by the side of the highway. There are two logging roads heading into the bush close together. Choose the left-hand one and arrive on Blue ski trail in a few minutes. Turn right.

This has to be the most delectable valley on the east side of the highway, containing within its boundaries all the finest components of mountain scenery: blue lakes, waterfalls, meadows, a karst pavement.

The prerequisite to heaven is a jaunt through Smith-Dorrien's network of skiing and mountain-biking trails.

Lower Headwall Lake.

Colour-coded logging roads make access to the valley easy. After this you follow an occasionally steep and well-used trail to the upper lake (which is also the scrambler's access to The Fortress).

Bike/push bikes to the end of logging roads and enjoy a fabulous run down at the end of the day.

FROM USUAL ACCESS
To Blue-yellow ski trail 1 km
If you want to be officially correct and add 2 km to the trip it's up to you. At least your vehicle won't be covered in dust when you return.

Your best bet is Blue lower leg, a ski trail which runs along the top edge of the parking lot from left to right and into the trees, heading in a southeasterly direction. It descends slightly, then turns sharp left and climbs a steep hill. At the top the trail turns right and meanders along to a T-junction with a road coded yellow. Turn left on Blue-yellow.

Just before this junction the shortcut route comes in from the right.

287

The cascade between the two lakes.
Photo Alf Skrastins

Waterfall on the west side of the upper lake. Photo Alf Skrastins

To end of logging roads 2.7 km
Blue-yellow ski trail/logging road winds uphill past a spate of skid trails to Blue upper leg. Keep right on Yellow. Yellow climbs to a logged area on a ridge, then continues more easily past Orange upper junction to Headwall Creek bridge. After the creek crossing, the road resumes climbing, zigging left, then right. At the top of the hill is a cutblock on the left side. At a cairn leave Yellow ski trail/logging road and turn left onto a single-track trail.

To Lower Headwall Lake 2.8 km
The trail heads into the forest and back to Headwall Creek Valley bottom. Continue along the right (east) bank through willows, more forest and then below a scree slope. Barely back in trees, the trail turns right and climbs, twisting up the steep side slope to treeline. At the top turn left and in two traverses separated by small step, arrive below the first headwall — a gleaming white wall of rock. The trail climbs up the right side of it on scree to a fascinating karst pavement scraped by a passing glacier. Just ahead and below you is lower Headwall Lake, cradled in a rock-girt bowl.

To Upper Headwall Lake 0.5 km
Follow the trail around the right shoreline. Then sidestepping crags, climb the second headwall on grass to the right of the tumbling stream that spouts out of the hillside at three-quarter height. Just over the top lies the beautiful blue upper lake, its setting austere amid screes and crags. At the head of the valley rises The Fortress.

Make your way along the east shore, looking across the lake to a waterfall tumbling down a cliff into the water. The upper valley beyond the lake is greener than you expect and there are many small waterfalls in the fledgling Headwall Creek to delight in.

Upper Headwall Lake. In the background is The Fortress, showing the route up the left-hand skyline. Photo Alf Skrastins

95 THE FORTRESS—map 4

Long day scramble
Unofficial trail & route
Distance 9.6 km from trailhead, 2.7 km from Upper Headwall Lake
Height gain 671 m (2200 ft.) from Upper Headwall Lake, 1128 m (3700 ft.) from trailhead
High point 3002 m (9850 ft.)
Map 82 J/14 Spray Lakes Reservoir

Access Hwy. 742 (Smith-Dorrien/Spray Trail). Via #94 Headwall Lakes at the upper lake.

The Fortress, which appears impregnable from Hwy. 40, is a walk-up from the back, accessible to hikers who can handle scree and a few metres of easy scrambling. There's even an intermittent trail. For vertigo sufferers there's certainly not much to be scared of. However, don't think of it as just a detour from Headwall Lakes; plan an early start from the parking lot and pick a fine day. In late October of 1997 two descending hikers went off route in thick mist, resulting in injury and a difficult helicopter rescue.

To Fortress/Chester Col 2 km
Follow the east shore of Upper Headwall Lake into the upper valley.

At a pool, start up low-angle scree, aiming for the low point on the ridge to the left (northwest) at 235314, which is the col between The Fortress and Mt. Chester. The slope steepens below the col, which, you discover, is not one, but *two* cols separated by splinters of rock with a cairn. What a situation! Apart from being able to look into two valleys at once, Mt. Chester, which normally resembles a pudding, has an east ridge built like a ripsaw.

To the summit 0.7 km
At the col turn right and follow the trail up the southwest ridge. The first rise is the crux: scree on top of slab. That

done with, the ridge broadens and the gradient eases slightly. The scree is still a trial, though, and you may find it easier to stick to the rocky crest and leave those gaudy orange slopes on the right for a fast descent. Higher up, after passing a couple of cairns, the angle eases even more as the ridge tapers and you become conscious of the drop on the right and then on the left.

Approaching the summit rampart, the trail cunningly turns left, traversing below the cliff band on broken ground. As you're about to drop off the edge of the world, scramble diagonally to the right up big blocks to a tilted platform of scree and walk to the summit (cairn, rock shelter).

The view is superb, taking in Mt. Assiniboine, of course, and the white fang of Joffre farther south, the whole of the Opal Range, Guinn's Pass and Fortress Mountain ski area, to name just some of the features. With care, Fortress Lake can be spotted 823 vertical metres below the eastern abyss.

OPTIONAL DESCENT

95A to Chester Lake

Chester and Headwall creeks share the same trailhead, so why not make a 17.2 km loop by descending from the Fortress/Chester Col into upper Chester Creek? While the odd party comes up this way, it makes a far better descent route.

Return to the Fortress/Chester Col. From the low point farthest south, drop down the concave west slope, 230 vertical m of steep black shale you can dig your heels into. Often there is snow. On arriving in upper Chester Creek Valley, boulder-hop to the sink and pick up the trail taking you down to Chester Lake. Then read #92.

View from The Fortress/Chester Col of the ascent route to the summit. Photo Niccole Germscheid

The easy scrambling just below the summit. Photo Roy Millar

The Fortress/Chester Col. Rising above it is the serrated northeast ridge of Mt. Chester. Photo Roy Millar

96 JAMES WALKER CREEK—map 4

Approaching the lake below the headwall. In the background is the south ridge of Mt. James Walker.

Day hike, bike 'n' hike
Official trail with signposts & coloured markers, unofficial trail with pink flagging and cairns, route
Distance 4.3 km to lake
Height gain 259 m (850 ft.) to lake
High point 2118 m (6950 ft.) at lake
Map 82 J/14 Spray Lakes Reservoir, 82 J/11 Kananaskis Lakes

Access Hwy. 742 (Smith-Dorrien/Spray Trail) at Sawmill day-use area.

Like Headwall Lakes, this valley is accessed via the colour-coded Smith-Dorrien skiing and mountain-biking network of logging roads. So it's a fairly easy walk to the lake. Once there, you're within reach of twin cirques divided by Mt. James Walker. This trail also accesses the scrambler's route up Mt. James Walker.

Biking the logging roads saves time.

To James Walker logging road 1.8 km
Start up the logging road to the left of the biffy (sign). After the gate is a T-junction. Go left onto Red/yellow. A boulder signals

waves of uphills to Upper Red junction (sign), which is also the snowshoe trail. Keep left on Yellow. Turn second right onto the James Walker Creek logging road. This is the road with tread closest to James Walker Creek crossing.

To lake 2.5 km
The logging road curves around into the valley of James Walker Creek, climbing through spruce forest to a levelling off where little spruce are beginning to infiltrate the road. Finally, in a patch of willows the road downgrades to trail.

The next 1.5 km is a beautiful walk that undulates at the edge of larch meadows strewn with boulders. Descend to the unnamed lake, which is quite attractive with a touch of deep azure, one tiny island and a surround of grass. In the background is Mt. James Walker, named in 1975 after Calgary's "Citizen of the Century." To your right rises 2000 feet of North Kent, from this direction a textbook example of an anticlinal mountain.

GOING FARTHER

96A The Cirques

Unofficial trail, route
Distance 3.9 km max
Height gain 320+ m (1050+ ft.)
High point 2438+ m (8000+ ft.)

A more strenuous trip up a headwall to the upper valleys. Anyone willing to sweat a bit is rewarded with meadows, waterfalls, tarns, karst, a remnant glacier and the amazing Grotto Spring.

The waterfalls at the forks.

The Headwall 1.2 km
There are two ways to start off, depending on water levels:

1. At low water walk round the right side of the lake to where the inlet stream pours into it. A trail starting in willows follows the right (east) bank of the creek. Jump a side creek, then take a flagged diversion around some deadfall.

2. At high water walk around the left shore to the inlet stream. Follow it up until a fallen tree across the creek gives easy access to the east bank trail.

It's not long before the trail starts climbing, following the noisy creek past many waterfalls. There's an increase in step-over deadfall prior to the forks where the creeks from their respective cirques meet in parallel waterfalls.

Here the trail turns away to the right. A left turn signals a short section of zigs—the steepest part of the route. This leads into the leftward traverse at the base of scree slopes below a high rockband. Cross the right-hand fork. Just past the crossing a side trail leads to the source of the creek at Grotto Spring—a photo opportunity not to be missed.

Continue the uphill traverse on scree into alpine meadows where the trail peters out. A decision has to made: which cirque to explore.

Grotto Spring.

The right-hand cirque with first tarn and knubbly rock with fossils.

The mouth of the left-hand finger valley.
Photo Allan Mandel

North (left-hand) cirque 2.7 km

Trail's end is in line for the left-hand finger valley, a long, stony wasteland pitted with sinks and two small tarns (sinks storing stagnant water). It has two interesting anomalies: a glacier beyond a mound of moraine, and no mountain at the valley head. The topo map is wildly wrong on both counts.

Northeast (right-hand) cirque 1.5 km

The shorter valley between mounts Inflexible and James Walker is the more attractive. To get there either climb over the large grassy hill, use the gap to its left or traverse around the hill to the right into a large area of meadow where innumerable tiny creeks from melting snow gather together, then sink, following some underground passage to the creek's resurgence below the headwall cliffs at Grotto Spring.

This right-hand branch holds a particularly beautiful tarn in a green and white setting of grass and limestone pavement. A string of shallow tarns can be followed up valley to a deeper pool hidden within the moraines of the valley head.

97 "NORTH KENT" — map 4

Day scramble
Unofficial trail, route
Distance 3.9 km one way
Height gain 1106 m (3630 ft.)
High point 2904 m (9530 ft.)
Maps 82 J/11 Kananaskis Lakes, 82 J/14 Spray Lakes Reservoir

Access Hwy. 742 (Smith-Dorrien/Spray Trail) at Sawmill day-use area.

The unnamed peak at 254256 anchors the north end of Kent Ridge and is the highest point along it, nearly 300 m (1000 ft.) higher than Mt. Kent, which I have always considered a mere bump along the ridge. Despite its height and ease of ascent, it's been a rarely climbed peak to date, with few entries in the summit register.

The Smith-Dorrien skiing, snowshoeing and mountain-biking network of logging roads gives access to open slopes, after which you're in for a relentless uphill slog. There's no real scrambling unless you

North Kent from Hero Knob, showing almost the whole route plus the route up the west outlier at bottom left.

count the push up a stoney gully. The one absolute essential is finding an overgrown logging road dating back to the 1970s.

Despite the prized view into Kent Creek from North Kent's summit, its western outlier is actually the more interesting trip! Combining the two is another option.

ACCESS NOTE The access via Sawmill Creek (thanks, Rod!) is different to Andrew's access in *More Scrambles in the Canadian Rockies* that heads up the west face of the outlier from Red-yellow trail.

Logging road section 1.6 km
The trail — a grassed-over logging road — leaves Sawmill parking lot just beyond the biffy at a signpost. Pass beyond the gate to a T-junction. Keep straight to a 4-way junction with Red ski trail to right and Red-yellow to left. Go straight on Sawmill Snowshoe trail with red marker.

Shortly the logging road starts climbing and heads right. On the left-hand corner, the upper leg of Red comes in from the right. Still following the snowshoe signs, zig left, then up the fall line to a T-junction. Here the snowshoe trail (also upper Red) turns off to the left. You zig right.

At the next bend and T-junction zig left (cairn). The road is becoming ingrown with mini-spruce. Zig right and follow

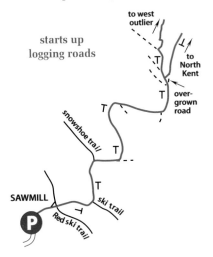

single tracks one side or the other of the road bed, being careful to stay left and up-hill. The road bends left and up the ridge line (the south ridge of the west outlier).

Coming up in 1.3 km, at about 244240, is a difficult piece of navigation where the road forks. Only the ridgeline road can be guessed at. There is absolutely no trace of your road to the right. What you do is this. Continue a little higher up the ridgeline road to a divergence of flagging at a wee cairn. Follow the flagging to the right along a narrow trail that joins the right-hand "road" in a minute or two. Go leftish following flagging through the trees. The roadbed is flat and becomes obvious as it traverses a steep slope to the right of the ridge line. After passing a crag on the left side, it sheds itself of trees and DESCENDS into the head of Sawmill Creek Valley. It ends a little way up from the creekbed below meadows sweeping down from the west outlier. Ahead you can see the next part of the route up the north fork gully between the west outlier and North Kent. Doesn't look too far.

The col at 246254. At left rises the west outlier (see #97A). In the background is Mt. Birdwood.

The summit. Mt. Inflexible at centre, Mt. James Walker at left.

To Col 246254 1.3 km

Continue on a trail to where it peters out. Then either follow strips of meadow in the valley bottom, veering left at the forks into the north fork, or make a slightly rising traverse of the meadow just above tree ribbons and on trail descend into the north fork.

Follow the north fork gully to the col, which is much higher and much farther away than it looks (all of 335 vertical m, 1100 vertical ft.). Alternate between the stones of the creekbed and the banks to either side; wherever you find remnants of game trails.

At 2484 m (8150 ft.) the col is cushiony with convenient hollows to sink into for a rest. To left the west outlier rises steeply with rock bands. Ahead are — weather instruments, though what they are doing here is one of K Country's mysteries.

To the summit 1 km

Turn right, up the billowy west ridge of the mountain. Dryas and heather with a few scattered larches give way to an endless scree slope, grossly foreshortened. After 424 vertical m (1390 ft.) of putting one step in front of another you arrive at the summit cairn perched above drop-offs. Early in the season be wary of a cornice on the east side.

Naturally the view is 7-star, with mounts Assiniboine, Sir Douglas, Joffre and King George all in one frame. Mt. Inflexible is the big yellow heap immediately to the east. To its left is James Walker Creek, its upper valleys separated by the ghostly pale peak of James Walker, which from this direction has an elegant bent to it. Spot the glacier in the left-hand finger valley?

What you have come for, though, is the bird's-eye view into the head of Kent Creek. Enjoy its meadows, larches and tarns vicariously, because getting to the valley head is a something hikers rarely aspire to. Bounding the valley to the east is Mt. Lawson, its incredibly long southeast ridge ending at #101, which looks "bloody miles away" as Tony likes to put it.

Return the same way unless you're a really proficient scrambler, in which case another 11 km of Kent Ridge is available. Just bear in mind that while everyone else will be stuffing their faces at Corkscrew Bills in Canmore, you will still be somewhere on the ridge.

OPTION

97A West Outlier 244254

Unofficial trail
Distance 2.9 km one way
Height gain 676 m (2220 ft.)
High Point 2536 m (8320 ft.)

A short, rather beautiful ridge that is bound to become more popular than the trudge up North Kent. And it comes with a trail.

The trail follows the top of the eastern cliff.

To the open slopes 1.8 km
At the flagged junction near 244240 continue uphill on the ridgeline road. Look for flagging at points of infiltration. After the gradient eases off and the road turns leftish, come to place where the road is blocked by branches. On the right bank is a cairn atop a stump and some flagging on a tree beyond. This is where you leave the road and take to the forested south ridge.

At first the trail is minimal. After you climb over two fallen trees, it picks up and follows the right side of the ridge above steep slopes. Squirm under a fallen tree onto open slopes.

The ridge 1.1 km
The ridge rises fairly gradually with steeper steps here and there, the grass of lower down giving way to slaty orange rocks harbouring a wide variety of alpines including roseroot and two types of yellow draba. Most spectacular are the big bunches of alpine cinquefoil. The ridge's main feature, though, is the vertical (even overhanging) cliff lining the east side.

The summit is capped with soft, tufty grass ideal for view gazing. Should the west wind be cold and blustery you can hunker down below the rock band that fortuitously peters out at the summit. Of course, the view to the east is blocked by the sprawling mass of North Kent. But to the west the whole of the Spray Mountains is displayed, from Tent Ridge to Indefatigable and across to Hero Knob.

OPTIONAL DESCENT

Possibly you want to climb North Kent on the same day, or return via the north fork gully for a change. So, first you have to descend to the col at 246254. (See the photo 2 pages back.)

This is not as easy as it looks from above, and if there's snow on it, forget it. (See photo on p. 223 of *More Scrambles in the Canadian Rockies*.) To find ways through two rock bands, go right at the first one and left at the second.

98 "HERO KNOB"—map 8

Day scramble
Unofficial trail, route, creek crossing
Distance 4.3 km
Height gain 710 m (2330 ft.)
High point 2524 m (8280 ft.)
Map 82 J/11 Kananaskis Lakes

Access Hwy. 742 (Smith-Dorrien/Spray Trail). Park by the west side of the highway at 240228, 540 m south of Sawmill access road.

Hero Knob is an eastern outlier of Mt. Smith-Dorrien at 228216. Extreme skiers doing the Black Prince traverse pass below it at the second col, which I hesitate to call a pass. K Country features it in their avalanche report, but spells it "Heros nob." The consensus of people asked about the name think it immortalizes not a Greek god's head, nor the Health & Education Research Operative Services, but some skier with a death wish—Sean from Canmore?—who was the first to ski one of those horrendously steep and narrow gullies off the summit.

In summer there is no need to be a hero. The approach is fast and easy via a logging road and trail up the unnamed valley between Warspite Creek and Murray Creek. The headwall offers up some scree, and while the summit ridge is decidedly knobbly, most of it can be avoided. Take Tevas and bear deterrents.

The valley 2.4 km
Head down the west bank into the forest, where the old logging road is obvious. It

View from Hwy. 742 of Hero Knob (left) and Mt. Smith-Dorrien.

trends downhill to Smith-Dorrien Creek and crosses it—an easy crossing. Some way before the crossing, put on the Tevas to slosh through marshy ground near a small pond.

On the west bank, the road is in remarkably good shape as it climbs gradually through spruce forest, then turns right, into the valley confines. Almost at once it narrows to trail width where it passes through a logged area (go either way at a split). As road it crosses a band of old forest with a fallen giant you skirt around. The line of it can then be traced across a grassy avalanche slope and into a final band of forest where the road ends close to the creek. A trail continues along the right bank, en route crossing a wash of stones, to a long, flat, willowy meadow at the valley head. Many trails lead through to the bottom of the headwall.

The headwall 0.6 km
The direct route works best. Don't be tempted by the creek to the left.

Starting you off is a trail climbing diagonally up the right slope of a small knoll. From behind the knoll, continue ahead through a grassy avenue onto the prominent grass slope where the gradient steepens. Pass a line of grizzly digs. You can hear the sound of water to your left.

Just below the rockband, a bit of a trail leads left to the centre creek. Don't cross. It's easier just to clamber straight up the rocks of the bed and through the gap into the bottom of a steep fan of scree, where the creek goes underground. During its brief re-emergence as a cascade, stay to its left, then traverse to the right above it, out of the fan and onto easier ground. Head left up a scree rib to the top.

The summit 1.3 km

You find yourself in a hanging valley below the formidable black walls of Leaning Mountain, a name coined by first ascentionist John Martin to describe the cornice-like profile of the summit rock ridge. The black chute to left is the skier's descent route from the first col!

Turn right and walk up the scree and meadow of the trough towards the second col. Higher up, climb onto the south ridge of the knob to your right. A trail of sorts winds through dense sub-alpine scrub harbouring masses of a snowy-white lousewort called parrot's beak (*pedicularis racemosa*). The going is faster when the ridge turns to grass.

Arriving below the first knob on the summit ridge, you make a decision. Hardcore scramblers can tackle the knobs,

One of the summit knobs. Leaning Mountain in the background.

which are exposed to a deepening drop on the left. Anyone who gets the wobblies in such places can traverse the right (east) slope on a scree/grass mix between the crest and a rockband, and at the obvious place work their way back up to the ridge not far from the summit. The actual top is quite narrow. (The knobs carry on down the far side a way and somewhere between them is the kamikaze ski gully.)

This higher vantage point gives a superb view of Leaning Mountain. Close at hand, the great northern cliffs of Mt. Smith-Dorrien, make Mt. Murray and Cegnfs look like pygmies. Across the valley rises North Kent and the whole of Kent Ridge.

Return

Back on easy ground, turn west and descend the west ridge towards second col. It's satisfying to look back at Hero Knob to view the vertiginous northwest flank you were walking above!

Before reaching the col proper, run black shale into the head of the trough, revelling in the many flowers dotting the slope, including beautiful big bunches of pink creeping beardtongue. At the bottom keep left and eventually join up with your ascent route.

99 BLACK PRINCE CIRQUE interpretive trail — map 8

Half day hike
Official trail
Distance to lake 4.1 km return
Height gain 122 m (400 ft.) return
High point 1820 m (5970 ft.)
Map 82 J/11 Kananaskis Lakes

Access Hwy. 742 (Smith-Dorrien/Spray Trail) at Black Prince day-use area.

A somewhat hilly trail leads to little Warspite Lake in a cirque below Mt. Black Prince. A grizzly frequents the area (possibly the same one that frequents the slopes of Indefatigable and Gypsum Creek) but keeps to himself and troubles no-one.

Carrying on to Black Prince Lake is a whole new ball game and is the scrambler's approach route to Mt. Warspite.

To Warspite Lake and back 4.2 km
The trail starts behind the garbage disposal unit. It crosses a logging road en route to a bridge over Smith-Dorrien Creek, then doubles back to the logging road on the southwest bank. Climb the hill to the cutblock. Where the road starts to bend left, a trail turns right to a bench (good view of Kent Ridge), then descends to Warspite Creek through menziesia and rhododendron bushes, Near the bottom of the hill, just after interpretive sign no. 5, is a T-junction with the return trail. Go straight (anticlockwise) around the loop.

After sign no. 6, cross Warspite Creek and meander along between berry bushes into a boulder field. In the midst of the boulders is Warspite Lake, its astonishing emerald-green colour caused by algae activated by strong sunlight. The outlet takes the underground route, the water heard gurgling deep down beneath the trail.

At sign no. 10 the trail winds its way back to the T-junction, recrossing the boulder field into the trees and recrossing a resurrected Warspite Creek. Turn right and return the same way.

Warspite Lake below Mt. Black Prince. The grassy ridge above the figure is the southeast rib above Black Prince Lake.

GOING FARTHER

99A Black Prince Lake

Unofficial trail with cairns, route
Distance from lake 2.6 km
Height gain add 503 m (1650 ft.)
High point 2323 m (7620 ft.)

The climb into a cirque below the north face of Mt. Warspite is a steep grind on game trail. Be alert for griz in the waist-high flower meadows below the headwall.

At interpretive signs #9 or 10 step off the interpretive trail onto an unofficial trail and, leaving the tourists behind, circle the lake anticlockwise. Before reaching the inlet, the trail takes you through a belt of spruce onto grassy flats—the runout zones of avalanche slopes, then crosses a boulder field with the help of many big cairns. You are aiming for a prominent black slit at the bottom of a cliff. Left of the slit, the old elk trail climbs diagonally left through flowery meadows towards the main fork of Warspite Creek. Then deeply entrenched, the trail climbs up the right side of Warspite Cascades to the top of the headwall. It's a climb to make you gasp.

(UPDATE FROM ALF: a less-steep secondary trail is developing to the right of the cascades on the more open slope.)

At the lip a higher cirque is revealed, with Mt. Warspite at centre stage. Continue on trail until past the trees on the right side. Then turn right and using one of many faint "trails," climb another 150 vertical metres up a grass and boulder slope to the top of a terminal moraine. Look down on inky blue/black Black Prince Lake, which later in the season dries to three tarns.

Those with energy to spare can wander up the grassy southeast rib of Mt. Black Prince to rockline. It's a great viewpoint for the cirque and for Warspite Lake a few thousand feet below your feet.

Warspite Cascades

Black Prince Lake from the southeast rib of Mt. Black Prince. Above the cirque rises Mt. Warspite (a difficult scramble). Photo Alf Skrastins

100 GYPSUM QUARRY — map 5

Day hike to quarry
Unofficial trail, creek crossing
Distance 7.4 to end of quarry
Height gain 457 m (1500 ft.)
High point 2133 m (7000 ft.)
Map 82 J/11 Kananaskis Lakes

Access Hwy. 742 (Smith-Dorrien/Spray Trail) at Peninsula day-use area, far parking lot.
Also accessible from #76A at the col between Indefatigable Outlier and the north summit of Mt. Indefatigable.

This is a long, easy and scenic walk up an exploration road to a gypsum quarry on the north ridge of Mt. Invincible. The "road" was brushed out recently during restoration work on the quarry, but unfortunately the temporary bridge over Smith-Dorrien Creek was removed when the work was finished.

So, crossing the rambunctious Smith-Dorrien Creek near the start is a problem. In mid-July the water can be thigh-deep and this is downstream of the bridge site, where the river is wider and calmer! You might think that fall is the time to go, but it all depends on water levels in Lower Kananaskis Lake. When the lake is full, the lake extends upstream of the bridge site. At such times the best bet is to canoe/kayak/raft across from the put-in near the kiosk at the parking lot. Another option is to follow a trail through the woods to the creek far upstream of the bridge site, wade across, then backtrack along the steep south bank.

More adventurous hikers can continue on to Gypsum Tarns and higher still to join with Indefatigable Outlier trail. If doing this route in reverse, it's essential you check the water level in Smith-Dorrien Creek first. Or you too can spend the night out on the south bank like our friends and be forced to hail a passing boat in the morning.

TRAIL NOTE 1. Since the last edition the shortcuts have grown in and are no longer used. 2. Carry bear spray.

HISTORY NOTE This particular gypsum outcrop was reported by the Geological Survey in 1964 (Report 65-1), and resulted in a 21-year lease being issued to CP Oil & Gas, who transferred it several times over to the Alberta Gypsum Company. After all the trouble in getting a road to the area — your road is the second attempt — they operated for just a few years until August 1970 when the lease was cancelled, the company having failed to make a cash deposit to cover land restoration costs.

By 2000 the quarry face was slipping down the hillside and in 2007/8/9 reclamation was carried out by A.M. MacKay Contractors Ltd. of Cochrane in partnership with Interior Reforestation Co. Ltd. It is they who have improved the access.

From the loop at the far end of the access road, transfer to the old quarry road (track) which is gated. Keep left and descend to Smith-Dorrien Creek at a meadow with rain gauge and shed, where you find out if the walk's a go. Maybe you'll meet people on the guided hike "Cut the Bull," which informs about Smith-Dorrien Creek's role as an important spawning bed for bull trout that live in Lower Kananaskis Lake.

Cross Smith-Dorrien Creek. On the south bank the track continues to a bend. The spruce-infested trail to left was the first attempt at getting a road to the gypsum deposit via Gypsum Creek, but came a cropper when it hit a series of rocky gullies. So you turn right.

The road slowly rises across avalanche paths below what snowshoers call Gypsum Ridge, then winds up the lightly treed north ridge of Mt. Invincible. Everywhere between trees grows the white rhododendron, a beautiful sight during blossoming. Below a steeper step the road runs in a

The quarry road headed for Mt. Invincible.

The trail along the quarry bench.
Indefatigable Outlier pokes up at top right.

straight line along the right side of the ridge towards the face of the mountain, at the last minute deking left through a gap to the quarry.

Walk a bench half way up the face to the far end of the quarry, where you're treated to an Opal Range panorama and views of Mt. Rae, the Elk Range and a glimpse of Lower Kananaskis Lake below Gypsum Creek. En route you can check out the methods used to restore this vast slope, which include the use of jute blankets to stabilize the soil, and straw and willow-weave waddles to "take the energy out of the water during runoff and heavy rains and promote a platform for growth to establish naturally or by planting." Already in 2008 the willows had taken root.

Return the same way, enjoying the views that were mostly behind your back on the way up.

GOING FARTHER

100A Gypsum Tarns

Unofficial trails
Distance 2.1 km from quarry
Height loss 91 m (300 ft.)
Height gain 152 m (500 ft.)
High Point 2179 m (7150 ft.)

Although the distance is relatively short, this cross-country jaunt from the quarry to the tarns in the cirque between mounts Invincible and Indefatigable is only for the experienced finder of game trails. Expect a rough, steep hillside to the first Gypsum Quarry road.

To first gypsum quarry road 1.6 km
From the far end of the quarry, follow hoofprints up a dirt ridge, then cut up left and through one or two trees to a gravel slope. Here pick up a definite trail that can be followed through the next tree ribbon to a shallow scree gully beyond. Rising and falling, but mostly falling, the trail crosses alternating tree ribs and stoney gullies all the way to first gypsum quarry road.

There are a few tricky metres where the trail disappears on a steep side slope, then reappearing, circles around a wider than usual gully manufactured from cement shale. But eventually you arrive on the first gypsum quarry road, which starts (or rather ends) on the far bank of the last gully.

The flat, easy road crosses below a humongous avalanche slope divided by a stream leaping down the headwall. Cross the stream (not marked on the topo map despite supplying 90% of the water to Gypsum Creek), then in trees cross the very much smaller creek from Gypsum Tarns. Just after the latter creek crossing, exit the road and turn right onto a small trail near the forest edge.

The largest Gypsum Tarn. In the background is Indefatigable Outlier at left, and Indefatigable Col at centre. Photo Alf Skrastins

To Gypsum Tarns 0.5 km

The trail heads upwards to the bottom of a boulder slope. Here intercept an excellent elk trail and follow it right back into trees. At a division climb either way to the lip of the cirque—a not too onerous task in larch and Glacier lily country. Cupped in grass at the bottom of scree slopes are three small green tarns.

Return

Someone is sure to ask: "Why can't I return via the first gypsum quarry road, because it's such a good road?" The dreadful thing is that from this direction the first couple of kilometres lures with a clear path through trees. Then, at the point where the road turns away from the valley, you hit a wall of prickly spruce, gooseberry bushes, 6-m-high alders and deadfall. You'll emerge looking like an escapee from the polar bear complex at the Calgary Zoo. Don't go. Return the same way via the quarry or consider the next option.

OPTIONAL RETURN

100B via Indefatigable Col

Unofficial trails
Distance 1 km to col
Height gain 304 m (1000 ft.) from tarns
High point at col 2484 m (8150 ft.)

Having made it to the tarns, it's definitely shorter to carry on through to North Interlakes parking lot via the Indefatigable trails, which of course requires that you have two vehicles. The question is: can you hack another 300 m of steep climbing?

Interestingly, predating guidebooks and K Country, this was one of those mythical routes known only to a few people. Only it was done in reverse and the first Gypsum Creek road was then available for walking and a bridge was in place over Smith-Dorrien Creek.

First, check the slope for the resident grizzly. All clear? From the larger tarn a very convenient trail heads southeast up the left bank of the inlet creek to treeline. While it's possible to climb direct to Indefatigable Outlier via its stony west ridge, the more attractive grizzly route tackles the grassy, shaley slope farther to the right. It leads straight to the col at 297329 between the outlier and Mt. Indefatigable North. Now read #76A Indefatigable Outlier, usual descent.

101 The "SOUTH END of LAWSON" — map 5

Day hike & scramble, bike 'n' hike
Unofficial trail, route
Distance 4 km
Height gain 762 m (2500 ft.)
High point 2393 m (7850 ft.)
Map 82 J/11 Kananaskis Lakes

The South End of Mt. Lawson from Hwy. 40, showing the two tops and the gap in between.

Access Hwy. 742 (Smith-Dorrien/Spray Trail). About 200 m north of Peninsula day-use area access road, park at the intersection of gated TransAlta roads. The road heading south leads to Canyon Dam, the road heading north leads to Kent Creek.

This refers to the southernmost tip of the ridge extending SSE from Mt. Lawson at 306209. Driving Hwy. 40 from Fortress Junction into Peter Lougheed Park, you see it as the last high point before the ridge drops to the flats.

I'm betting this route up the south ridge will become enormously popular with experienced hikers: there's a rudimentary trail most of the way; the gradient is gentle with occasional steep steps; a rock ridge at the top adds spice; the summit is an unusual viewpoint; and lastly there's the option of going farther.

NOTE The first 0.7 km along the TransAlta road can be biked.

Kent Creek section 1.2 km
Head north on the TransAlta road alongside a diversion ditch built in 1956 to divert water from Kent Creek to Lower Kananaskis Lake. This is also a part of Penstock loop snowshoe trail.

Around a bend the pointy lower summit of your objective comes into view, the ascent ridge looking very foreshortened. Then several things happen within a short distance: the ditch is replaced by a metal flume; at a red sign the snowshoe trail turns off to the right across the real Kent Creek (no bridge); opposite a bridge over the flume, Kent Creek pours out of a pipe; and the water issuing from the canyon is swallowed by an intake structure.

The road ends at the canyon's mouth. (Farther along is a waterfall only attainable by a paddle.) The canyon and cliffs staggered across both hillsides are the reasons why entering Kent Creek Valley is so difficult.

To Kent Creek junction 0.4 km
Just before the intake, cross boulders in the dry bed to the far bank and turn right. After the slope on the left loses its crags, look for a trail climbing steeply onto the lower south ridge.

The gradient eases right off, the trail keeping mostly to the right side of the ridge crest. Just past a boulder it steepens again, zigging up easy ground between the big cliff on the left and the escarpment on the right. At the top in pines is an unmarked Y-junction. Go straight up the fall line. (The easier-angled trail to Kent Creek forks left at 10 o'clock.)

To lower top 1.8 km
The ridge trail continues to climb moderately steeply, but then the angle eases and for a kilometre you stride along above the eastern escarpment in pines with almost no understorey. Down right you can spot unsuspected ponds amid the forest and buildings that were once a minimum-security work camp (the Kananaskis Correctional Centre).

So easy is the going that the trail is almost redundant, and in fact it disappears temporarily just before a very small dip. After this the pattern is short steepish climbs alternating with long easy stretches. A longer-sustained uphill, where you must look harder for the trail, leads to a grass ridge and a narrowing. Look back for

a first thrilling view of Lower Kananaskis Lake glinting in the noonday sun. At the top of the slope the lower summit is decked out in larches.

To summit 0.6 km
The trail heads gently down at the edge of a big rock gully to a col.

Coming up is the day's steepest climb, along the rim of the gully and onto a wide, flat ridge of scree and grass. The knob of scree at the end of it is not the summit, merely the lead-in to an entertaining rock ridge, where for a few metres you traverse the left side while hanging onto the ridge crest. After this the ridge broadens to grass and you walk through a few trees to the true summit (cairn).

What a place to view the Opals! Scramblers can pick out the route up Mt. Hood and hikers the route up King Creek Ridge opposite. To the west is the incredibly long Kent Ridge anchored by North Kent at the head of Kent Creek Valley. Looking down into the valley's dark forest reminds you that sticking to ridges is much more fun.

A flat stretch of ridge between the two tops. In the background is Lower Kananaskis Lake.

Going farther

The next section of open ridge—another nameless bump on the way to Mt. Lawson—is a come-on if you don't mind losing nearly 100 m (328 ft.) in height, and plodding through a lot more trees. Initially the ridge is broad, but soon narrows and undulates, becoming the realm of the scrambler/climber.

OPTION

101A Kent Creek

Long day hike, backpack
Unofficial trail, then route
Distance to end of trail from trailhead
1.8 km, to valley head 11 km
Height gain 808 m (2650 ft.)
to valley head
High point 2484 m (8150 ft.)

Meadows and tarns at the head of this long, straight, dead-end valley are extraordinarily hard to get to. Climbers can drop in from the heights, but the rest of us must bushwhack. This description only gets you the 1 km beyond the canyon to the start of the valley proper. Because of the canyon's cliffs, the access trail described here starts from some distance up the south ridge of Lawson and descends in.

NOTE I have yet to check out game trails along the southwest hillside. So stay tuned.

Trail to valley bottom 0.7 km
From the junction as mentioned, turn left onto a rising trail that crosses the hillside above a big cliff. Step over much deadfall. A gradual descent above another drop-off precedes the plummet—a definite design fault in trails. At the bottom, traverse right above a third drop-off, then angle fairly steeply down to the valley bottom.

Going farther
For much of the way the valley is dark old-growth forest, mossy bumpy with pools of standing water, beautiful in its way, but not conducive to easy travelling. Expect tiny snippets of game trails going nowhere and lots and lots of deadfall. Most people will have given up long before they reach the meadows.

The rock ridge below the summit.

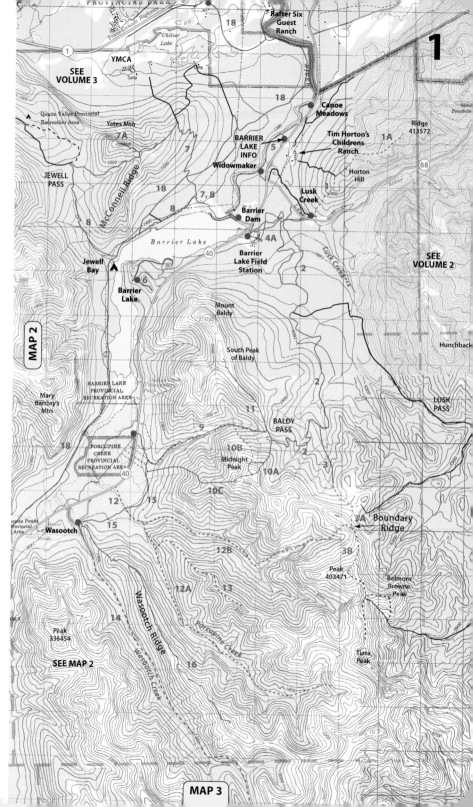

PROVINCIAL PARK

Rafter Six
Guest
Ranch

18

Chilver
Lake

Trans Canada Highway

1

SEE
VOLUME 3

YMCA

Camp

18

Canoe
Meadows

Quirk Valley Provincial
Recreation Area

Yates Mtn

Ridge
413572

7A

7

1A

BARRIER
LAKE
INFO

Tim Horton's
Childrens
Ranch

5

68

Widowmaker

McConnell Ridge

JEWELL
PASS

18

7, 8

Horton
Hill

Lusk
Creek

8

Lusk Creek Area

Stony

8

Barrier
Dam

Barrier Lake

40

1, 4A

Jewell
Bay

SEE
VOLUME 2

6

Barrier
Lake

Barrier
Lake Field
Station

2

Mount
Baldy

MAP 2

South Peak
of Baldy

Hunchback

Mary
Barclay's
Mtn

BARRIER
LAKE
PROVINCIAL
RECREATION AREA

2

11

LUSK
PASS

18

9

BALDY
PASS

PORCUPINE
CREEK
PROVINCIAL
RECREATION AREA

40

10B

2

Midnight
Peak

10A

3

12

15

10C

3A

Boundary
Ridge

Wasootch

15

12B

3B

Peak
403471

Belmore
Browne
Peak

12A

13

Peak
336454

14

Wasootch Ridge

Porcupine Creek

16

Tiara
Peak

SEE MAP 2

Wasootch Creek

MAP 3

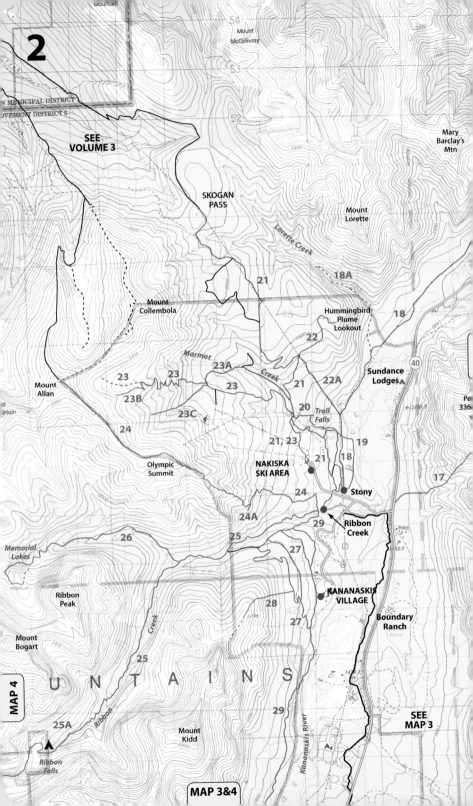

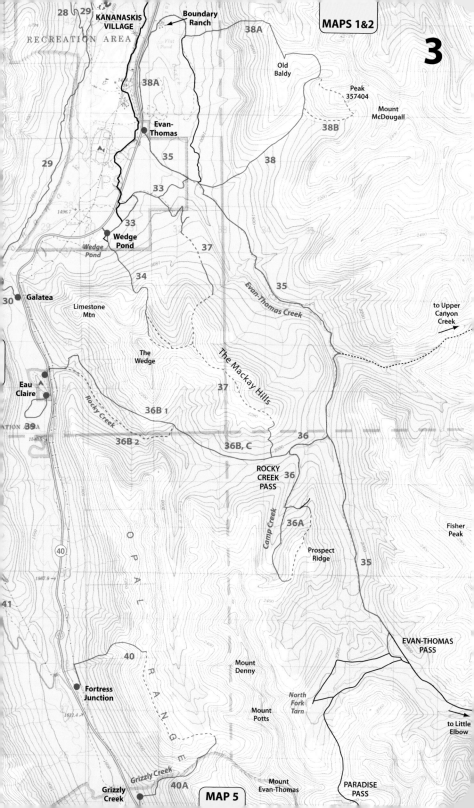

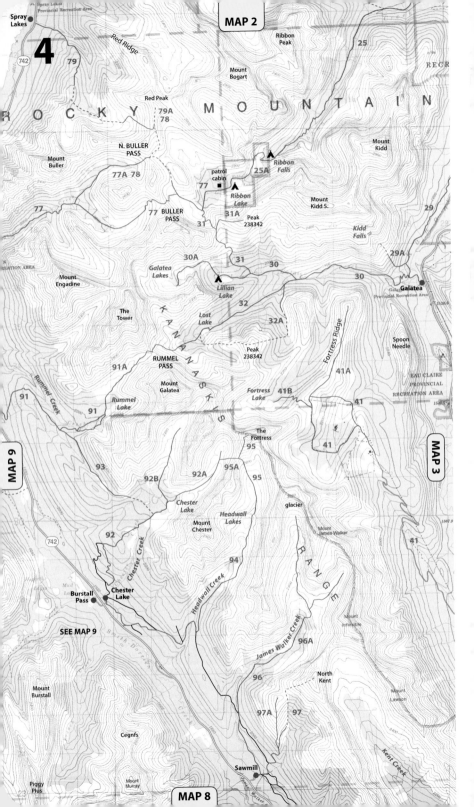

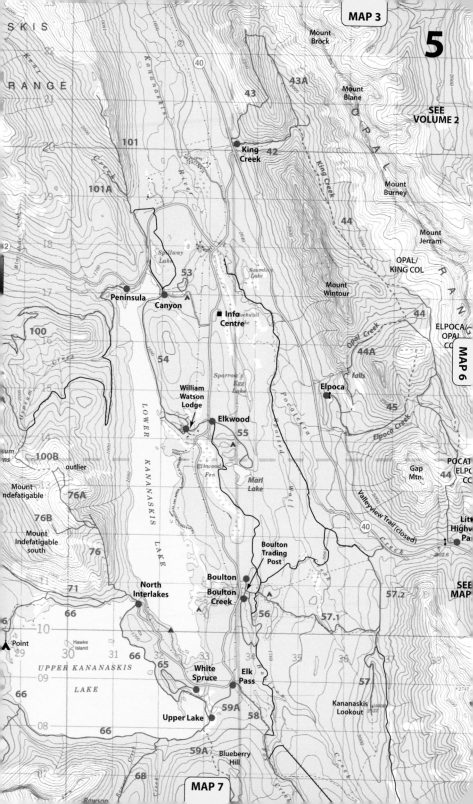

MAP 3

5

S K I S

R A N G E

Kent Creek

22

21

Mount Brock

Kananaskis River

40

43A

43

Mount Blane

SEE VOLUME 2

101

King Creek

42

King Creek

Mount Burney

101A

Blackstone Creek

18

44

Mount Jerram

Spillway Lake

53

Soundiss Lake

OPAL/ KING COL

O P A L

12

Peninsula

Canyon

Info Centre

Rockwall Lake

Mount Wintour

R A N G E

44

100

17

16

54

Sparrow's Egg Lake

Opal Creek

44A

falls

MAP 6

ELPOCA/ OPAL CO

Cypress Creek

William Watson Lodge

Elkwood

55

Elpoca

45

Elpoca Creek

POCAT ELPO CC

sum ns

100B

outlier

14

Elkwood Fen

Marl Lake

Gap Mtn.

44

Mount Indefatigable

76A

13

Pocaterra

Dotted Wolf

Mount Indefatigable south

76B

76

L O W E R   K A N A N A S K I S   L A K E

Valleyview Trail (closed)

40

Litt Highw Pa

6

71

66

North Interlakes

Boulton Trading Post

Boulton

Boulton Creek

56

57.2

57.1

SEE MAP

Point

29

10

30

Hawke Island

31

66

32

33

65

White Spruce

34

35

36

37

57

Kananaskis Lookout

U P P E R   K A N A N A S K I S
L A K E

09

Elk Pass

59A

58

66

08

66

Upper Lake

59A

Blueberry Hill

68

Rawson Creek

MAP 7

6

MAP 5

SEE
VOLUME 2

SEE
VOLUME 4

SEE
VOLUME 4

SEE
VOLUME 5

MAP 7

Tombstone
Mtn

Piper Creek

Elpoca
Mtn

patrol
cabin

Tombstone

Sheep
Lakes

to Little Elbow
recreation area
Hwy. 66

Little
Highwood
Pass

Elbow
Pass

Elbow
Lake

47

47A

Rae Lake

Rae
Creek

to Juncti
day-use a
Hwy. 54

52

Rockfall
Lake

Pocaterra Ridge

46

Rae
Glacier

Mount
Rae

44

45

46

47

M
I
S
T
Y

Mount
Arethusa

48

R
A
N
G
E

Burns

Creek

LITTLE
HIGHWOOD
PASS

52

49

Grizzly
Peak

Highwood
Pass

51

Storm
Mtn

EAST
ELK
PASS

Mount
Tyrwhitt

GRIZZLY
COL

50

50A

Highwood Ridge

40

50B

Paradise Valley

51A

Storm Creek

Mount
Lipsett

Mount
Lipsett

40

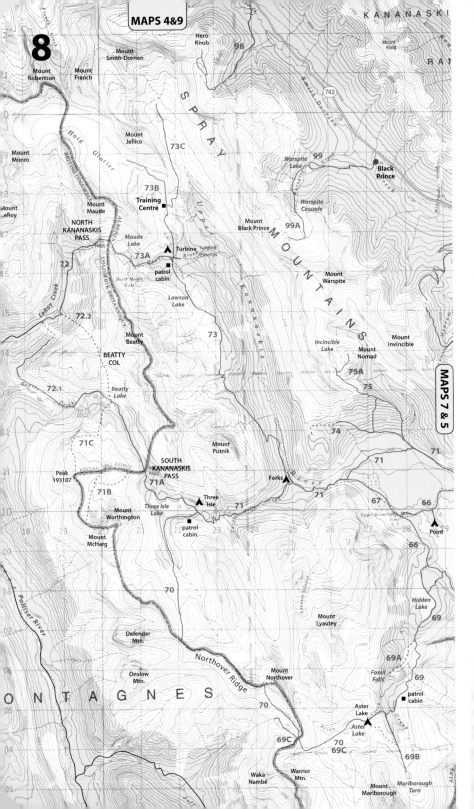